D0394655

Law in Brief Encounters

LAW IN BRIEF ENCOUNTERS

W. MICHAEL REISMAN

Yale University Press   New Haven and London

The following are reprinted with permission: W. H. Auden, "Postscript" to "Prologue: The Birth of Architecture," in W. H. Auden, *Collected Poems*, ed. Edward Mendelson (New York: Random House, Vintage International, 1991), p. 688, and lines from *My Fair Lady*, based on *Pygmalion* by Bernard Shaw, adaptation and lyrics by Alan Jay Lerner, music by Frederick Loewe (New York: Coward-McCann, 1956), and *Fiddler on the Roof*, book by Joseph Stein, based on Sholom Aleichem's stories, music by Jerry Bock, lyrics by Sheldon Harnick (New York: Crown Publishers, 1965, © 1964).

Set in Adobe Caslon type.

Library of Congress Cataloging-in-Publication Data
Reisman, W. Michael (William Michael), 1939–
Law in brief encounters / W. Michael Reisman.
p. cm.
Includes bibliographical references and index.
ISBN 0-300-07569-3 (alk. paper)
1. Law—Social aspects. 2. Law—Psychology. 3. Law and ethics.
4. Law—Philosophy. I. Title.
K380.R445 1999
340'.11—dc21   99-13730   CIP

Printed in the United States of America.

A catalogue record for this book is
available from the British Library.

The paper in this book meets the guidelines for permanence and durability of the Committee on Production Guidelines for Book Longevity of the Council on Library Resources.

10 9 8 7 6 5 4 3 2 1

In memory of Erving Goffman, 1922–82,
for "developing an apt terminology for the
interactional tasks that all of us share"

Contents

Preface / ix

Introduction / 1

CHAPTER 1
Looking, Staring, and Glaring / 21

CHAPTER 2
Standing in Line and Cutting In / 51

CHAPTER 3
Rapping and Talking to the Boss / 97

CHAPTER 4
Amending Microlaw / 149

Conclusion: Microlaw and the Good Life / 174

Notes / 177
Acknowledgments / 221
Index / 223

PREFACE

This book is the product of almost twenty years of research and reflection on the details and implications of the myriad and ephemeral legal arrangements that weave our lives together and affect who we are. The inquiry, which was by its nature inductive, was reported in a series of papers; in each I discussed a particular microlegal system and tentatively linked it to a larger theory about law. Each paper was perforce tentative in key parts and sparked reconsideration of its predecessors. With the research phase completed, I was able to rethink all of the studies and to see them in relation to some of the urgent challenges to liberal democracy. Several new essays, published here for the first time, were the result.

The research for each of the original papers (Chapters 1, 2, and 3) largely appears as it was at first publication, but the text of each has now been substantially revised in the light of the others and their public policy implications. "Looking, Staring, and Glaring" was originally delivered as the Myres S. McDougal Lecture at the University of Denver in 1983. Parts of earlier versions of Chapters 1–4 were originally published as follows and are reprinted by permission: "Looking, Staring and Glaring: Microlegal Systems and World Public Order," *Denver Journal of International Law and Policy* 12, nos. 2–3 (1983): 165–82; "Lining Up: The Microlegal System of Queues," *University of Cincinnati Law Review* 54, no. 2 (1985): 417–49 © University of Cincinnati; "Rapping and Talking to the Boss: The Microlegal System of Two People Talking," in *Conflict and*

Integration: Comparative Law in the World Today (Tokyo: Chuo University Press, 1988), 61–104; and "Autonomy, Interdependence, and Responsibility," *Yale Law Journal* 103, no. 2 (1993): 401–17, reprinted by permission of the Yale Law Journal Company and Fred B. Rothman and Company.

Law in Brief Encounters

Introduction

Ubi societas ibi jus.

Early in my teaching career, Abraham Goldstein, dean of the Yale Law School, sent me to a number of South American countries. One weekend in Peru, I flew to Cuzco, high in the Andes, and took the single gauge railway train that runs along the wild Urubamba River to the mysterious ghost city of Machu Picchu. Late the same afternoon, back in Cuzco's airport, dense fog had grounded all flights to Lima. The waiting area was crowded, and with the impunity of a tourist (and perhaps the arrogance of an American abroad), I was looking about at the milling Quechua and Aymara Indians when I realized that I had been staring at an Indian woman who now glared back at me. I turned away in confusion and embarrassment and with a certain amount of anxiety, wondering whether the woman's husband or father or brother was now going to confront me. Like many in my culture, I took for granted that the target of my improper staring, a woman, would only glare at me, whereas her male companion might well escalate the protest. As I sat and reflected on the exchange, I realized that nothing further had happened precisely because the visual exchange had occurred within a microlegal system, with a shared recognition of the governing norm, shared acknowledgment of its violation, application of an understood and adequate sanction, and, as a direct result, correction of the offending behavior.

It occurred to me that afternoon in the Cuzco airport that the way we gather visual information about others is facilitated by a microlegal system that permits some looking at others while protecting them from intrusive staring through the application of an effective enforcement system. Detailed analysis of this microlegal system became a project for me, and I decided subsequently to expand my research into other microlegal systems that are critical in our lives.

Mainstream contemporary legal theory—with its emphasis on the state as the centerpiece of any legal system and, for many theorists, its primary, if not exclusive, source of law—misdirects our attention from the full realm of law. The law of the state may be important, but law, *real* law, is found in all human relations, from the simplest, briefest encounter between two people to the most inclusive and permanent type of interaction. Law is a property of interaction. Real law is generated, reinforced, changed, and terminated continually in the course of almost all of human activity. This law, which I refer to as microlaw, also manifests a constitutional dimension or, to put it more dynamically, a constitutive process: part of every decision is concerned, not with the immediate decision, but with the structure of decisionmaking itself. Microlaw is effective and sanctioned, although those who look for the familiar enforcement mechanisms and litmus tests of conventional legal theory will not find things like microarmies, micropolice, or microprisons. They will, however, find functional equivalents.

Without the existence and operation of microlaw, we could not interact in business meetings, in seminars, in crowded buses or subways, nor even engage in transactions that we may value but may still think are wrong and try to conceal, for example, bribes, criminal conspiracies, and extramarital affairs. Each of these events involves a social organization, and such organizations ineluctably include legal systems in their structure. Some of the situations may be durable— for example, a nuclear family, a long-term collaboration between scholars, or an extended space mission. Others may be extremely brief, indeed, evanescent—for example, two strangers glancing at each other.

Many of these situations are face-to-face, but that does not mean that they may not be extraordinarily complex and difficult to understand. Mary Douglas has remarked that "in small-scale, face-to-face society the gulf between personal meanings and public meanings cannot develop; rituals are not fixed; discrepancy between the situation being enacted and the form of expression is immediately reduced by change in the latter."[1] Her observation may be accurate for village society, where life consists of a series of microsituations almost always with familiar people, but it is not correct for face-to-face encounters in a mass society. Life in a mass society is also a series of microsituations, but often with strangers—people of different cultures, classes, and, indeed, language groups. What is so fascinating about many microsituations in mass societies is that they involve two strangers, surrounded by others yet momentarily isolated with each other. Shared public meanings between them are likely to be conjectural or illusory. The personal meanings of each actor with respect to the other may be full of gaps. Yet each person must interact with the other for the duration of this brief social organization.

Microlaw warrants study for a number of reasons. It may shed light on how legal systems that are not formally organized operate, and it may provide other insights into general properties and operations of law that may clarify our understanding of conventional legal systems. Study of microlaw may also facilitate a better grasp of the important distributive functions of law: the allocation of the things people want and desperately don't want. An accurate picture of who gets what can be gained only if the lives of the various whos are examined in a textured microlegal sense and if the highly localized but often powerfully focused social processes that operate on them are understood. Only these sorts of inquiries enable the inquirer to assess the effects on people of the aggregate of the legal systems under which they live. When such assessments yield discrepancies between what people want and what they can expect to achieve, macrolegal changes may not be effective. Microlegal adjustments may be the necessary instrument of change. In everyone's life, microlaw has not only *not* been superseded by state law but remains, as Walter Weyrauch has said, the most important and continuous normative experience.

The only person I ever met who saw the State was an elderly professor. "I have seen it," he assured me solemnly. Did he really? Do we see the State, the Government, the Town, the Church, the Army, the University? Terms for these entities are repeated so often in political as well as mundane discourse that we begin to take them as referents for something tangible. But the whole is not more than the sum of its parts. Human interaction is no more and no less than people interacting with one another, often in very small groups, many of them composed of only two people and lasting a very short time. Those other grand terms are abstract symbols. Human beings do not interact with symbols, nor are they injured by them. They interact with—are helped, reared, robbed, raped, killed by—other human beings, who relate to them in various patterns of equality, subordination, and superordination.[2] Persistently overlooking ineluctable human agency and blaming the symbol becomes a technique of amnesty for individual perpetrators and a continuing invitation to impunity.

I am not saying that the symbols for these larger collectivities are devoid of meaning or are socially or politically unimportant. Far from it. Grand terms such as "the Masses," "the Proletariat," "das Volk," and "the Nation" may have little empirical correspondence with ordinary people, but they can be critical to doing great good or harm. Big symbols are frequently used by elites to legitimize themselves and to validate the use of the authority over the rank-and-file without consulting them. Bitter experience has led to a deep suspicion about symbols of this type and those who wield them. But the symbols are a part of our destiny, for the modern period is also, inescapably, an era of authentic mass society in which macroeconomics and macrosocial planning properly command our attention. Collective symbols are, and always have been, a glue. Even ancient mass societies like China required such symbols for their governance.[3] The larger the collectivity, the more generalized and abstract the principles and symbols of governance.

The problem is not the symbols but the confusion that their use may engender. When the manipulation of the great contemporary collective symbols obscures individual people, who in all social interactions are the ultimate and only actors, critical human values can be jeopardized. Fascisms of various kinds can be the result of the uncritical abstraction and elimination of real people in favor of emotionally charged mythicized collective symbols. I believe that the conception and focus of microlaw can serve, at least at the intellectual level, as a corrective to these dangerous tendencies, for microlaw yanks us back to the activities and texture of our lives.

The symbol of the State has loomed large in jurisprudential inquiry and formal legal theory and has had a pernicious effect on the study of microlaw. John Austin,[4] the great nineteenth-century legal theorist, is usually indicted for forcing jurisprudence into the straitjacket notion that real law, "law properly so called," is exclusively positive law, or the law posited by the state. All the rest is, at best, what Austin styled a jurisprudential consolation prize, "positive morality": "rules set and enforced by *mere opinion*, that is, by the opinions or sentiments held or felt by an indeterminate body of men in regard to human conduct" (Austin's italics).[5]

Since the Romans, jurists in Western civilization have systematically studied the generation of custom, which is law produced by people through informal interactions, sometimes without the intention of legislating. But even Austin's contemporary critics, some of whom were Romanists, were captive to the idea that law, to be law, requires some governmental hierarchy. The difference between Austin and his critics was that some, like Sir Henry Maine,[6] the great Cambridge legal historian who pioneered the study of primitive law, were willing to find in enduring non-state structures the hierarchy that Austin had insisted on and to pronounce that these structures, too, might constitute legal systems. Others, like Lassa Oppenheim, grappling with the reality of international law in the absence of a formalized hierarchy, found theoretical support for law in a balance of power, with states checking and restraining one another.

Few jurisprudential writers, however, have addressed microlegal systems. Leon Petrazycki, with his essentially psychological approach to law, did some work in this area, much of which remains unavailable to English-language readers.[7] Eugen Ehrlich, teaching legal theory early in the century in Czernowitz, Austria-Hungary, resisted the state-centric concept of law. He sent his students into the field to map the legal systems of non-state arrangements, like factories and peasant collectives. Given his interest in law that neither derived from nor was enforced by the apparatus of the state, Ehrlich would have been amenable to micronormative inquiries.[8] Unfortunately, neither he nor his students seem to have made such investigations. Contemporary legal anthropologists have examined microsituations but have generally focused on more durable territorial and nonterritorial communities, not the brief encounters of interest to us.[9] Writing from the legal standpoint, Burns Weston has insisted on the "law" quality of micronorms.[10] Walter Weyrauch, an astute and innovative observer at the Universities of Florida and Frankfurt, has even described the constitutive process and constitutional outcomes in microsituations.[11] No one has recommended policies to change microlegal systems.

Legal Positivists' narrow conception of law has had implications beyond the formal study of law. Over several generations many prominent anthropologists, under the influence of the Austinian notion, studied "primitive" societies that, according to the definitions that the anthropologists imported from Legal Positivism, could not have real legal systems. The scholarly intentions may have been pure, but the political implications of the statist theory of law were rapidly and decisively felt in the lives of the "natives" who were being anthropologized. If primitive societies did not have law in this proper sense, then colonial governments, as part of their *mission civilisatrice,* could fill the vacuum by importing the law from their own "advanced" culture to the everlasting benefit of those under their tutelage. And fill it they did. The social scientists of the day, who were, by the nature of their task, concerned with the texture of the lives of the individuals whom they studied, did not compile an account of the consequences of the application of this theory precisely because they were convinced that their function was to advance civilization rather than to preserve culture.

Scholars in other disciplines that have largely ignored legal theory and have escaped these distortions have also lost whatever benefits jurisprudence might have offered them. Traditional sociologists and small group psychologists, for example, have rarely used the potential insights of legal theory in examining what are, in effect, legal systems. Following the seminal work of Arthur Bentley, the central role of small groups in both local and mass politics has been appreciated and studied widely. But the role of *law* in very small groups, especially in very evanescent ones—the way law affects the behavior of the individuals in them and in the outcomes of much larger political conglomerations—has not received comparable attention.

More recently, sociologists have fruitfully explored norm generation in informal situations.[12] A few names stand out. Erving Goffman, the Canadian-born sociologist to whom this book is dedicated, was unparalleled in exposing the reticulate network of reciprocal normative expectations that operate in microsituations.[13] Eric Berne was able to unpack the intricate and rapid exchanges between people in some evanescent encounters and relate them to psychopersonal issues.[14] The work of Georg Simmel,[15] who taught in Berlin and Strasbourg at the beginning of the twentieth century, shows great sensitivity to microsocial systems, whose structures he tried to generalize. Simmel was also alert to problems of injustice at this microsocial level.[16] Phoebe Ellsworth, who studied nonverbal communication at Yale, produced a number of studies pertinent to this inquiry.[17] Ethologists have examined the norms in the primate kingdom; more than a few have noted their similarity to our own.[18]

Some other civilizations have been more focused on the microsocial level. Traditional Japanese social arrangements with their intricate, hierarchical dyadic relationships, so brilliantly described by Chie Nakane,[19] and traditional Confucian legal conceptions[20] certainly escaped the mass symbol distortions considered above and should fit with the conception of microlegal relationships. But these microlegal relationships were enduring rather than evanescent and were often supported and, if need be, sanctioned by national law and culture.

I believe that the persistent inability to focus on microlaw is due, in no small part, to the continuing tyranny of conceptions of law that relate law to the formal structures and apparatus of the state. Western political and legal conceptions have been profoundly influenced by Thomas Hobbes and Jean Bodin, who were at pains to demonstrate that social order depends on a strong centralized state apparatus, with its attendant legal system. Of the contemporary options available to deal with the rampant disorder of their time, what Hobbes and Bodin were proposing may have been the best alternative. But the theory that they propounded to buttress their political goal has been transformed into a virtual iron law that obscures and skews legal conceptions about the effective operation of law in non-state settings that the modern state is also committed to preserving. For the most part, there is manifestly no "state" governing an ordinary conversation between two of us, the way we look at each other, wait in lines, conduct our love affairs (and hate affairs), the ways (if not with whom) we have sex, the way we control such socially disruptive behavior as laughing or crying in public, manage unavoidable and otherwise intimate physical contact in crowded public places, and so on. The state may—and, many would argue, should—intervene in some of these microsituations when microlaw is not operating satisfactorily or when injuries within these spheres cry out for remedy. But the official custodians of justice will not know if and when to do this without understanding the existence and operation of microlaw.

When legal scholars have a problem, they ordinarily head for the library or, increasingly, to their computers, which link them to the libraries of the world. But research into microlegal systems is different from other legal inquiries. The norms are not only uncodified but often operate below levels of overt consciousness. In situations that do not appear to be novel to the actors, the appropriate norms are known, though knowing is often at an unconscious level so deep that the actors whose behavior is being influenced by those norms are unaware of knowing, acting on, and reacting to them. Yet the norms are there, and it may become apparent, even painfully apparent to sensitive travelers, whether they are venturing abroad or into a different stratum in their own country or a deeper stratum of a social relationship they already have, that they are ignorant of those norms. Handbooks of etiquette, guidebooks, and books of folklore may codify and promulgate some of the micronorms. Folklore may supply them. Even if people are aware of the pertinent microlaw, they may not characterize it as law. Awareness, in any case, is often limited to a particular norm and not to its systemic aspects—hence the need for a certain importunate style of inquiry. An investigator must press an informant until, with exasperation, the informant bursts out with "Well, you're just not supposed to . . ." It takes considerably more questioning and probing for informants to dredge up to awareness and analyze their responses and to appreciate that these responses have been serving as sanctions for the microlegal system in question. As soon as each informant begins to do that, the lineaments of a real legal system become apparent.

One indicator of the presence and operation of a microlegal system may be found in rather consistent sensations of irritation or anger over the actions of another in certain microsituations. If you tease apart these outbursts, you discover, among other things, that (1) A's irritation derives from the perception that B has violated some expectation that A believes he or she was entitled to rely on, or (2) A's willingness to express that irritation openly—which is always an event of social significance—derives from one of the following beliefs:

the ordinary social restraints on expressing anger are suspended, and A is entitled to the momentary release available through erupting, though in an appropriate way; B shares this expectation and will not turn on A for actions that might in other circumstances warrant a response; or B shares the expectation to the point that A's eruption will lead B to apologize and/or adapt his or her behavior so that it conforms to the expectation.

Once informants grasp the object of the inquiry, each may become an active investigator, with certain possibilities for enhancing knowledge and self-knowledge and growth, if not self-empowerment, effectiveness, confidence, and pleasure in microsituations in which participation was theretofore awkward, embarrassing, or painful. When I read early drafts of these essays to students, their reactions were consistent. They saw the relevance of their personal experiences and volunteered them. But in addition, in almost every case, the experience had been awkward or even painful, yet was now recounted with a certain surprised amusement, and each anecdote was followed by a pause for reflection. Infractions of microlaw or ignorance of other microlegal systems may cause distress or embarrassment to both parties because the microlegal systems are imperfectly understood by the person committing the violations. The painful mistakes may be attributed to personal deficiencies or fecklessness, and this, in turn, may have a subtle, corrosive impact on self-esteem, health, and subsequent behavior.

What accounts for the jurisprudential resistance to microlaw? As yet, no one seems to be paying for opinions or legal guidance on microlaw, but there are deeper ideological reasons than the lack of an economic incentive to study microlaw.

Lawyers and scholars who are concerned with the effective operation of a social system, its conformity to certain preferences, and its production and distribution of values in equitable ways frequently overlook mundane situations in favor of more general normative analyses.[21] This is unfortunate, for a moment's reflection will confirm that the lives of human beings in modern societies are involved largely with these situations. The skeptic may point to those who run afoul of the law of the state and occupy its jails as witnesses capable of giving testimony of what "real" law is and does. But even prisoners must contend with microsituations. In some instances, the microlegal system may supersede or inform inconsistent "macro" laws. Consider, for example, the long period of explicit racial segregation in the United States and the federal constitution with which such behavior was inconsistent. Some social scientists contend that informal rules of a microsituation may have more force than formal rules because the informal rules are easier to enforce, provide social support for compliance, and are developed by the group itself.[22]

Writers who identify law solely with the apparatus of the state must, by definition, dismiss microlaw as law. At the core of most state-based theories of law is an assumption of enforcement only through a hierarchical institution: a sheriff. This assumption confuses the function of enforcement with the institutions of enforcement. Although sanctioning and enforcing are indispensable characteristics of law, these functions need not be carried out by a particular institution or type of institution. Many systems are characterized by the development of specialized enforcers, but in many other systems, as Bronislaw Malinowski observed, law is enforced coarchically—in other words, by the actors themselves rather than by a specialized enforcer—and is sustained over time by expectations and, when necessary, by actions of reciprocity and retaliation.[23] In the international system, as Myres McDougal put it, the essential understanding is, "You scratch my back and I'll scratch yours. You kick my shins and I'll kick yours." Georges Scelle of

Paris, grappling with the same phenomenon, coined the term *dédoublement fonctionnel,* a "doubling of functions": the same actors are, in rapid alternation, actors and deciders.[24] Decades before Scelle, Lassa Oppenheim, at Cambridge, as we saw, made this dynamic the basis of his theory of international law: governments alternated between claimant and enforcer roles.[25]

What must exist in order for us to speak of a legal system is not a *formal* enforcer but an *expectation* accompanying a belief that there is a "right" way to act, that someone, possibly even the injured party, may properly respond, in ways that might otherwise be improper, to infractions of that expectation. It is this factor that helps sustain the norm. The durability of norms through time is what makes law, including microlaw, significant in our lives.

Statists also defend their restrictive theory by reference to a certain threshold of severity for sanctions. "De minimis non curat praetor," they intone gravely. "The law does not trifle with minor issues." The comparative triviality of the sanctions applied in microlegal situations has led some writers to dismiss their importance, if not to disregard them as law. That is why John Austin called them nothing more than positive morality. Level of severity is a useful, perhaps inescapable, classification in statistical descriptions in a mass society, for there it is convenient, if not necessary, to assign numerical values to the otherwise unmanageably abundant fragments of human experience that the student of mass society must deal with. But in designing and implementing events to make people retain or change certain behavior, it is self-defeating for policy purposes and wrong for scholarly inquiry to assume that "one size fits all" or to succumb to some arithmetical assumption that more of something painful or pleasurable will generally and proportionately induce or deter in desired ways. Behavior is more complicated than that.

It is reasonable to assume that people will avoid deprivations and secure indulgences and thus to incorporate threats of deprivation and promises of indulgences to support norms. This is what jurists mean by sanctions. Severity of sanctions is a useful criterion for distinguishing effective from merely semantic norms, but only insofar as there is a real correspondence between the *amount* of deprivation entailed in a particular sanction and the *sense* of deprivation that it evokes in all those susceptible to it. For many sanctions, the actual sense of deprivation varies with the condition of the person being sanctioned. Deprivations of respect, no matter how great, may be effective deterrents in one culture or stratum and utterly useless in another. Class can have multiplying effects on the bite of monetary sanctions. A $200 traffic fine, mildly irritating to a wealthy person, may be devastating to the poor person who takes home that much each week. A $200,000 fine for dumping hazardous wastes may may be a trivial bookkeeping inconvenience to a corporation, far less than the cost of complying with the law by detoxifying waste and disposing of it in an environmentally safe way. In any case, the corporation will try to pass the cost of the fine to its customers.

The bite of a sanction is a function of the subjective universe of the target and not of the sanctioner. The critical question is not the magnitude of the sanction but its effect. The bite is adequate if it is enough to sustain the norm; it need not secure the implementation of the norm in every case. The trivial sanctions of John Austin's positive morality may be very effective. Indeed, the microsanctions of microlegal systems may be much more significant determinants of our behavior than conventional macrosanctions, which loom portentously in the minds of theoreticians but may be ineffective and, in any case, will in all likelihood never be applied to most of us.[26]

Sanctions do not consist only of the limited repertory of

techniques of domestic criminal law, the most dramatic of which are marked by tangible physical deprivations. Every negative sanction includes in its mix of intended deprivations— of liberty, of wealth, of life opportunities—a significant deprivation of respect. The sanction is "shaming"; it involves "loss of face." The bite of respect deprivations varies and is sometimes relatively mild. Respect deprivations are key ingredients of microsanctions.[27] In the end, the issue is not whether the sanction is intense but whether it is effective.

Micronorms and their sanctions may be significant factors in the shaping of personalities in ways that have civic impact and social importance, not to speak of effects on an individual's autonomy, self-assurance, sense of self-worth, and capacity to develop affection for others. Knowledge of micronorms and facility in their use can empower. Most generally, microlegal systems and how we use them may influence our ability to be happy. Microlegal systems, like international law, may be near "the vanishing point of jurisprudence,"[28] but their low visibility and hitherto disdainful rejection by scholars of the law should not obscure the significant effects they can have on social order, the quality of individual lives, and the formation of personalities.

For the divinely inspired totalitarian, it is axiomatic that "the earth is the Lord's."[29] But in all totalitarian theories of power, whether secular or based on divinity, the state claims the authority to subject every feature of social order to governmental regulation. Jacek Kurón, a Polish dissident, described state rule under communism as a concentration of power "so total that if citizens gather freely and discuss freely a matter as simple as roof repairs on a block of flats, this constitutes a challenge to the central authority."[30] The great contribution of Western civilization has been the legitimization of the "partial" state, a conception of social order in which the power of the state is intentionally limited so that what some scholars call a private sphere or "civic order" exists outside of and is protected by public power.

The civic order is not a spatial sector but consists of "the features of social process that are cultivated and sustained by recourse to relatively mild rather than severe sanctions. It is the domain of social process in which the individual person is freest from coercion, governmental or other, and in which a high degree of individual autonomy and creativity prevails. Civic order thus includes all of the processes and institutions of private choice, as distinguished from public decision."[31] In the civic order, individuals may conduct their own lives as they wish. They must regulate their relationships, but they do so by microlegal arrangements in which the sanctions are much milder. Microlaw is the way individuals in the liberal state provide order in their lives in the private sphere. Civic order is not a legal vacuum; there is no such thing. This point is a critical one for all the chapters that follow: the area of the civic order, or privacy, is not an area in which there is no law, for social relationships cannot operate without law. The Roman maxim *Ubi societas ibi jus*, "Find society and you find law," the epigraph with which this chapter opens, is as true now as it was when it was first expressed, and it is true for every level of social organization. The law, the *jus*, in the civic order is microlaw.

There is nothing magical about the word "privacy." The civic order is not a zone of natural justice. Serious injustices can be done to individuals and groups through the medium of microlaw in this private sphere. This is one of the reasons why, early in the twentieth century, liberal societies, despite their commitment to the maintenance of an autonomous civic order, began moving inexorably into it. The provision of welfare to citizens necessarily drew government officials deep into aspects of the recipients' lives that until then had been deemed inappropriate for state intervention. The civil rights revolution in the United States extended government regulation into areas of private business and recreation that had until then been insulated from such governmental action. Sexual harassment in the workplace is now acknowledged as a problem and regulated by macrolaw.[32] Some of these movements appear to have reached their high point and have now begun to recede. Inspired by Prime Minister Margaret Thatcher in the United Kingdom, a movement to privatize many governmental activities was instituted and was quickly replicated in settings as diverse as Sweden, South Korea, Japan, and the United States.

The boundary between the public and private sphere in liberal systems is moveable; it shifts according to the objectives and policies of the community. Yet the abiding preference, indeed, characteristic of a liberal system is for civic order or microlegal arrangements rather than governmental regulations, because the latter require the creation of new governmental departments and government officials, perforce operating in bureaucratic mode and intervening more and more in the lives of the individual, however laudable the social goals. In this respect, the decision to arrange for macrolegal intervention in areas previously regulated by microlaw is a grave one. It is sometimes necessary, but it should always be taken with great caution. Even when the targeted violation is egregious, there are ineluctable unintended consequences whenever governmental officials expand into an area that had been subject to microlaw, a point that will be examined in detail in Chapter 4.

I believe that an appreciation of microlaw can be empowering to those who feel weak or who are imposed upon or violated in certain situations. "Weak" has both a physical and an emotional meaning. The amorphous feeling of inadequacy felt in such situations often arises from a distressing sense of anomie or from that awful presentiment that there is no justice. Because there are apparently no norms in a particular situation, the person who is stronger, bolder or less inhibited, more vulgar, or more privileged seems to be able to do whatever he or she wants. But if there *are* norms, and they can be invoked by the person whose "rights" have been violated, the possibility of nonviolent self-protection returns.

The point was illustrated for me by an anecdote that a former student, a trial lawyer, recounted. X had been taking the deposition of a critical witness for the other side. Depositions are not taken in the presence of a judge. Ordinarily no one is present but the witness, the lawyers for each side, and a reporter who makes a verbatim record. The transaction usually takes place in a law office. Without a referee, there is a certain potential for moral hazard; one counsel's abusive behavior is likely to escape the judicial sanctions whose prospective application would otherwise deter it. In this deposition, the opposing counsel had interfered with many questions; muttered remarks and asides had disturbed X's train of thought while conveying guidance to his witness. Yet because the comments were muttered, the reporter was not transcribing them, and they were not becoming part of the record. Finally, X, exasperated, slammed the table and said in a loud voice that the opposing counsel's behavior was inappropriate and unacceptable and he would not put up with it. To X's astonishment, the opposing counsel reddened, swallowed hard, apologized with apparent sincerity, and did not interfere further.

In retrospect, X concluded that his protest had not called forth more disruptive behavior from opposing counsel because the words that he selected without even thinking about them invoked a normative standard for a situation that opposing counsel acknowledged. X had no additional sanctions at his disposal. Had the opposing counsel jumped to his feet snarling, X would have had to make a statement for the record (which would have had little effect), then proceed with the deposition.

The continuing demand for etiquette manuals and the repetitive national debate about "civility" are essentially searches for the appropriate norms for microsituations that seem new and unregulated. Without such guidance, people may not enter situations that are otherwise desirable, or they may enter them but pay high costs in emotional pain because they do not know how to act. In some cases, macrolegal changes may overcorrect problems in microsituations and create new problems. Consider the belated efforts to address sexual harassment the way other civil rights were addressed. Overt and sadistic harassment (of which there is no shortage) aside, there is now confusion about the acceptable norms for initiating erotic relations in the workplace in a heterogeneous mass society. Yet it is the workplace where we spend much of our time. Much of the increased confusion may be due to the absence of or uncertainty about microlaw there. In many microsituations, particularly the most intimate ones, many ego defenses are down. Without a sense of the normative expectations of the situation, a participant may innocently injure the other and put stress on or possibly end the relationship. In other sectors, microsituations may be venues of serious injustice, even zones of human indignity. Their investigation—in terms of microlaw—may expose the injustice and indicate not only the need for but the method of remedy.

The possible pragmatic application of the microlaw perspective should not be overlooked. One of the tasks of the lawyer is to advise others on how to adjust their actions to achieve whatever objectives they seek in particular environments of normative expectations. Because many of the situations in which they operate are in effect the evanescent microlegal systems considered here, understanding of them and their sanctioning components can increase the realism and utility of counsel and the effectiveness with which lawyers operate. As it is, microlawyers, people who have an intuitive sense or possibly some empirically based knowledge of microlegal dynamics, can assist those of us who may be running afoul of microlaw, and they may on occasion make judgments about infractions.

For all concerned with the formulation and appraisal of individual responses and social policies that can contribute to a good life, microlegal arrangements cannot be overlooked.

I

Looking, Staring, and Glaring

*Eye engagement is like touch with its mystic and magnetic quali-
ties. As in touch, a spark seems to pass between two persons whose
eyes meet—sometimes a spark of recognition, sometimes one of love,
sometimes one of conflict.*
—Nancy M. Henley, *Body Politics: Power, Sex, and Nonverbal
Communication (1977)*

As I stand in a public place, scanning casually but looking at no
one for more than a moment, I become fascinated by a particular face. Without quite realizing it, I find that I am studying it
intently.[1] Subtly and imperceptibly, looking has modulated to
staring.[2] I have no interest in meeting the person I am looking at and do not want to expand the exchange in any way,
nor do I want to be looked at or studied in return.[3] My target senses my gaze and may ascribe to it an unsolicited sexual
message.[4] (There is no way to minimize the sexual element in
looking at others, which Freud characterized as "a component
of the sexual instinct," *Schaulust,* the delight of looking, or, in
its bizarre English rendition, "scoptophilia."[5] A latent sexual
element is present in all interaction, but, as we will see, it is
particularly significant, especially in our culture, in visual exchanges.)[6] The target almost always senses the staring.[7] That
prompts him (or her) to turn and look briefly at me. His eyes
meet mine, a contact that, if maintained, requires acknowledgment of each other as meetable individuals, so I and sometimes
both of us quickly avert our eyes.[8]

If we have averted our eyes, my target almost always looks

back as if to check out the sensation he had of being observed and to verify whether it is continuing. If I am staring back at him, I may wish our exchange to continue.[9] At this point, he may avert his eyes to reflect on his next move. If he does not keep them averted, he has signaled that an explicit exchange may occur.[10] That outcome may well terminate the silent visual exchanges; the encounter could then move toward verbal modes of communication, for which the looking performed an instrumental scouting function.[11] But if he keeps his eyes averted, he has signaled two things (depending, of course, on context and on any accompanying smile or frown or glare.). First and obviously, he has indicated that he does not want an exchange.[12] Second and more subtly, he has indicated that he does not want me to continue to look at him.[13]

At this point, I seem to be permitted one or two quick looks, apparently justified as a way to check whether I have read my target's reaction correctly. And so, like a squirrel hastily stuffing its cheeks with nuts, with the intention of scampering off to feast at a safe remove, I visually gulp in as much as I can and then stop looking.

Until now, the implicit norms of a generalized "looking" situation have been complied with.[14] An overly long and intent look at another, neither intended to be noted nor animated by a conscious wish for more contact with the target, was interpreted as an invitation to establish a broader exchange and was refused, all in a series of very rapid nonverbal moves. That overextended look was not an invitation, but in this context, the fiction retroactively disarms a stare and renders it socially innocuous. Without realizing it, our exchange, the likes of which may occur many times a day with different strangers, has affirmed a larger social norm that balances the need of human beings both to gather visual information about others and to preserve the exoself, the defensive perimeter of the self, from visual penetration or intervention.[15]

STARING AS UNLAWFUL LOOKING

But the encounter may not end here. The original looker may persist in looking or, having stopped, may resume looking. At this point, the character of the exchange modulates: it is no longer plausible for the target to characterize the looking as innocuous. It has become an unwelcome intervention, the invasion of the exoself of another for the gratification of the looker. Looking has unquestionably become staring.[16]

A look that has been protested can be retroactively rendered innocuous in a number of ways. A gentleman, in days past, might have lifted his hat to the lady or gentleman he stared at and then continued on his way. Lifting one's hat in that context is what we may call a "disarming" communication, akin to saying "sorry" when one bumps into another in a crowd.[17]

Some looking situations may have special disarming norms. Tourism, for example, is a transaction in which demand for various sensory experiences is supplied for a price. Tourists may be expected to pay a certain amount for the privilege not only of photographing but even of staring at a local citizen. In Khartoum, the capital of the Sudan, I witnessed a vivid instance of a demand for payment for such unauthorized looking. Two tourists were watching a man ride by on his donkey. When he saw that he was being looked at, he raised his stick in acknowledgment and salute. When the tourists continued to stare at him, he turned around, dismounted, and asked for money.

In some cases, even this sort of staring can be disarmed — with a verbal explanation, whose veracity is never put to the test. "I'm sorry I'm staring; you remind me of so-and-so"; "I'm certain I know you from somewhere," and so on. Excuses like these are implausible when there is a great divergence in the class or ethnic background of the parties, and it can be an irredeemably hackneyed line when a man says it to a woman. And disarming statements are not available when there is no common language.

The uncodified, reticulate network of norms governing looking and staring has certain affinities with the way people deal with the complex rules of games. Many individuals are uncomfortable with games, because they fear unpredictable outcomes or a loss of esteem and self-esteem following a defeat (a deprivation that can be viewed as catastrophic by the insecure). A person who is wary, if not fearful, of encounters with strangers in which the sexual potential is indeterminate may worry that even the initial eye play—looking that is permissible under the norms of the microlegal system—may be assigned a sexual message, so they may focus on the ground and rely on and become quite skilled in using peripheral vision. A journalist in New York, whose friends must think she loves concrete, writes, "I look at it so much, as we all learn to do, to avoid looking into people's eyes."[18] Another complex self-defense mechanism involves the use of sunglasses, including photosensitive lenses, which, whether warranted by brilliant sunshine or sensitive eyes or not, allow the wearer to stare but also provide an effective defense against looking. All of these are examples and props for what Erving Goffman called "civil inattention," those things that, though perceived, are not deemed to have been seen or heard.

The response of people who are unwillingly looked at is often a type of cultivated autism. Those being looked at may affect not to realize that they are under observation or may be shy and thus intently bury a nose in a book or study something else.[19] Women may have very good reasons to feign not to realize that they are under observation by strange men, and in uncertain circumstances it may often be the least costly response available to them. But people who inhabit different microlegal systems are puzzled and puzzling when they cross their normative frontier and encounter behavior that is appropriate in a situation but inexplicable to them. A farmer from North Dakota visiting New York City felt uncomfortable that people in the big city did not make eye contact or make small talk the way they do back home. "I was walking up Broadway and saying 'Hi' to people as I passed them," he said. "And some people looked back at me like, 'What are you, nuts? I don't know you.' "[20] Some such cross-cultural misunderstandings may reinforce other misunderstandings. The European pioneers' construct of the "shifty-eyed Indian" was, as we will see, a failure to understand Native American micronorms about looking.

Legal arrangements are purposive: they should facilitate human exchange. From the perspective of a person in a looking and staring encounter, as well as that of an observer studying the making and applying of looking and staring norms for their utility to social exchange, defensive responses, such as the cultivated autism mentioned above, may be viewed as undesirable social responses precisely because they impede fulfillment of one of the basic social functions of all the micronorms of looking: to permit the initial gathering of visual information by two people without committing themselves to further interaction.

Sanctions for Staring

Thus far we have teased out of a mundane and characteristically evanescent microsituation a normative system that characterizes some visual information gathering as lawful (I have referred to this activity as "looking") and some visual information gathering as unlawful ("staring").[21] When an intervention such as staring cannot be disarmed or otherwise rendered innocuous, it creates a crisis for the person being stared at, possibly for the starer as well, and for the microlegal system of looking and staring itself. The particular act of staring may not technically violate rules about looking. Some violations do not cause injury. In modern secular and nonformalistic legal systems, so-called technical violations of norms may be immaterial and can be ignored in that they do not impair the pertinent norm or the general perception of its continuing validity. Staring, even in a microlegal system, is different. Openly and brazenly violating the pertinent rule by staring puts into question the very existence of the microlegal system, thereby causing that special sense of distress and anxiety that people experience when their normative universe begins to crumble.[22]

One cannot speak of a legal system unless the distinction between licit and illicit behavior is supported by certain sanctions. If a microsystem contains no mechanisms for characterizing the violation (in this case, staring) as unlawful and for reinstating the sense of order that has been disturbed—in short, it has no sanctions—then to treat looking and staring norms as a legal system would be inaccurate in any save the most metaphorical sense. A legal system as such must provide for responses sufficiently forceful (1) to clearly characterize offending behavior as unlawful, (2) to confirm the norm in the face of its violation, and (3) to prevent, deter, correct, or effect whatever other sanctioning goals there may be.[23] In microlegal systems, these sanctions must be commensurately low-key and are often nonverbal. But they must be present and operating if we are to speak of law.[24]

There are two species of sanctions for staring offenses in microlegal settings. Nonverbal sanctions aim at terminating the staring with minimum disruption to the microsystem. They involve primarily silent protests by the target. In looking situations, these sanctions are initially visual communications from the target to the violator. Let us provisionally refer to such responses as "glaring" to distinguish them from "looking" and "staring."[25] Sometimes the grimace or look of distaste that a woman being stared at will flash across her face is enough to stop the staring. Since this is a comparatively aggressive response, many may be too timid to resort to it or may consider successful application of the sanction unlikely. Where glaring back is physically possible and socially feasible, the more timid target—woman or man—may still simply turn around. A woman may seek the arm of a male companion, implying that if the staring does not cease she will invoke his response. Or she may say to him, "That man is staring at me," and her companion may glare at the starer. Through such direct or vicarious means, the target protests the stare, with the expectation that it will cease.

The second species of sanction, verbalization—"Stop staring at me"; "Would you please stop staring at her"—is a substantial escalation, as is inevitable whenever the ambiguity of communication by behavior cedes to the comparative clarity of words. An informant recounted a case, part of her family lore, which involved such sanctions, though escalated. Her grandfather was traveling by train in the American West at the end of the nineteenth century. Apparently he had the curious habit of dozing off with his eyes open and fixed on some distant point. The point in this instance was the nose of the passenger sitting opposite him. After what we can assume were a few minutes of fruitless glaring at the staring sleeper, the man being stared at drew his revolver, pointed it at her grandfather's head, and said, "If you don't stop staring at me, I'm going to shoot you."

Nonverbal responses may be so subtle that the parties themselves are not aware of them at a level of overt consciousness; an exchange of looks permits starer and target to adjust their relationship without disruptive embarrassment precisely because looking may be accomplished without the need for operating in that state of overt consciousness in which words are the common coin of exchange. Verbalization is an escalation because it transforms ambiguous behavior, which is so woven into the situation that the actors themselves are often not aware of it, into something express and unequivocal. Verbalization, once used, precludes silent settlements that incorporate accommodations that need not be acknowledged nor, indeed, perceived. Verbalization has another important consequence. Because words may often involve other people who, until that moment, were not involved in the microsituation, they raise and expand the stakes. They may also increase the embarrassment of starer and target and leave a residue of unpleasantness in each for hours. Microlegal sanctions, when verbalized, are often like overly destructive and disproportionate reprisals in the law of armed conflict: lawful in inception and effective but more socially disruptive than would have been desired.

Nonverbal sanctions operate *within* a microsituation by reinstating the norms about defense of the self, permitting the pattern of social interaction to continue—minus the untoward staring. Verbalized sanctions, because of their overt character and comparatively high intensity, are responses *outside* the immediate microsystem of two people; although they often put a stop to the offending behavior, they are also likely to disrupt the microsituation and involve what the law calls third parties. If one posits a general community interest in facilitating or maintaining interaction, verbalized sanctions may be viewed as counterproductive, although there may be situations, as we will see in the fourth chapter, in which moral, developmental, or microlegislative advantages to disruptive sanctions may outweigh other social costs. But because the situations we are considering—chance encounters that may occur innumerable times each day—are fungible, no great social consequence follows from the termination of a single one. In this respect, these escalated sanctions in microsituations cannot be analogized to macrosocial situations, where the external sanction may either restore public order to a disturbed situation or precipitate greater disruption and even widespread deprivation of third parties. In looking, though not necessarily in other microsituations, the deployment of verbalized sanctions may cause collateral damage, creating awkwardness for others who may have been unaware of the improper staring and the subsequent visual exchanges that it engendered but without creating any corresponding benefit to the operation of the microlegal system.

THE SOCIAL DYNAMICS OF LOOKING

We now have some sense of the basic rules about looking at others. But before I generalize about microlegal systems, let me make some observations about the social and psychological dimensions of looking, for they condition legal arrangements at all levels.

A stranger, for purposes of our discussion, may be taken to mean someone we do not know, someone therefore about whom visual information will be a useful and in some circumstances indispensable preliminary to making decisions about whether to seek any association and, if so, how to go about it. Nothing would seem simpler than looking at strangers, yet there are, as we have already seen, many inconsistent cultural norms and social policies in this apparently mundane act. Many animals orient themselves by hearing or smelling, but we gain much of our information in face-to-face encounters by looking. Walter Benjamin observed that "the manner in which human sense perception is organized, the medium in which it is accomplished, is determined not only by nature but by historical circumstances as well."[26] The author J. P. Mayer, in his insightful *Sociology of Film*, surmises that the modern city dweller's sensorium is considerably more visual than that of his pre-urban counterpart;[27] for Marshall McLuhan, this assumption is a fundamental variable in accounting for changes in social structure and individual personality.[28]

Looking is important as a pre-engagement scouting activity, a type of intelligence gathering; the looker is able to acquire information from afar without having to acknowledge the existence of the target or to engage the target verbally. After a verbal exchange, extrication by ignoring the other is more difficult. In some circumstances, it could be viewed as an insult and could engender strife. Looking was almost certainly an important natural selection feature and continues to have some advantages over other long-distance and mid-distance sensory methods. Visual orientation at its most mundane is common sense; the folk wisdom is expressed in sayings like "Look before you leap," "Use your eyes," "Open your eyes," "Are you blind?" "Why do you think God put eyes in your head?" and so on. But that granted, looking is much more than a pragmatic activity. We also gain aesthetic and sensual pleasure from looking, and in many groups the human face and figure are considered objects of beauty, and looking at them is encouraged.

Where the looker's object is not an image but another person *in corpore*, looking becomes an important *social* activity, for the object also has eyes and knows that he or she is being observed.[29] This is not a light matter in our culture. In a curious and often disturbing essay, "The Struggle for Law," Rudolf von Jhering, the great German legal theoretician of the nineteenth century, observed that "property is but the periphery of my person extended to things."[30] The poet W. H. Auden, with his antic humor, put it best in his "Postscript" to "Prologue: The Birth of Architecture":

> Some thirty inches from my nose
> The frontier of my Person goes,
> And all the untilled air between
> Is private *pagus* or demesne.
> Stranger, unless with bedroom eyes
> I beckon you to fraternise,
> Beware of rudely crossing it:
> I have no gun, but I can spit.[31]

What I have called the exoself,[32] the external image of the self-system, that part of us that is ineluctably available to the eyes of others, is a psychocultural creation, a type of psychosocial carapace or integument.[33] As a personal creation, one of its functions is protective. "Each of us," wrote Martin Buber, "is encased in an armour whose task is to ward off signs."[34]

A person's image is necessarily an interactive construct, but in many ways the exoself is proprietary. The property notion is expressed in subtle ways, including the rules about how others may gather visual information. People may look, but they are expected to look at those parts that the owner of the exoself wants them to look at, at appropriate times and following certain procedures. Minimally polite behavior often dictates that others accept, at least publicly, the exoself as presented by its owner. In mass democracies, the politician's spouse—whether he or she, under relentless public glare, ingratiates aggressively or, like the late Pat Nixon, tries to protect a core of integrity behind a glazed smile—feels entitled to be taken at "face value." For all people, there are proper ways of looking at another's exoself, although the proper ways may vary according to culture, class, gender, and social function. Improper ways of looking may range from penetration through objectification to exploitation and may vary according to time and situation. What woman cannot attest to the difference between a look of respectful admiration and a leer or ogle?

But the exoself also comprises interactive elements, for in complex and contradictory ways, it[35] is at once the private property of the self and a public good, a *res communis*. The character and the appropriate normative regime for looking at an exoself are determined by many features of the context. The emotional experience distilled in Jhering's remark is one that most of us undergo. Beautiful people, as well as deformed people, whose psychic makeup does not include sufficient narcissism and exhibitionism suffer more than the rest of us, although only the scoptophobic find being looked at unbearable.

Our sensitivity to being looked at may be less intense with intimates, but even with them, there may be unspoken rules whose violation may be destructive. This seems to be what one of C. S. Lewis's characters means when he says, "Do you not know how bashful friendship is? Friends—comrades—do not look at each other. Friendship would be ashamed."[36] Lovers, too, whose tacit compact includes taking, allowing, and sharing delight in each other's physical beings, may resent being looked at in certain circumstances in certain ways or at certain times. That should occasion no surprise. Jude Colter asks: "Where else are we as vulnerable as we are during sex? We are naked, physically and spiritually, and there's an obligation to be sensitive to that vulnerability."[37] Violations of space by an intimate, whether made visually or physically—marital rape is an extreme example—are distinctively injurious.

Families are asymmetric settings for looking rules. Relatives, who are even less restrained than strangers, look at children without any of the restraints practiced when looking at others. This can be an excruciating experience for the children, the more so because they cannot effectively protest. Alas, children enjoy no reciprocal privilege. For them, tender years notwithstanding, unrestrained gathering of visual information is deemed uncouth. Children exhibiting a healthy curiosity often drift into absorbed staring; adults regularly admonish them not to stare. Adults who are targets may be initially amused by the immature violation, but not for long. As children grow older and try to construct for themselves the unexpressed code about gathering visual information, they may err on the other side and be rebuked for "sneaky" looking and "peeping" until they learn the appropriate balance and techniques.[38]

Amy Vanderbilt, whose work is a useful cache of micronorms, alerts her readers to subcultural variations. "Etiquette, too, is obviously geographically influenced. In cities thousands of families live under one roof, yet most never speak to one another on meeting. In the country not to speak to one's neighbor on encountering him would be very rude. In some parts of the South girls are quite accustomed to young men asking for late dates, a date—usually with an old beau—following one that may end at about eleven. Elsewhere such behavior might be considered questionable."[39] Her observation applies to looking and staring, not only through space and time, but in terms of culture, class, and gender as well. There are subcultures where the general norms considered above[40] are inverted: long and lingering eye contact is considered courteous; aversion of the eyes, rude.

An interesting example of the implicit restraints on looking in situations of comparative intimacy is offered by Scandinavian practices of eye contact. Earlier, when courtship had to be conducted under close supervision or in public, courting couples could be distinguished by a distinctive pattern of looking into each other's eyes. In the Nordiske Museet, the Swedish Museum of Ethnology, the section on courtship is composed largely of photographs of this stylized looking, and some of the scholars surveyed in the endnotes have observed the greater eye contact of those with affectionate attachment. In some of the Nordiske Museet pictures, eye contact and body posture are so distinctive that plainly, one of the functions of looking is to show onlookers that the lookers are a courting couple.

In noncourting situations, otherwise unacceptable eye contact is permitted in the Scandinavian countries in the practice of "skoaling," or toasting, which can involve a direct and intimate male-female visual exchange. The norms regulating skoaling are complex and vary with the size of the group, among other things. The skoaler lifts a glass, addresses the skoalee by name, often gravely, and is acknowledged with eye contact and a warm smile. Eye contact is held for an instant, then the skoalee lifts his or her glass and drinks; the skoalee drinks at the same time. The skoalee puts down the glass, acknowledges the toast with a brief nod, breaks eye contact, whereupon the skoaler puts down his or her glass. Direct eye contact that lasts too long is a basic violation of the norms of skoaling. Informants explain that this causes embarrassment to both the skoalee and other diners. Two options are available to the offended skoalee: breaking the stare by drinking and thus concluding the toast, a response that does not disrupt the gathering but which in some contexts may have a certain sanction potential. A second, more overtly sanctioning response is glaring.

In Cassadaga, Florida, a spiritualist village that I observed,[41] increased eye contact is not delictual; instead, it appears to be a bland and noninquisitive looking, passive rather than aggressive, concerned more with conveying polymorphous affection, openness, and tranquillity than with gathering information.

In some encounter groups or environments where explicit, vigorous, and sometimes aggressive exploration of the self and others is the norm, more eye contact will be tolerated, although certain types of restrictions may still operate.[42] But the permissive norms do not travel. Members of the group who meet outside the group will comply with the more restrictive norms of the larger society.

The license to stare is a function of power. In an exchange between a man and a woman, the superordinate—generally the man—stares without restraint; the subordinate perforce lowers her eyes. In an account of racial superordination, Patricia Willaims considers the taken-for-granted right of whites to stare at blacks: "I decided to go on a walking tour of Harlem. The tour . . . except for myself, was attended exclusively by young, urban, professional real estate speculators. . . . The guide asked the group if they wanted to 'go inside some churches.' The guide added, '. . . We'll probably get to see some services going on. . . . Easter Sunday in Harlem is quite a show.' . . . What astonished me was that no one had asked the people in the churches if they minded being stared at like living museums. I wondered what would happen if a group of blue-jeaned blacks were to walk uninvited into a synagogue on Passover or St. Anthony's of Padua in the middle of High Mass."[43]

This generic looking situation has also been studied in terms of respect and affection. Albert Mehnabian correlated eye contact with the attitude toward the person visually addressed. He found that eye contact is "lowest for intensely disliked addressees, increases to maximum value for neutral addressees and diminishes slightly to a moderately high value for intensely liked addressees."[44] Disrespect can also be expressed by bolder looking, even leering, or completely ignoring the other person.

People are sensitive to being looked at by strangers, perhaps because personal experience so dictates, perhaps because our culture teaches us to be wary of strangers, perhaps because the child's profound fear of the stranger persists, perhaps because there are phylogenetic reasons.[45] To some degree, everyone is sensitive to being looked at. In our civilization, this sensitivity may be an aspect of psychopersonal organization linked to a society and an economy that encourage individuation. Formal authority prohibits certain types of "peeping," or unauthorized looking. It may enjoin photographing people in certain circumstances and may even allow tort suits or criminal actions against paparazzi for some violations of looking restraints. But precisely because of the cultural and policy antinomies that we have considered, the code will be ambiguous, in part contradictory.[46]

Eye contact plays an important, ineluctable, and distinctive role in the repertory of face-to-face communication techniques, yet there is, as we have seen, a uniquely explosive potential to the gathering of information visually. Whether or not, in Leibniz's lapidary phrase, "the eyes are the windows of the soul," key phases in sexual invitation and the initiation of courtship are effectuated in many circles by looks rather than by words.[47] In some stratified societies, including societies that stratify according to gender, looking may signal equality or dominance; looking away or lowering the eyes may signal deference or appeasement.[48] The meaning of a refusal to look at someone who is talking to you may vary with context, sometimes signaling deference, sometimes insult, sometimes asserting the worthlessness of the other person or even a denial of his or her existence.[49]

Two vivid examples show this. William Fields has remarked that most Native Americans consider it rude to look someone directly in the eyes. In exchanges with the dominant culture, in which eye contact indicates candor and earnestness, the Native American practice was interpreted in terms of "white" or "Anglo" perspectives, which completely mischaracterized it—hence the derogatory stereotype of the "shifty-eyed Indian."[50]

Conversely, the virtual banishment of a person from a microlegal situation of looking is a powerful verdict of what French law calls civil death. Yoram Binur, an Israeli journalist who disguised himself as a Palestinian Arab in order to test Israeli attitudes and behavior toward Arabs, recounts an experience from when he worked as a dishwasher at the Hatuki Cafe in Tel Aviv.

There was one night at Hatuki that brought home most strongly all the feeling of frustration and humiliation that I had experienced as an Arab worker. Ofra's sister, Michal, had a boyfriend, a handsome man with an athletic build, who used to come to the pub during work hours in order to help out or just sit over a drink in his girlfriend's company.

It was about two in the morning and most of the customers had already gone. I was in the kitchen washing dishes and returning leftovers to the refrigerator so they could be recycled the following day, when Michal and her boyfriend, laughing excitedly, pushed their way into the kitchen—which hardly had enough room for one man alone to move around in. They squeezed themselves into a small corner between me and the refrigerator and proceeded to kiss each other passionately.

I lowered my eyes and concentrated on washing the dirty dishes in the sink, carefully going over each plate, so I wouldn't embarrass them with my presence. The breathing got heavier as they got bolder, and for a fleeting moment I thought I might as well enjoy the little scene that had come my way. I ventured a peek at them out of the corner of my eye.

Then a sort of trembling suddenly came over

me. I realized that they had not meant to put on a peep show for my enjoyment. Those two were not the least bit concerned with what I saw or felt even when they were practically fucking under my nose. For them I simply didn't exist. I was invisible, a nonentity! It's difficult to describe the feeling of extreme humiliation which I experienced. Looking back, I think it was the most degrading moment I had during my entire posing adventure.[51]

Depending on the context, eye communication can convey explicit content and also secondary or metacommunicative information. When strangers look at each other in nonroutinized situations, there is considerable possibility for misinterpretation. These considerations can hardly outweigh the need to gather information visually. Indeed, visual information may be even more urgent where routine is absent. But gathering it can introduce special complexities and even hazards to participants in the looking exchange. In routinized situations, in contrast, only gross departures from the norms will require fresh and potentially hazardous interpretation.

Because of these antinomies, the general normative regime for looking and the characterization of certain visual techniques in certain circumstances as unlawful is necessarily complex. Microlaw here must balance the social benefits gained from visual observation against the social benefit of protection of the self. The challenge to the normative regime is further complicated when distinct codes, each of which assigns a different value to one interest or the other, are often being applied to the situation.

The Microlegal System That Regulates Looking

This discussion of looking, staring, and glaring has brought us to the point where we may essay some generalizations about law in microsocial settings.

In a microsituation, a very small group of people have the opportunity to interact as a result of their social, if not physical, proximity (they may be proximate telephonically or sequentially by mail or in cyberspace). Physical proximity is an important, though not indispensable, variable for these situations, for it permits multiple opportunities for nonverbal communications and misunderstandings about them. Like every other social situation, mundane microsituations—even those with only two actors and of the shortest duration—have the complex and significant normative components that are characteristic of law in its conventional usage:

1. expectations, shared by the people in the situation, that in that situation, there is a "right" way of acting, a "norm";
2. expectations that defections from the "right" way will lead to a shared judgment that the defection was "wrong"; and
3. expectations that the injured party is authorized to undertake certain responses that may hurt or sanction the offending actor but at the very least must reaffirm the norm that has been violated.

We may speak here of a legal *system* because we are encountering more than those imprecise yearnings, the innumerable "you oughts" and "you shoulds" that we hear and ignore every day. There is a rulelike formulation—a "do this" or "don't do that" statement—but such statements are common in ordinary discourse. What distinguishes a microlegal system from conversation is that it has an attendant set of expectations about proper subjective and objective responses to norm violation, intimating some sort of system for enforcing the norm. And there is enough of an expectation that those norms are effective to sustain belief in them as effective norms through time.

Very complex microlegal systems are found embedded in language reflecting and reinforcing policies about relations between classes, castes, and genders. There are microlegal systems about looking at people, touching them accidentally, standing in line, laughing in public, talking, and so on. Wherever microlegal systems occur, they are important as much for their obvious function in microsituations as for their contribution to more general systems of community order. Some of what Amy Vanderbilt means by etiquette is microlaw. "The word 'etiquette' for all the things I have tried to discuss is really inadequate, yet no other will do. It covers much more than 'manners,' the way in which we *do* things. It is considerably more than a treatise on a code of social behavior. . . . we must all learn the socially acceptable ways of living with others in no matter what society we move. Even in primitive societies there are such rules, some of them as complex and inexplicable as many of our own. Their original *raison d'être* or purpose is lost, but their acceptance is still unquestioned."[52] In response to her own question "Who needs a book of etiquette?" she answered, "Everyone does."

Amy Vanderbilt is right about etiquette and microlaw. Alas, no code book can cover every contingency. No current etiquette handbook codifies the microlaw of the many different strata and groups an individual is likely to encounter in a mass and heterogeneous society.[53] Even with such a handbook, some social situations will seem so novel to the actors in them that even if they are intuitively aware of the importance of micronorms, they will be uncertain about the appropriate norms in that setting and how they are to be applied. Novelty is not to be confused with unusual or even exotic settings. What makes a situation novel is the uncertainty about the norms that govern it. Stanley and Livingstone could meet in the bush and interact without introduction as naturally as they might bump into each other in the Atheneum Club in London, whereas a white and a black may cross paths daily in a New York subway station yet be unable to establish an easy pattern of interaction. The character of novelty can be introduced by variations in or uncertainties about identity, class, gender, culture, or language, the nature or purpose of the encounter, its location, and so on.

Anthropologists, by profession, venture into settings in which they do not know the norms. We all can recall acute "anthropological" moments when we realized that the others in a situation could not know how we expected them to act, while we were uncertain about how they expected us to behave. Sometimes the stakes are low, but in some instances the possibilities of misunderstanding can disrupt the encounter or even lead to violence. When there is uncertainty about norms appropriate for the situation or the suspicion that there are no common norms, the situation will not be disrupted if the parties seek jointly or in parallel fashion to prescribe or make law. Would extending the right hand be viewed as a proffer of friendship based on equality, or would it be viewed as hostile or insulting? Would reciprocating a bow seem respectful, obsequious, ludicrous, or mocking? If there is no common language and no mediator, each of us must seek to determine appropriate norms by tentative analogy from similar situations or by the complex process of nonverbal claim and deference that accompanies the more manifest exchanges. In the situation I have described, isn't that exactly what happens? We move tentatively, watching face and body movements for clues or confirmation that we are doing the appropriate things. These exchanges have a certain play aspect, and, as we saw earlier, personalities too insecure to risk even the minor losses in games or the possible reductions in respect may find it extremely difficult to interact under conditions of increased uncertainty. For people willing to take chances generally, at least in bounded situations, these opportunities may be exhilarating.

Failure to successfully identify or prescribe norms appropriate for the situation will result in what may be objectively described as anomie but is subjectively experienced as awkwardness or loss of balance. That feeling can impede interaction or further ostensible noninteraction, as when two people pretend to ignore each other in an exquisitely reciprocal civil inattention. Both of these outcomes may be deemed socially undesirable, for we may assume a general interest in modern secular societies in facilitating exchanges.

To reiterate: the distinguishing feature of a legal norm is not words in an "ought" formula. The feature of a legal norm that distinguishes it from all the depreciated "you oughts" and "you shoulds" of daily conversation is its *sanction,* a communication accompanying the ought that indicates that the speaker or the community, through some specialized agent, is willing to invest something of value to see that the norm is followed. The investment is the cost necessary to punish or deprive the deviator or to reward the conformer. Rewards may be no more than symbolic approval or disapproval, or they may be substantial—money, time, life—given, withheld, or taken away. Often sanctions are woven into a social situation with an instinctive cunning, and work without those subjected to them appreciating what is happening.

Consider interviewing, which takes place in a hierarchical and manipulative microlegal system in research, business and law, and many informal settings. In a manual of interviewing, Stephen Richardson, Barbara Dohrenwend, and David Klein note that some interviewers use social pressure "directly and

forcefully." "One method is to urge the respondent to participate by classifying him with a group which he respects. This
approach is embodied in such statements as 'I have been interviewing a number of leading citizens and, to complete my study,
I should like to ask you . . .' or (to a physician respondent) 'I am
interviewing all members of the county medical society, and I'd
like . . .' Such an approach exploits the desire of the respondent
to conform to the behavior of others in the reference group or,
conversely, his reluctance to refuse to participate in an activity
which the reference group apparently endorses or approves."[54]

For our purposes, it is important to note that these contingent "social pressure" communications function as sanctions.
Where normative communications are also accompanied by
indications that they are authoritative or that those issuing
them have authority to do so, they may properly be called legal
norms. But such norms, though an indispensable part of law,
are not synonymous with law. The distinguishing feature and
sine qua non of a norm that is law is that it is deemed of sufficient importance for someone to expend personal effort and
social resources to ensure that the behavior of others will conform to it. The effort and resources need not be sufficient to win
full or even partial compliance in every instance of infraction.
They need only be enough to sustain the expectation support-
ing the norm as law.

Microsituations are governed by microlaw and must have
sanctions, although they may be "microsanctions." In the introduction to this book, I considered the jurisprudential significance of trivial sanctions. Students of customary law at the
international or subnational level appreciate that behavior embedded in a situation and stimulated by nothing more considered or profound than some sense of irritation may function
situationally as a sanction. Take a simple example: If X fails to
play by the rules in a two-person game and Y, out of a sense

of indignation, disrupts the game by withdrawing, Y's behavior has sanctioned X. It has deprived X, and, more important, it has affirmed the norm that has been violated. Conversely, Y's failure to leave, in addition to permitting the game to continue, might have resulted in termination, erosion, or modification of the norm that X violated.

Neither explicit motive nor consciousness that sanctioner and target are playing those roles is a requisite characteristic or property of a sanction. Actors in microlegal systems are, as we have seen, usually unaware of the legal quality of the experience and oblivious to their own functional roles as decisionmakers or sanctioners. They view their own behavior, insofar as they are overtly conscious of it, as an expression of irritation or indignation or as an act of personal defense. They would hardly see themselves as having been deputized *pro hac vice*, as lawyers would grandly put it, to sanction a lawless starer. Nonetheless, their responses may be sanctions, for here, as in all macrolegal arrangements, it is the *systemic* effect rather than the motive or even consciousness of actors that renders their reactions a sanction. In the result, microlegal norms have microenforcers, whose ranks include, potentially, each and every one of us in the myriad ephemeral microsituations that we live through each day.

Routine situations may have distinct, though unverbalized, norms. If you are a member of a group, which means you have been acculturated to its basic postulates, you know the norms and even the norms about norm making. "I may be doing something wrong," says a character, a solicitor by profession, in one of George Bernard Shaw's plays. "But I'm doing it in the right and proper way." Hence we can extend the postulates to new situations by a type of generative and analogizing logic. If we do not know the micronorms of the situation, the usual method of learning them is by trial and error. We must learn the new norm through what may be to some an exhilarating experiment, to others a task. Still others experience it as a series of embarrassing and even socially paralyzing failures.

When outsiders enter a group with a distinct microlegal system, it takes them time to learn the rules. Until then, the social transient is like a child, without, unfortunately, the limited tolerance allowed to children. And in a cruel correspondence, ignorance of microlaw may synergize with other fears of the stranger, confirming in-group members' conviction that outsiders are uncivil, if not crude and barbarous. Recall the Euro-Americans' derogatory perception of Native Americans as shifty-eyed Indians.

In fleeting, nonroutinized interactions, norms may be established in a tentative manner but then fade as the interaction ends. In more routinized fleeting interactions, such as looking or waiting in line, the norms are known and to some extent have been refined by the experience of the members of a more inclusive group. Although these interactions may seem trivial and the sanctions evanescent, even unreal, the situations have occurred often enough for the observer to assume that both the norm and the response are consistent with and expressive of more general social values. Curiosity and further investigation may be warranted if they are not, for the discrepancy could be important. Components of a social system that impede the realization of its larger social values and goals should be viewed — as I will suggest in the fourth chapter — at least provisionally as counterproductive arrangements that should be changed.

A Tentative Code of Looking

Because looking norms vary with culture, it would be a formidable task to try to establish a universal concordance. Indeed, as we have seen, even within a single system, significant variations may occur because of differences in culture, class, gender, and crisis exposure. But with these caveats, let me essay an articulation of the general substantive looking and staring rules in the United States, based on the material we have considered.

The basic norm is that short-term looking is permissible, but staring is not. The temporal length of a permissible look does not vary contextually as much as one might expect. There are, however, a number of very important exceptions.

1. *Professional "stareables."* In American society, certain classes of people, including actors, politicians, dancers, athletes, and musicians, intentionally place themselves in the public eye with the expectation and, indeed, demand that they be stared at while they are performing. The performance may in fact be no more than a prop for staring opportunities. The public pays for the privilege of staring at them with an intensity and penetration and for a duration that would otherwise flout the general micronorm.

Whether members of this group can be stared at outside the structured atelier of performance is controversial. Fans seem to feel that, in return for their loyalty, they are entitled to stare at their idols anywhere that they or their proxies—journalists, paparazzi—can find them. Many stars or would-be-stars cultivate this adulation; they may retain specialists to arrange appropriate photo opportunities. Others complain about the lack of privacy. The institutions of formal legal decision establish a special standard for "public figures"—the "cafe society," as C. Wright Mills called them.[55] Public figures are assumed to have struck a Faustian bargain, bartering their privacy for the ecstasies of fame or notoriety and the accompanying cascade of material indulgences. Politicians are members of this particular group of stareables, as, it would appear, are their spouses and children.

Yet there are some interesting limits on staring at stareables.

One may stare without restraint at all parts of the exoself of such stareables as dancers and strippers. Although it is permissible to stare boldly and intently at the exposed groin of a nude disco dancer—that is, after all, the point of that looking transaction—comparable staring at a politician's exoself is impermissible.

2. *Intermittent stareables.* Nonprofessional stareables, people who are momentarily in the public eye, become stareable as long as they are discharging a public function. But the duration and focus of the staring are micronormatively limited. If I lecture in class or rise to speak at a Parent-Teacher Association meeting, the ordinary primary rules of looking are suspended, and those present may stare at me as long as I am speaking. The moment I stop speaking, the ordinary looking rules come back into operation, and the intense observation that was lawful an instant before now becomes unlawful. At a panel discussion, likewise, the audience may stare at a panelist who is speaking, but must be restrained in looking at the panelists who are not speaking, arrayed though they are in front of a roomful of people.

In some social strata, women may fall into this group of intermittent stareables, unless some specific attribute, such as age or wealth or association with power, mitigates their unequal social status or gives them a vicarious one. Visual abuse of women, especially women unaccompanied by men, may be due to an expectation on the part of the starer that they will not glare, either because of timidity or fear or the cultural idea or knowledge derived from experience that glaring would be ineffective.

3. *Children.* Young children accompanied by adults may be stared at, but a special species of smile must be exchanged with the accompanying adult in the course of the staring to render it innocuous. The children themselves cannot glare, and if they are unaccompanied by an adult, they can be subjected to staring

with impunity. But when they are accompanied, the presence of an adult conversant with and capable of applying the microsanctions makes them partial beneficiaries of the adult standard.

4. *People with infirmities.* Malformed or retarded children accompanied by adults may not be stared at. Indeed, they are not even looked at but are part of that tragic category of social invisibles. If unaccompanied, the same children or malformed or retarded adults are usually unable to fend for themselves by effective glaring and hence are likely be the targets of stares. Each of these exceptions demonstrates the relevance of an expected effective sanction to compliance with a rule and, over time, its content.

5. *Foreigners.* Foreigners, including people from other castes and social strata, may be stared at, but they will be treated as social invisibles if they seem in some way ominous or threatening. Who knows whether that tough and dangerous-looking kid sitting on the subway and presumably from the slums may conclude that a brief look, permissible by the general code, amounts to "dissing." Because foreigners may not know local looking rules and may not content themselves with a glare, it is prudent to pretend not to see them at all.

Every micronorm can be influenced by variables such as class, age, and culture. But looking norms appear to be particularly sensitive to gender and may require adjustments if account is taken of that variable. How we feel we are obliged to look at others can depend on whether the visual exchanges are between male and male, male and female, female and male, or female and female.

The Importance of Context

It is hardly a matter of surprise that the *content* of looking norms may vary widely in different microsocial situations within a particular community. Perhaps more interesting is that individuals readily adapt to the different looking norms as they move from situation to situation in the course of a day, from visual exchanges with a lover, to encounters at the elevator,[56] to visual orientation in other public transportation among strangers,[57] to visual exchanges in the office setting where an assertive bonhomie conceals a complex stratification system with caste-like elements,[58] to aggressive business encounters in which bold eye contact may be cultivated less for information gathering than as a metacommunication of candor, control, decisiveness, and self-assurance, to a cocktail party among peers at a business convention, replete with lapel tags announcing "My name is ———," where all micronorms seem to facilitate rapid and superficial contact with strangers, and on and on. That an individual knows and can operate with diverse micronorms about looking is no more cause for comment than the fact that the mature speaker of a highly stratified society's language, let us say Japanese or Persian, knows the terms and body language appropriate for exchanges with peers as well as with people at many different levels of superordination and subordination.

The extreme variety of the different norms in these and hundreds of other distinguishable situations does not mean that some are right and some are dysfunctional. There is no absolute or Platonic content to a looking norm. Looking norms are instrumental; the basic question is whether their content and systemic operation adequately fulfill the immediate objectives of an encounter, are consonant with general cultural values, and conform in their effects to certain transcultural standards concerned with protecting the integrity and dignity of the person.

(I will take up this question in the fourth chapter.) Norms of widely varying content may be appropriate in widely varying contexts. Transposed to other contexts, those norms will impede the fulfillment of the purposes of the exchange and the realization of more general social values.

2

Standing in Line and Cutting In

We stand in line until our hearts break.

—Sign carried in a Polish demonstration (*Time*, 10 August 1981)

Whether people are waiting for a bus, tickets to a show, a turn to vote, a table in a crowded restaurant, sacramental communion with God, a few moments in a public toilet, even a turn in the gas chamber or a Swedish or Japanese visa to avert that fate,[1] they tend to line up. When a resource is scarce and aggregate demand cannot be met simultaneously nor the resource divided up, they seem to queue.[2] This chapter focuses on the microlegal system of the archetypical queue: persons standing in an approximation of an actual line, in the order of their arrival, for the primary purpose of receiving some distribution of goods or services.[3] Terminology for the phenomenon varies. Americans "stand in line," except for New Yorkers, who "stand on line"; the British "queue up."[4]

A queue is a linear community with some unique, even peculiar features. Whether the queue is apparently spontaneous or has been explicitly signaled, its common characteristic is that it has no manifest decision structure. That does not mean that there is no such structure. In many organizations that lack institutionalized law-making and law-applying procedures, norms can still be efficiently established, modified, and changed, characterizations of behavior in terms of the norms can be made, and sanctions can be meted out. All of these can be done without formalities and, in some cases, without the participants even appreciating that they are making and applying law, indeed, that there is law.[5]

Queues would appear to stretch the conception of microlegal systems for a number of reasons. Queues do not seem to be groups in even the broad sense in which the term has been used for microlegal analysis. Queue members do not face each other. They do not interidentify through a leader or a communicator, as do the members of a dispersed radio or television audience, creating a group identification through a highly refracted and intense common focus. Each queue member sees the people immediately in front and behind.[6] Yet even without face-to-face contact, queue members know they are part of a tapewormlike organism.

Some contemporary equivalents of the archetypal queue perform the distribution function but lack the serial, spatial organization. In a "number queue," for example, an authorized steward or a machine serving as the steward's functional equivalent distributes numbers sequentially, and the number holders are then called in numerical order.[7] There are also "sitting queues." In many waiting rooms, people do not stand in a line and confirm their relative place by their location but sit at random and hence must recall their own queue positions relative to their competitors'.[8] There are "mail queues," whose members are informed of their place by letter. There are transportation queues: In airports, planes line up for their turn to take off. In the air above them, planes circle and wait their turn to land.[9] Ships line up in busy ports, and cars queue for the privilege of paying a toll and crossing a bridge. There are also "automated queues." In the Netherlands, for example, callers are told, by recording, their place in a queue whose members, perhaps scattered throughout the country, are waiting for telephone assistance. In the United States telephone queuers are not told their place; a recorded voice states soothingly at programmed intervals that "your call is important to us."

Some very ancient civilizations apparently developed queues. The steles at Persepolis portray kings and chiefs lining up to present tribute to the King of Kings, and one would speculate on similar spatial arrangements for, say, maize distribution in the Incan civilization. But the aesthetic factor should never be excluded from the catalogue of potential reasons explaining why human beings organize themselves or are organized in a particular way, especially in visual artistic renditions. Some people may have enjoyed seeing others in lines, as they still may. Ancient Egyptians, who appear to have used lines for distribution, also used linearization of objects in graphic art and hieroglyphics. Yet some of the ancient examples were of mechanisms used exclusively for distribution and are thus wholly consistent with the modern queue phenomenon.

Other queues may be spatially and sequentially organized but are not queues in the contemporary meaning of the term, for they lack the distribution function as their raison d'être. The animal world provides many examples of apparently spontaneous spatial arrangements that look like queues, from lines of ants to the celebrated tree trunk stratification of howler and rhesus monkeys. Salmon in the Pacific Northwest swimming upstream to spawn have been described as waiting in line.[10] In the human world, there are many examples of people who are spatially staggered but constitute a queue only in a figurative sense: slaves shackled together, workers pulling a hawser, and so on. We are concerned here with the more conventional distributional queue: a social organization with a unique microlegal system formed when people literally stand in line.

In the previous chapter, I used the word "microsituation" to mean a very small group of people who, as a result of social, if not physical, proximity, have the opportunity to interact. Like most other social situations, even the most mundane micro-situations — indeed, a situation with only two actors and of exceedingly short duration — can have the complex and significant normative components that are characteristic of law in its conventional usage.

Law, as we have seen, does not require special organs or expressly articulated codes. The normative components of micro-legal systems are strands of intertwined expectations shared by the people in the situation. The expectations are, first, a belief that under the circumstances, there is a "right" way of acting; second, the idea that defections from that "right" way will lead to a common response among members of the microsituation that the defection was "wrong"; and, third, a consensus that authorizes the injured party to respond in a way (otherwise impermissible) that may hurt or sanction the offending actor but, at the very least, will reaffirm the norm that was violated.

To refer to these microsystems as authentic legal systems is appropriate, as we have seen, because, for all of their evanescence and informality, there are rules and an attendant set of expectations about proper subjective and objective responses to norm violation, intimating some sort of system for enforcing the norm. Enforcement is significant: without an expectation of enforcement, microlaw devolves into nothing more than a synonym for the tiresome flow of "you oughts" and "you shoulds" of daily conversation. Enforcement, however, does not require formal control by an authority; sanctions may be embedded in the situation and may be no more than symbolic approval or disapproval of something substantial, like money or time.

Complex microlegal systems are found embedded in languages reflecting and enforcing policies about relations between and within classes, castes, and genders. There are microlegal systems about the way people look at each other (the subject of the previous chapter), the way they touch each other accidentally, laugh, act as audiences, and stand in line.[11] These microlegal systems are the building blocks of a society, though not of its macrolegal system.

Like other evanescent microlegal systems, queues involve complex normative systems, but queues are particularly interesting because of their informal yet recurring ways of ruling on lawful exceptions and imposing microsanctions. Without these processes, queues could not operate. In light of the indispensability of queuing to distribution in mass societies, public order requires that queues have appropriate microlegal systems.

CULTURAL, SOCIAL, AND ECONOMIC FACTORS IN QUEUING

Queues are frequently the butt of popular criticism, as the epigraph to this essay indicates. As with many other problems of social and personal organization, Americans tend to assume that other states and economic systems suffer from queues more than they do. Western observers of socialist countries frequently reported on the prevalence of queues there for the most basic items and suggested, often with a certain air of superiority, that queues were a humiliating, onerous product of those social and economic systems.[12] Hedrick Smith, a keen and always entertaining observer of the former Soviet Union, made the following report.

> The accepted norm is that the Soviet woman daily spends two hours in line, seven days a week, daily going through double the gauntlet that the American housewife undergoes at her supermarket once, maybe twice a week. I noted in the Soviet press that Russians spend 30 billion man-hours in line annu-

ally just to make purchases. That does not count several billion more man-hours expended waiting in tailor shops, barbershops, post offices, savings banks, dry cleaners and various receiving points for turning in empty bottles and so on. But 30 billion man-hours alone is enough to keep 15 million workers busy year-round on a 40-hour week. . . .

. . . Lines can run from a few yards long to half a block to nearly a mile, and usually they move at an excruciating creep. Some friends of ours, living in the southwest part of Moscow, watched and photographed a line that lasted two solid days and nights, four abreast and running all through an apartment development. They guessed there were 10,000–15,000 people, signing up to buy rugs, an opportunity that came only once a year in that entire section of Moscow.[13]

In a popular poem, "A Chorus of Nymphs," Andrei Voznesensky wrote:

I'm 41st in line for Plisetskaya,
26th for plaid blankets from Czechoslovakia,
30th for a ticket to the Taganka,
35th for a place in Vagankovo Cemetery,
whoever wants to see the Madonna sign up
at Seaport Hall hey, you with the kid,
you weren't in line before!
Whoever was ninth goes back to tenth,
Rimskaya becomes Korsakova,
I'm 16th at the optician's,
and 75th for Glazunov,
110th for an abortion
(not pregnant now, but ready when my turn comes).

You with the kid, you weren't here before,
47th for spare car parts
(they signed me up at birth).
No. 1000 for a new car
(signed up before birth).[14]

Yet if an American traveler examines the United States with
the eager, open eyes of the tourist abroad, he or she is likely to
discover a comparable prevalence of queues with many functional equivalents: the two-hour lines at the White House, the
half-hour lines at movies and theaters, the lines for buses, and
so on.[15] When publicly financed apartments become available
and when restrictive guild-type trade unions open for a limited number of new candidates, people in the United States are
willing to queue for days. The *New York Times* has editorially
lamented indigenous and mundane queue situations that, some
years ago, would have seemed quintessentially Eastern European or socialist:

> One of the great myths about New York is that
> it's big enough to be spontaneous. There's a sub-
> way at the corner. Broadway's dazzle is just a short
> ride away. Restaurants and street life abound. The
> opera doesn't come for a one-week stand; two of
> them live here. This is not Kansas City.
>
> And yet . . . the shows are downtown all right,
> but you have to get your tickets weeks, months in
> advance. Want to go to the U.S. Open to watch
> tennis? Too late. Bad luck. There are, of course, un-
> sold bargain tickets to Broadway shows available in
> Times Square, but you'll have to wait a few hours
> in line to buy one. That's what New York is really
> all about: not spontaneity but lines.
>
> Consider the city's banks. They invested heavily

in money machines, open day and night, to allow customers to avoid the lines during bankers' hours. Look at some of the machines now. The wait at some is a half-hour long and 20 people deep. Not so long ago it was fairly easy to get to work in Manhattan in a half hour from anywhere in the boroughs. Some days now it takes that long to buy a ticket.[16]

Plainly, the queue is not a pathology unique to socialism but is a distribution phenomenon characteristic of complex mass civilizations that require plans to distribute things. The spatial arrangement of queues also means that they are part of the complex "linearization" that cultures becoming civilizations seem ordained to undergo.[17] For it is clear that queuers must think in terms of linear time and space to participate in this type of organization.

Some contrivances, though human made, we still assume to be "as eternal as air and water," as Jorge Luis Borges said of his beloved Buenos Aires. As with arrangements in other parts of our lives that seem indispensable and inevitable, the very prevalence of queues makes them seem to be what the Russian-American jurisprudential theorist Nikolai Timasheff called "natural uniformities": social arrangements that do not result from either imitation or enforcement but seem to take place naturally.[18] But the fact that queues seem peaceful and queuers seem to accept violations of queue norms with comparative equanimity should not mislead the observer. Queues are not natural.

Any behavior that requires the deferral of satisfaction when the means for gratification are so tantalizingly close at hand cannot be deemed natural.[19] At some level of consciousness, there is in every queuer a nucleus of fury at having to wait.

When others openly violate the norms of the queue, that fury can grow intense and malignant. The shootings that took place at gas station queues during the 1973–74 petroleum shortage are an extreme example. And anyone can call to mind the innumerable times that people grumble, jostle, and argue in the mundane queues of life. Such latent dissatisfaction should neither surprise nor disquiet. When people queue patiently for a public toilet, despite the pain and potential for public humiliation, when even young children queue in fire or air raid drills or, more remarkably, in the actual calamities, when people queue for bread during shelling, as they did in Sarajevo, when people queue for anything, we are encountering a learned behavior that imports both the rules of a complex society and, on the personal psychological level, powerful internalized control mechanisms.

We are trained to queue from an early age. Learning to stand in line is an important part of preschool and early-grade curriculum. Consider one example: "Rather than promoting early reading, for instance, the program tries to give the children experiences that will make them more likely to succeed when they encounter normal first-grade work. Often this means socializing the youngsters, teaching them to be part of a group. The need for such training could be seen last fall when the children were asked to wait in line. Many did not know what was meant by 'waiting in line.' The teacher knotted a rope every foot and a half and asked the children to hold onto the knots, keeping the rope straight between them. Soon they could form a line without the rope."[20]

One consequence of this early training is the inculcation of both queue behavior and, as we shall see, queue ethics.[21] Other latent and ancillary objectives may also be realized in these types of queue instruction: self-discipline, reinforcement of the social need to be able to defer gratification, and so on. Sometimes these may be the educators' primary objectives, with queue training being only a learning tool. Close-order drill in military training, for example, is ostensibly aimed at refining a method of moving large numbers of people through space as rapidly and in as organized a way as possible. That is manifestly necessary for infantry. But close-order drill in, say, the air force would likely be more concerned with inculcating immediate and full obedience to orders. Whatever the manifest objective, exercises like these reinforce queuing norms.

Through socialization, queuing may become the style of a civilization, the normal way people arrange themselves and others in space. In the same way that we speak generally of national styles of accent and information, of personality and neurosis, of posture and architecture, we may speak of styles of microsocial organization.[22] In a military organization, for example, recent inductees quickly learn to organize themselves sequentially in virtually every situation.

After a while, queuing behavior may become self-regenerating and self-enforcing, even in situations in which there is no pragmatic reason for queuing. On a number of occasions in the former Soviet Union, I observed officials instructing people to line up when it seemed to me that neither the officials nor the people they were directing were certain why they were lining up. Such "automatic queuing" occurs because queuing behavior has been internalized. At that point, people will feel uneasy about breaking a queue and, as we will see, become indignant when others do so, even if the violation harms no one in the queue. Much of the microlegal system of queues rests on this feeling, which functions as a type of basic norm, or "*Grundnorm*," in the sense in which Hans Kelsen, the formulator of the so-called pure theory of law, used the term.[23] Queuing with little expectation of receiving the good in question[24] is sometimes recognized by the queuers as repetitive, almost neurotic behavior, as with the man in Kafka's haunting parable "Before the Law," who waits hopelessly, to his death, in a queue of one at a door intended only for him.[25] In Gdansk, Poland, in 1981, a woman lamented, "Waiting in line is a national sickness."[26] When queuing becomes internalized and automatic, people may require explicit directions to ignore the norms of the microsystem. In a self-service cafeteria line in the airport in Minneapolis–St. Paul, a neat sign embossed on a plastic card has been posted to inform entering queuers that "it is not impolite to pass others if there is space ahead."[27]

People may form a line without a clear current distributional function when the queue performs a latent social function or when queuing has acquired a ritual dimension. Adherents of the Melanesian cargo cults line up at symbolic wharves or airfields to await the arrival of cargo from supernatural sources. Sometimes the implicit assumption is that if we, too, stand in line, we will increase the likelihood of receiving what we want. Such "cargo-queuing" may evoke the absurdity of a Beckett play, but it is not necessarily as irrational as most of us would label the cult from which its name has been borrowed. In a mass capitalist society, resourceful distributors may locate themselves precisely where an existing queue or an incipient queue promises to make their operation more efficient.

Latent functions and covert objectives are sometimes part of modern queuing. A slow-moving line is a reasonably respectable setting for initiating a conversation and, given constant, authorized spatial proximity, an extremely convenient one. Socializing with strangers under other circumstances would probably be considered rude or dangerous, for it could violate the so-called norms of noninvolvement that govern most daily contact with strangers.[28] But these norms can hardly operate with the same force when the people standing in line are focused on the same objective. Thus, in some circumstances, men and women may stand in a line—for example, at a ski resort—where the prospect of socializing in the line may enhance the good being distributed or be the good actually sought.[29]

In some instances, a queue's latent function of providing opportunities for socializing may produce an intense queuing community. Even if the people standing in line do not all share culture, class, or gender, they share at least one common demand, manifested by their presence in the queue. If that common demand is focalized, it may become the basis for a significant operational, though perhaps ephemeral, shared identity. The specificity of the items being distributed is a key factor in the formation of the identity. Some distribution points—for example, a supermarket—offer a wide range of goods at varying prices to a relatively undifferentiated consumer group. Because those standing in line at a cash register are likely to be equally heterogeneous in their wealth, status, and value orientation, the likelihood of their forming a more intense queuing community is small.

When distribution points are focalized on distributing a distinctive good, they are more likely to create evanescent but very intense communities.[30] People who queue for a particular item among all the goods in the universe are communicating to each other that they share at least one value important enough to them to warrant waiting in line. That convergence of demands may be reinforced by dress codes, posture, language, dialect, and so on, cultivated externalia that function as metacommunications facilitating interaction. If the item being distributed is expensive or an acquired taste, it may in itself serve as a functional class-screening device, akin to the admissions committee of a private club.

My daughter has remarked to me that young people who line up for tickets for local rock concerts, sold at a downtown record store in New Haven, treat the line, not as a nuisance, but as a kind of spontaneous party. At Yale, I have observed that undergraduates line up more than an hour ahead of time to wait for tickets to certain movies. The queuers come in groups, sometimes with beer and food. The "line party" that ensues seems as important an event as receiving the ticket. Leon Mann's study of the long ticket queues for soccer games in Melbourne, Australia, describes a social system in which small groups form, and establish divisions of labor for mutual help; some hold places while others go for food, and so on.[31]

In spite of the ritual and social purposes of queues, much queuing is considered primarily an economic distribution device by the participants. From the perspective of the spatial serialization of supply, queuing presents itself, at first glance, as a rational arrangement for both distributors and consumers when (1) a resource must be and is being distributed from a central point or a number of central points less than the number of consumers seeking the resource; (2) there is a presumption if not an expectation that enough of the good is available to go around among the queuers; and (3) the distribution system has compelling policy reasons not to distinguish between consumers.[32] But the apparent balance of benefits between distributors and consumers does not survive a second look, for existence of a queue usually signals that the distributor is imposing—"externalizing," as economists put it—the costs of distribution onto the consumer. The consumer is paying a supplementary price for the good or service in "dead time," the opportunity costs lost in waiting and the exasperation that often attends it.

When the three conditions obtain, queuing becomes rational for distributors. The opportunity to pass on to consumers the cost of distribution is not infinitely elastic, however, especially in circumstances of competition. When consumers are conditioned to arrange themselves spatially and then to present themselves serially or sequentially, distributors can economize far more on the number of distribution points established and maintained than if (1) consumers stampede distribution points on a first-come, first-served basis or (2) an operational distribution outlet had to be available for every consumer whenever one signaled an interest in securing the good or service in question. We might call the first anarchic possibility "stampede" or "mad rush" distribution and the second possibility "homologous distribution."

Intricate mathematic models have been developed in the field of queuing theory to help rational distributors predict which combination of number and location of servers will produce the most efficient system of distribution. Simply put, queuing theory rests on the assumption that given a "service model," such as a "single queue–single server" or "single queue–multiple servers," and a "queue discipline"—different rules for queuing, such as appointments, first-come, first-served, and according to need—variations in queue size and waiting time are determined by (1) the arrival distribution of an organization and (2) its service time distribution. Queuing theory then allows derivations of waiting time estimates "for any value or combination of values or specifications with regard to these parameters." [33]

As a practical matter, distributors attempt to create a system that will reduce their overhead costs without reducing demand. Thus, if consumers have been conditioned to queue, a distributor can externalize some of the costs of distribution and impose them on the consumer as a concealed nonmonetary time supplement added to the manifest price. The distributor will prefer that option unless the costs of maintaining the good or the value of the lost opportunity of using the money the consumer would exchange for the good exceeds the costs of more rapid but more expensive distribution. Lines may also serve distributors by functioning as a latent form of advertisement, for they attest that something is being distributed to people who value that something enough to wait in line for it.[34]

But even when consumers have been conditioned to queue, there is a limit to their "patience," a term that in this context means their calculation that the value of the item being distributed warrants investing more dead time waiting in line for it. The trick for the supplier is to gauge where this breaking point is and to provide a sufficient number of separate distribution points so that individual queue time does not exceed the consumers' patience.[35] The electronic simultaneity of a large technological and consumer-oriented civilization offers unique possibilities in this regard. For instance, twenty-four-hour 800-number telephone distribution service for a country divided into several time zones permits the distributor to establish maximally efficient queues.

Queues work best for distributors and consumers when the good or service to be distributed is fungible, demand is constant, and the market is continuous and undifferentiated. The distributor then has no interest in identifying and treating one class of consumer better than another. After all, the price will be the same for each, and everyone will still have to buy the good or service. Even when the distributor has some incentive to discriminate in favor of particular consumers, perhaps to build up goodwill, swap indulgences, or give a return on bribes, the queue provides a regularized environment in which special favors may be covertly and cost-effectively dispensed at the discretion of the distributor. Because order is the precondition for cheating, queues provide putative violators with the most economic method for selectively violating the rules of queues. Indeed, even the rest of the queue-abiding consumers may be better off with a queue that is being selectively violated than with a stampede mode of distribution.

Like the distributor who wants to reserve the capacity to violate the basic rules of the queue, the queuer who is disposed to engage in private violations of the queue by bribing, special pleading, or pushing to the head of the line will find that such private programs are substantially facilitated if the conditions for those not receiving preferred treatment are standardized. After all, who pays a headwaiter for a table if the headwaiter cannot or will not prevent nonpayers from benefiting from the same special treatment?

This ironic aspect of queues applies even to the more violent queue violator, the thug. In Plato's Dialogue *Gorgias*, Callicles,[36] anticipating Friedrich Nietzsche[37] by more than two thousand years, remarks that "those who lay down the rules are the weak men, the many. And so they lay down the rules and assign their praise and blame with their eye on themselves and their own advantage. They terrorize the stronger men capable of having more; and to prevent these men from having more than themselves they say that talking more is shameful and unjust. . . . But I think that if a man is born with a strong enough nature, he will shake off and smash and escape all this. He will trample on all our writings, charms, incantations, all the rules contrary to nature. He rises up and shows himself master, this slave of ours."[38] Although Callicles' strong man may "trample under foot all our formulas and spells and charms," he would be well advised to maintain for others the microlegal system of queues even as he reserves for himself the privilege of violating them at will.

From the perspective of the consumer, queuing may also appear to be a rational economic arrangement serving common interests: it provides orderly access to a distribution point. But it provides access at a cost, part of which, as we have seen—and possibly a substantial part—is borne by the consumer. For the person standing in line, the cost of the queue is the amount of dead time expended to get the value being distributed. That cost can be measured in lost opportunities and emotional pain.[39]

In some cases, the allocation of cost is manifestly fair to the consumer, as when a street vendor sells at substantial reductions, part of which probably derive from the extremely reduced overhead costs of the vendor. Then consumers can freely decide that it is worth standing in line for a bargain. In other cases, the allocation of cost is less intuitively fair. Queuing may be imposed to ration goods that consumers feel should be more readily obtainable or at least have its availability governed by the market rather than by state law.[40]

Keeping People in Line:
The Social Distribution of the Queue

Queuing has profound ethical implications in civilizations whose myths emphasize democratic equality. Because timely access to something one values is a value in itself, in places where only the market operates, the richer will wait less than the poorer.[41] Queuing should reverse that, for one of the key resources distributed in latent fashion in the queue is time itself. But no observer can miss the innumerable queues that crisscross poorer peoples' lives like the bars on a basement window: lines for work, for unemployment checks, for food stamps, for emergency medical treatment.

The lower the economic stratum, the more prevalent queues are and the longer the wait is likely to be. From the perspective of a welfare agency, client queues[42] help welfare officials by "maximizing worker efficiency, clarifying client dependency, and creating the impression that waiting is necessary and just." From the perspective of the queuer, long waits, usually in demoralizing settings, are an example of "mortification rituals," those punishments imposed as part of the price of public assistance.[43] The popular notion that richer people are busier, hence richer, and that the poor are lazy, hence have more time may reverse causality. Much of poor people's time is not leisure but *tiempo muerto*, as I heard someone sigh in the emergency room of a New Haven hospital: "dead time," minutes and hours interred in lines. Lance Morrow has observed that "one of the more depressing things about being poor in America is the endless waiting it entails." So there is more than a grain of truth in the observation that "standing in line is a literal embodiment of social control—'keeping people in line.'"[44] The higher one scrambles in the social heap, the more likely it is that one's only queuing experience will be in the buffet line at the local country club, where everything is made as pleasant as possible and where diners are encouraged to return for second helpings.[45]

In a rigidly and overtly stratified society or in a caste system, the norm requiring that one yield for one's "better" is no different in a queue than in any other setting. With some exceptions, which we will consider below, queues are not supposed to work this way in a democracy. If no one is better than anyone else, why should anyone go to the head of the line? Where the myth of democracy coexists with a queuing system whose rules allow for substantial and manifest exceptions to democratic equality, tensions and complex dynamics are likely to be at play in the queue, and they may reveal much about the society.[46]

To a remarkable degree, the members of the queue community are aware of the rights and duties of group membership and understand the common interests that they share with all the other community members. But there is a paradox. When queues work, those who participate in them ordinarily have contacts with only two other queue members—the one in front and the one behind. These direct links, the building blocks of the queue's legal system, make queuers reciprocally police their own role behavior.[47] There are, nonetheless, obligations owed to others farther away in the queue, and they owe rights to other queuers even though there is no face-to-face contact with them. These obligations are those of an authentic community.[48] Yet attempts to initiate contacts with more distant members of the queue are inherently suspect because they could be a prelude to cutting in, a blatant violation of a key queue norm. When queuers make such contacts, they are likely to proceed in a public and even ostentatious way, as if to confirm the innocent purpose animating them.

MICROLEGAL AND MACROLEGAL QUEUE SYSTEMS

Looking, as we saw in the first chapter, is a quintessential microlegal system. Queuing, by contrast, may be a microlegal system, but there are also examples of state-enforced or "macrolegal" systems of queuing. In this respect, queuing may reveal some of the factors that determine which social arrangements can be spontaneously microlegal and which must be macrolegal.

Supertankers line up when they enter a harbor. One would not expect to find this queuing regulated only by an informal microlegal system. Supertankers do not respond quickly to pilot controls; unless the pilots act well in advance of directly gained visual information, they may do little more than watch from the bridge or on their monitors as their vessels glide inexorably toward disaster. Even the most refined electronic instruments will not avail, for a pilot cannot know the plans of other pilots in the queue. Each pilot is locked in an insoluble "supertanker dilemma," with dramatic consequences in case of a "misqueue" in the line of supertankers. We may hypothesize that where the social and economic costs of a violation of a queue system are high in terms of property and life, the operators of the legal system will insist upon an explicit legal arrangement, supported, in some instances, by intense criminal sanctions. Conversely, microlegal systems will regulate activities whose economic and social impacts, if not their emotional ones, are considerably smaller.

Relatively few of us navigate supertankers, but in advanced industrial and science-based cultures, most adults drive automobiles. Automobiles at tollgates manifest queue behavior and queue problems. Drivers often change lanes, cut into lanes, and create traffic jams, violating incipient queues. Yet the dynamics of the microlegal system of queues do not operate with respect to automobiles. Some of the face-to-face features of a queue as well as the opportunities for protest that are critical to the operation of any microlegal system—for example, an insistent sounding of the horn—do obtain. But in contrast to the microlegal systems that we have considered so far, misqueues and expressions of protest by drivers of automobiles are likely to involve more than dented egos; they may lead to serious damage to the automobiles and injury to their drivers.

I would hypothesize that where queuers are not face-to-face, the spontaneous enforcement system of the microlegal queue is unlikely to operate. Yet the demands of the drivers of vehicles for queue behavior in "autosocial" interactions may still be high. In Israel, in 1997, a member of the Knesset found the violations of queue systems by automobiles so frustrating that he introduced a draft law to provide criminal sanctions. The draft law would have amended the criminal law by introducing a new section under the rubric "Failing to Stand in Line": "A person waiting to receive a good or service in a public place who does not wait in line shall be punished with three months of imprisonment."[49] The explanatory note that accompanied the draft amendment is instructive of the circumstances under which people, vainly or otherwise, seek to transfer to the realm of macrolegal regulation some activity that was, until then, subject to a microlegal system: "This draft law seeks to deter and to punish people who are accustomed to cutting into lines rather than waiting their turns patiently. Waiting in line is a self-explanatory usage in every civilized state, but from time to time it appears that in Israel it has not yet taken root. It is proposed therefore to fix in the criminal law . . . a special crime for failing to wait in line in order to educate the Israeli public. It is proposed to enable the courts to impose a punishment of up to three months' imprisonment, even though it is reasonable to assume that if indictments are submitted, the courts will satisfy themselves with requiring the payment of a fine."[50]

Where microlegal sanctions are perceived as failing adequately to regulate an important social activity, operators of the legal system will be pressed to take the matter up at the macrolegal level.

The Formation and Transformation of Queues

Signals to form a line may be express or implicit. They may range from a sign indicating where the queue should be, to a person with authority indicating that a queue should form, to no more than a rope or a pipe or some other type of barrier strung along a hall, or to a distribution point, such as a bus stop or ticket window.[51] Whatever the initial signal, once queues have been established, they generate a queue process by their own example or by instructions from queuers who are performing informal "steward functions."[52]

Queue stewards indicate amiably or with asperity that a line should form, and where. But the formation of queues does not require or depend on express signals. Sometimes a queue steward will recommend or order that people line up. At other times, one clot of people will queue, and others will imitate. Sometimes the line forms spontaneously. We are not concerned now with "heterarchical queues": queues established and maintained by some outside authority, such as a police officer, a uniformed attendant, or a maître d'. We will return to them in considering the problem of special treatment that heterarchical queues allow. Our primary interest is in the coarchical queue, one without a heterarchical decisionmaker.

The stability of a coarchical system of queuing depends on a perception shared by each person standing in line that the time spent waiting is worthwhile. For each person, the value of time spent in line is relative to the value attributed to the thing being distributed, and the value, in turn, is influenced by the culture, stratum, and individual preferences. When the time spent in the line becomes too long, and the queuer comes to believe that the cost is thus no longer reasonable or commensurate, a special sense of anxiety and even outrage develops, not over lost money but over dead time, killed time, lost opportunities. "Waiting is a kind of suspended animation. Time solidifies: a dead weight."[53] This feeling, which all people who stand in line have felt, was captured in the city of Lodz, Poland, where a caravan of vehicles displayed banners bearing messages such as "We stand in line until our hearts break."[54]

The student of law is particularly interested in that point at which the individual feeling of impatience becomes a shared collective presentiment and either transforms the queue and its microlegal system or disrupts the distribution system. Is there a certain amount of time required for a subjective and undirected feeling of impatience to become a sense of outrage and injustice that begins to acquire a political vector? Is this question susceptible to a quantitative analysis? [55] I would guess that even when queuers attribute approximately the same value to the item being distributed, the degree of subjective impatience each will feel will vary. My observations suggest further that taxing a queuer's patience is ordinarily likely to induce an individual defection from the microlegal situation, but not an effort to foment a revolution to change it. The dissatisfied individual will simply leave the line. Acute dissatisfaction may, however, induce a microlegal transformation in the queue. This may occur in two ways.

Transformation from within the queue depends upon a leader who expresses the anger of the other queue members at the right moment, has sufficient skills or status to influence others, and develops alternative options that seem reasonable to others in the queue.[56] They may all leave the queue, insist that other windows or distribution points be opened, stampede the distribution point, or develop an alternative queuing system. Two examples of transformation are instructive: Helen Quinn, an avid Metropolitan Opera goer, set up a number queue for the Saturday morning line for tickets at the point at which the wait had begun the preceding Friday afternoon. She produced and distributed the numbered tickets, and ticket holders vigorously enforced their priority in the later line.[57]

Another transformation that was arranged by lawyers incorporated, not unexpectedly, a contract. The attorney Beaumont Martin "was instrumental in negotiating what immigration lawyers in Houston always refer to as the Agreement of May 17, 1982—an agreement that gave immigration lawyers their own line, on one side of the entrance [of the Immigration and Naturalization Service office]. Before that, they had to stand in line with the general public, across from the fish wholesaler.... Before May 17, 1982, a lot of lawyers got to know one another well standing in line in the pre-dawn hours outside Immigration. ... Under the Agreement of May 17, 1982, a lawyer can use the special lawyers' line and file papers with a special clerk on one predetermined day of the week, according to the first letter of his last name."[58]

In securing transformation, timing is critical. Even when the self-appointed leader steps forward, he or she often discovers well-wishers and sympathizers but no followers. Even those who share the would-be leader's impatience may resent being presented with the verbalization of that impatience and cling more tightly to the legal system of the queue. The other queuers are likely to resist the self-appointed leader if following the leader requires them to abandon an advanced place in the queue and if that queue is, at that moment, the only place to secure a particular good. People may grumble, but observers of queues are struck by the patience with which they generally wait. Patience here apparently has little to do with the question of whether there will be enough of the good to go around. Some people will continue to wait even when that expectation is low.

Where high demand puts extreme pressure on the queuing system, and queue violations are frequent, a second type of reinforcing transformation of the legal structure of the queue may be effected by an external authorized agent. Intervention may take the form of creating a new queuing system—for example, a number queue—or a list or a formal appointment schedule. Alternatively, intervention may merely arrest incipient efforts at effecting transformation from within the queue.[59] Whether transformation from within or intervention from without will occur depends in part on the patience of the members of the queue.

Because patience is always influenced by the time-value attributed to the item being distributed, *relative* patience can be predicted with some precision when we have a fair idea of what time-value the queuers attribute to the item they are waiting for. The same people who, several days before a performance, will wait at a box office for hours for tickets to hear the Spice Girls or Pavarotti, will push and shove and even riot if they are waiting (or still waiting) as curtain time approaches.[60] The point is obvious: the commodity being distributed has a time-value that, at a certain moment, begins to rise. As showtime for any performance approaches, the accelerating decline of the patience curve and the rapid rise of the anxiety curve increase the propensity to violate queue norms. In contrast, for goods that do not have a terminal or irreplaceable time-value, the patience curve should be steadier; and a steadier patience curve should contribute to producing a more stable and durable queuing system.

The coarchical queue system is self-enforcing[61] to the extent that and as long as most of its members believe that they will be better off with the queue than without it. Thus, an important factor in the early stages of spontaneous queue formation is a shared, though not identical, perception that, in terms of the distribution of the scarce and desirable resource, the queue will benefit everyone. Because the perception is most likely to be more strongly held by those closer to the distribution point, who realize that without a queue they may be pushed from their preferred places, spontaneous queues generally grow from the distribution point outward. For the same reason, queues that do not appear to be advancing and, by implication, cease to promise distribution to those toward the end of the line generally break down from the tail to the front.[62] The persistence of people close to the distribution point is a thoroughly rational calculation, for they may believe (correctly) that they can still get served, or at least that their chances are better where they are in this queue than they would be in a new one where they will have no priority and their location is undetermined.

Once the basic pattern—establishment of the queue or its disintegration—has taken discernible form, the queue may be expected to continue to replicate itself, like a tapeworm, until the cogency of the queue system in that context is challenged by a new perception.

Sequential Priority and Its Corollaries

As soon as a queue has been formed, a number of norms come into play. The primary norm is "sequential priority": One holds to one's place and respects the sequential priorities of those in front and behind.[63] One does not push ahead of those in front or try to cut in. Ambiguous situations in which two parties are abreast of each other are usually resolved by subtle maneuvering with peripheral observation but no eye contact. If, however, one of the queuers feels that a queue norm has been violated, the injured party will glare or grumble, actions that constitute spontaneous sanctions.

The unit rule. Queuers may not abuse their position by putting friends ahead in the line, because the norm of sequential priority also incorporates respect for the priority sequence behind. But there are a number of exceptions to this aspect of the priority principle. The first is what we may call the "unit rule."[64] Priority may be extended to include a spouse, a companion, and, in some cases, two or even three other couples if they came as a group, as long as the group is popularly conceived of as a unit. There seems to be no limit on the number of children who may join a parent, but presumably a busload of couples or children would excite protest from other queuers further back in the line. If those behind grumble a bit, a latecomer may offer a justification, turning and remarking to whoever is immediately behind that "we're together" or "I was parking the car."[65]

Substantial social-scientific data confirm a direct correlation between personalization and the reduction of sanction severity. Whenever personal contact has been established—whether with a jury, a meter maid whose pen is poised to write a traffic ticket, or a teacher whose deadline has been passed—the sanctioning authority is more likely to reduce the severity of the sanction. Speaking directly to the protester establishes a human contact. But that correlation should not operate in the queue, because it is manifest to all the other members of the queue that when the de facto sanctioner yields to the ingratiation or hard luck pitch of the person cutting in, he or she violates the community obligations that are still owed to everyone farther back in the queue.

The corollary norm implicitly invoked in these remarks seems to be that preexisting groups are entitled to be taken as units in establishing priority but spontaneous groups are not. The point may be demonstrated by considering a violation. Imagine a couple in the middle of a long line waving excitedly and saying, "Oh, there's Jim and Sue. Hi. We didn't know you were coming here. Come on and stand with us." This is likely to be met with substantial grumbling from those behind, which should be sufficient to deter the latecomers from cutting into the line in this fashion. The grumbling, as we will see, performs sanctioning functions in the microlegal system of queues. In contrast, an excuse of "we came together," meaning "we are a preexisting and not a spontaneous group," will spike any protest.

The unit rule is also applied when one member of the unit leaves the line temporarily. The place may be held by the other member or members of the unit, and the leaver can resume the same place simply by rejoining the the line. This aspect of the norm is closely related to another rule about "holding places," which we will consider presently.

The clarification rule. Another exception to the rule of sequential priority is the "clarification rule." Someone may go to the head of the line *momentarily* if the purpose is only to seek clarification from the distributor or queue steward—for example, to ask whether the queue is the right one to stand in or whether special documents are required. But clarification can be abused, and other queuers, jealous of their sequential priority, will become noticeably tense if someone advances on the distribution point. They will certainly protest if the person who was ostensibly seeking clarification tries to transact queue business at the same time. Beneficiaries of the clarification rule generally demonstrate good faith if they stand away from the server and call out their question, indicating by their spatial location that they are not cutting into the queue at its most advanced point and do not intend to. Even with this nonverbal disclaimer, a general uneasiness will grip the rest of the line, for the server, who is effectively above the microlaw, could wave the ostensible clarifier over and serve that person out of turn. For a moment, the line is on the verge of becoming heterarchical, but people cannot grumble at the server, who is immune to the queue sanctions and may even capriciously violate queue rules with impunity.

Protests of violations of the clarification rule demonstrate the normative force with which everyone in the line insists on the rule of sequential priority. When the clarifier temporarily leaves a place in line, those standing behind that place protest as vigorously as those in front, even though they will not be deprived of either access or the item being distributed if someone already ahead of them is served out of turn.

The new-line rule. A further exception to the principle of respect for priority of place becomes evident whenever a new line is suddenly formed. If an additional cash register in a supermarket or an additional box office window is opened in a theater or airport, one might expect the principle of sequential priority to require that those who move to the new line keep the order and respective priorities established in the old line. Logic notwithstanding, the priorities in a new line are established on a first-come, first-served basis. There is a flurry of dashing when the new line is opened, often resulting in a distribution of sequential advantages and disadvantages quite different from the distribution in the original queue. When a queuer in the new line is considerably farther back than in the other line, he or she may show some irritation but is otherwise unlikely to try to wangle a more advanced position on that basis. The "new line" rule indicates that sequential priority is queue specific and may not be taken from line to line in a public place. This exception does not operate in queues that are nonspatial—for example, a telephone queue.

The hold-my-place rule. Another corollary to the principle of sequential priority is the rule that may be referred to most conveniently by the words with which it is invoked: "Hold my place."[66] If someone standing in line leaves for one reason or another, that person is deemed to have relinquished his or her place and must go to the end of the line upon returning to the line. But if, before leaving, the queuer turns to the person behind and says "Hold my place" in any number of variant formulations, that person may return to that place in the queue up to the moment when the person holding the place reaches the distribution point.

The line leaver need not say "Hold my place" in so many words, but clarity of expression and an explicit commitment from the person behind make return to the same place more certain. When the queue is slow moving or when the line leaver intends only a short absence, a shopping cart or suitcase can be left where the line leaver was standing, and that is sometimes honored as a symbolic placeholder.[67] But the line leaver may discover that the cart was pushed aside as the queue advanced, in which case the place cannot be regained. Social scientists have found, however, that the more personal the item left as a marker, the more effectively it will serve as a placeholder. Likewise, a verbal request followed by a commitment from the person behind might have prevented the place being lost. In both instances, more personalization is more effective.

If intruders ask neighboring queuers if a marker is saving a place, the neighbors will usually defend the space. If intruders merely take the place or question the neighbor nonverbally, there will be little defense of space, even if the neighbor and the original spacetaker interacted before that person left.[68] The general validity of the hold-my-place rule can be confirmed by examining responses to protests. If someone farther back objects when the line leaver reappears just as the person holding the line leaver's place reaches the distribution point, the response "I'm holding his place" or "She was here" is usually enough to silence the protest.

The hold-my-place rule allows savvy queuers to make more refined use of time when scarce items are being distributed in several simultaneous queues. Hedrick Smith describes this practice as having been highly routinized in the former Soviet Union, where it permitted people to advance toward distribution points in several queues simultaneously.[69]

> In a dairy store one Saturday morning, I found that the game is both simpler and more complex than that. I went in to buy some cheese, butter and bologna sausage which were, unfortunately, in three separate departments, each with its own line. *Nine lines!* I groaned inwardly. But rather quickly, I noticed that veteran shoppers were skipping the first stage. They knew what most items cost, so they went directly to the cashier for their receipts. After a bit of studying prices, that was what I did, too. Then, receipts in hand, I went to the cheese line, the longest—probably 20 people—to get the worst over with first. But I was in line less than a minute when the lady in front of me turned around and asked me to hold her place. She darted off to

the butter-and-milk line. The cheese line was moving so slowly that she got her butter and milk and returned before we had moved forward three feet. I decided to take the risk, too, and got back with my butter while the cheese line was still inching along. Then it dawned on me that the entire store was churning with people getting into line, holding places, leaving, returning. Everyone was using the cheese line as home base. That was why it was barely moving: it kept expanding in the middle. So once again, I got the elderly gentleman behind me to hold my place and went off to buy my bologna. Once again, it worked. In the end it took me 22 minutes to buy butter, sausage and cheese and instead of being furious, I felt oddly as if I had somehow beaten the system with all those shortcuts.[70]

In the northeastern United States, where I have observed the operation of the hold-my-place rule, it is used for more limited purposes. Someone in a supermarket line realizes she has forgotten something, invokes the formula to the person behind her, often leaves her cart (a constructive personal presence that may be important), scurries off to get the item, and returns to resume her place. I would doubt that the Soviet application of the principle that Smith describes would be acceptable to queuers in the United States.[71] Indeed, Smith notes that even in the former Soviet Union the hold-my-place rule was suspended when really scarce and sought-after items were being distributed.[72]

The "hero" rule. Heroes may go to the head of the line. This exception is inculcated early. In an episode in Marc Brown's "Arthur" series, televised stories for three- to six-year-olds broadcast on PBS, Arthur's friend Buster saves a treed cat and becomes a hero. When he and Arthur go to the movies, Arthur goes to the back of the line. Buster walks confidently to the head of the line, pulling a doubtful Arthur with him and explaining that, as a hero, he is entitled to do this. The queue steward waves them in, and no one in the line protests.

Sometimes exceptions are institutionalized. In the former Soviet Union, writes Smith: "At railroad stations, signs at civilian ticket windows state that Deputies in the Supreme Soviet (which automatically includes the most important Party and Government officials), war invalids, Heroes of Socialist Labor, and others honored by "socialist orders of the third degree or higher" can buy tickets ahead of the line. At military ticket windows, Heroes of the Soviet Union, generals, admirals, colonels and majors are accorded this privilege. This works at airports, theaters, hotels and untold other public institutions. Each of the 15 individual republics has its own hierarchy of VIP's granted such privileges within its territory."[73] In the United States, too, hero exceptions apply. At Ronald Reagan Airport, in Washington, D.C., for example, signs award comparable privileges to Supreme Court justices and members of Congress with regard to proximate parking places.[74] Others can sometimes bootstrap into the category of hero. Celebrities are likely to be hurried to the front of the line, often by their paid retainers, one of whose functions is to validate that their employers are heroes.

The hardship rule. There are other general exceptions, but some are more ambiguous because they vary according to contextual factors. In a queue for a public toilet, pregnant women may be moved to the front of the line amid general approval; but the same woman and the same queuers are not likely to make or yield to the same exception in a cinema queue. Yet in a queue outside the Children's Museum in Manhattan, I observed a line, whose members were standing outside and in the rain, yield to a mother who pushed her little child through the door with the explanation "He has to go."

The general tolerance for exceptions like these is often a function of the nature of the commodity being distributed, the urgency and validity of the need of the person who will benefit from the exception, and the extent to which others in the queue share the expectations and demands of the person petitioning for an exception.[75] This last factor is critical. If queues are to survive, exceptions must be collectively approved and policed, for when one individual in a queue decides to make an exception, that individual is not merely giving up his or her place in favor of someone else or inserting an additional person (or group) but violating the principle of sequential priority with regard to everyone behind that place in line. It is evidence of the healthy demands for microlegal order in a queue that exceptions not deemed licit will arouse intense negative reactions on the part of those affected. Queues are an unusual microlegal system in that they are not isolated dyads, like many other microlegal systems, but aggregates of more people. In the absence of a heterarch, many members of the system must participate in decisionmaking.

The political styles of nondemocratic societies also infect their queues. The restraints of the microlegal system operate for ordinary people, but when an elite member violates the norm, collective decisionmaking and sanctioning are confined to muttering and grumbling. This confirms the continuing validity of the norm despite its violation, but it provides no remedy to those who have been deprived. In Tashkent, Hendrick Smith reported that he "watched a line of tired people grumbling curses at a high-ranking military officer for going to the head of a long taxi line and seizing the first vacant cab for himself, but no one made any vocal protest or physical move to stop him."[76] The general sense of grievance at these violations of microlaw was captured in popular Russian songs by the dissident poet Vladimir Vysotsky.[77]

The resignation that Vysotsky evokes may be contrasted with an American reaction. In Houston, where attorneys negotiated a special line for themselves at the Immigration and Naturalization Service office, an annual lawyers' meeting was

> dominated by a discussion of relations with Immigration—particularly concerning the special line for lawyers. Someone had been at the district office one morning that week when there was a scuffle between the gate guard and an out-of-town lawyer who thought he had a right to enter a public building. Someone else had been present when an Iranian who was handling his own case complained loudly that the two lawyers ahead of him in line at the clerk's window had not been in the line outside. Someone had been present when there were complaints outside Immigration that lawyers were being allowed through the gate while old people and women with babies remained outside in the cold. . . . [One lawyer] who had that very week heard an I.N.S. official say something that made him think the entire system was in danger of being scrapped, summed up his response to that prospect in one sentence: "I had the feeling the sky fell down."[78]

Every queue has a context that has some influence on the way the queue rules will be applied.

The Sanctioning System

An important test of a legal system is whether it can sanction violations. In some spontaneous queues, functional decision-makers do emerge. I have been referring to them as "queue stewards."[79] Their authority derives from their ability to capture, at the right moment, the indignation of other queue members over the violation of a basic norm and their courage in expressing that indignation. . The protest may be cryptic: "This is a line," "I was here first," or, more persuasive because of the absence of self-interest, "He [she] was here first."

Sanctions may range from physical violence, to verbal threats and protests, to nonverbal expressions of disapproval.[80] Protest sanctions may be delivered to the queue violator in a variety of different ways. The most moderate defensive or deterrent protest is postural or positional: those in the queue who feel that their rights are threatened move more closely together so that the person suspected of trying to cut in is or seems to be physically blocked. Another form of protest is visual: those in the queue who feel their rights are threatened glare at the would-be violator. Verbal protests incorporate specific references to the microlaw of the queue and explicit characterizations of what the person trying to cut in is doing as a violation. In heterarchical queues, verbal protest invokes the decision or sanction of the queue steward.

In many cases, the mere expression of indignation and its confirmation of the normative demands of other queue members will suffice to deter the queue breaker and, at the same time, will reinforce for everyone the basic rules of the queue. Even when it does not, the queue breaker, while persisting in the violation, may seek to justify herself in ways that acknowledge the validity and even the applicability of the basic norm;

for example, she might insist, however implausibly, that she was there first or that there is a "higher" reason that justifies cutting in.[81] I observed an unusual effort at justification in the airport at Montego Bay, Jamaica. A Jamaican cut into a very slow line of American lawyers and law professors returning from a conference. In response to shouts of indignation from the queuers behind, the Jamaican said truculently, "This is my country," an assertion heavy with unmistakable racial implications. The shouts of protest continued, but the line breaker held his place and laughed. When a queuer announced loudly that she was going to inform airport security, the line breaker retreated.

Where common indignation and verbal protests have failed to shame or frighten the queue breaker into conformity, the effectiveness of the application of a sanction by the queue steward to a particular deviation will turn ultimately on the steward's physical size relative to the queue breaker, the steward's credibility or unpredictability as a threat, and perhaps the support of proximate queue members. The sanctioning-deterrent system may be most effective near the head of the line, where people share a powerful group solidarity that derives from the common perception that those closest to distribution have a virtual property right. To protect this right, people may close up the line. After all, those near the head of the line have the greatest investment and the most to lose if a queue disintegrates into a stampede and a new first-come, first-served line.[82]

Protests serve many functions in the microlegal system of a line: as a corrective sanction, a punitive sanction, a deterrent sanction, a confirmation of authority, and catharsis.

A corrective sanction is an authorized reaction that corrects the behavior of the nonconforming target. It is, in analogues of macrolaw, the admonition of a judge or the warning ticket of a state police officer. In the coarchical system of the queue, one function of a protest is to force or shame a violator back into a prescribed place, possibly the end of the line.

Protest may also serve a punitive function, which may accompany the correction but which operates even when the protest fails to correct. A public denunciation, even in the short-lived microsystem of the queue, is likely to embarrass many violators and may cause real anguish to some.

Even when the punitive protest fails to correct, its public manifestation may deter those in the queue who, like clones of Justice Oliver Wendell Holmes's "bad man," will act oblivious to law if they think they can get away with it.[83] Without deterrent sanctions, "bad folks" will calculate whether their own violation of the norm might yield real benefits without significant costs.

Protest also confirms authority and its prescriptions by a public indication that a norm exists and has been violated.[84]

Finally, protest provides a socially beneficial catharsis, a release of the pent-up anger experienced by the law-abiding queuer at the violation of the norms. Providing licit opportunities for release of indignation is a subtle but important function of legal systems. Popular indignation over norm violation is, as Harold Lasswell observed, critical to the support of the legal system, for it is in large part what impels people to invoke law and to demand its application. Successful application of the law provides a release for that indignation.

The act of deciding frequently includes critical acts before and after the final act of decision. One prior act is a preliminary and often only partly authoritative characterization that something that was done or is being done is not right and requires a decision. This provisional characterization of norm violation triggers a formal community decision process, which may lead to the application of sanctions if it concludes that they are appropriate. On the macrolegal level, a crusading columnist's denunciation of a travesty is akin to a queuer's protest, but the journalist may stimulate legal processes—the convening of a grand jury, prosecution, a trial, a conviction, legislative reform.In coarchical and unorganized systems like the ordinary queue, protest is an effort toward a complete microsanction, at once an invocation and application of law. In the heterarchical queue, however, the same protest is not a decision in itself; like the journalist's column, it only invokes a possible decision—in this instance, by the queue steward.

The queue breaker may still ignore the queue steward, or there may be no queue steward, no one who step forwards to characterize certain behavior as a queue violation. This lack need not destroy the queue, as a personal experience shows. When I was a law student in what was then the Israeli sector of Jerusalem, I was standing in line at a movie theater on a Saturday night. (Cinemas were then the only public entertainment available, and films were much in demand as the Jewish quarter roused itself from the Sabbath, a twenty-four-hour period during which virtually everything was closed.) Some thirty people were in an orderly line; I was about twentieth. When a burly fellow about my age barged in and placed himself at the head of the line, the other people in the line grumbled and looked at each other, and I found myself walking to the front of the line and confronting the queue violator. "Zeh Tor!" I said. "This is a line." This short protest was common in Israel then, when queue behavior was neither as spontaneous nor as self-policed as in the United States or the United Kingdom. The queue violator looked at me, perhaps measuring me for potential conflict. He said, "If you don't like what I'm doing, you do it, too." In fact, I did nothing but look exasperated and disgusted to conceal my confusion, then resumed my place in the queue. The queue breaker did not relinquish his, and we all continued to stand in line.

Where the queue steward is ignored or no queue steward emerges and a norm violation, witnessed by most of the queue members, goes uncorrected, the queue, as a specific microlegal system, not only need not disintegrate. It may continue and may actually be reinforced. The reason has to do with a rarely perceived aspect of all legal systems. In every type of legal system, the primary or principal function of the formal application of a norm is not—as the language of judgments and verdicts frequently suggests and most of the community may believe—to punish or to otherwise do justice or to give the gods their due by penalizing or securing penance from the violator of the law or some surrogate, if blood penance is deemed necessary. The most urgent objective of a legal application is to maintain the credibility of the system of which it is a part by reaffirming the norm that has been violated and demonstrating the efficacy of the decision process and its commitment to continuing to police the norm. *This increases the likelihood of conformity to the norm in the future.* Characterization of certain behavior as criminal, punishment for that behavior, and the rituals attending both characterization and punishment are only instruments to that end. All the objectives of application can be achieved without involving the alleged deviant. Our notions of justice may be offended when a deviant escapes punishment for violating a norm, but this is not a central, systemic concern. The real social calamity is not the violation of the norm. That event is inevitable, and if the violation is repaired, the violation is actually a system-strengthening event. The calamity would be the deterioration or disintegration of the entire decision process as an effective system.

These general observations have particular reference to the

microlegal systems of queues. In spontaneous queues, the latent and probably most important function of legal application is not to punish the queue breaker but to reaffirm the basic norms and ethics of the queue so that others do not violate it as well. When those in the queue perceive that a violator is doing wrong but themselves remain faithful to the principle of sequential priority, that particular instance of its violation does not undermine the microlegal system of the queue.

The tensile strength of queues under the stress of norm violations does have its limits. As long as people in a queue believe that the queue serves their interests, queue behavior may hold even in the face of violations. If a substantial number of people who are close to the distribution point conclude, out of timidity, physical weakness, or commitment to what they think is the need for community order, that they cannot operate in a stampede, they may hold their places despite queue violations. Curiously, their behavior may, of itself, generate a type of mimesis among waverers behind them, which may prove sufficient to maintain the queue, for it is the nature of a queue, given its spatial organization, that those farther back realize that they have less information about distribution options than those farther forward and can infer from the persistence of those before them that, violations notwithstanding, the queue is still working.

But violations shake that conviction, and there will be an uneasy interim during which many queuers will be watching carefully to determine whether the queue is disintegrating. The moment they sense that it is, they will stampede, creating a new system on a first-come, first-served basis, oblivious to preferred positions in the old queue and securing as much priority for themselves as they can. For the ordinary person in the queue, this interim poses the quintessential dilemma of navigating between Scylla and Charybdis: If I move too quickly and violate the queue norm but the queue holds, I'm exposed as a queue breaker, and, worse, I lose my place and go to the end of the line. If I move too quickly and the queue breaks, I'll feel, in addition to the condemnation of others who would have still waited, that my early defection from the norm made disintegration of the queue inevitable. But if I move too slowly and there is a stampede and then a resumption of a queue system, I'll end up at the back of the line and, worst of all, feel like a sap. In such a situation, as in so many others, the middle of the group is a desirable location.

Violation of a queue norm in a particular setting may lead to the disintegration of that queue, but, as with many other constantly replicated microlegal systems, violation does not appear to erode the general expectation that in appropriate and easily recognizable situations, one is expected to queue and demand that others do, too. Virtually every reader will have encountered this phenomenon on numerous occasions. Shortly before curtain time, a queue for tickets will disintegrate into a stampede. Those who fight their way to the box office and get inside will dutifully line up at the cloakroom or the bar during intermission. The alternative, a societywide breakdown of queuing habits, is scarcely imaginable to them because queuing has acquired self-evident validity in our civilization, that validity is reinstated on each occasion that people queue. It would take traumatic queue breakdowns to shake that expectation. The result would likely be a drastic change in the organization of our personalities and our social order.

Heterarchical queues have a much more conventional decision structure. They cannot be characterized as dictatorial—decision systems in which the superordinates can do anything they want—for the queue director, though able to introduce variations in the application of queue norms, must still defer or appear to defer to some norms. But the mere presence of a heterarch, like the cop on the beat, tightens the discipline of the queue and tends to deter some potential deviation. This results in a much more effective and overt policing of the basic queue for observation of the norm of sequential priority. Ironically, the heterarchical queue generates—along with the more efficient maintenance of the normative code of all queues—a discreet "operational code,"[86] a normative code which those in the know apply to their advantage but which is not congruent with the formal code. Those who understand the operational code of the heterarchical queue appreciate that it is now possible, while publicly affirming the basic norm of sequential priority, to make discreet, private deals with the heterarch in order to move ahead in the queue in violation of the rule of sequential priority.

Take as an example a queue in a restaurant in which demand for tables exceeds supply. In addition to the ubiquitous velvet-covered rope, the heterarchical queue is kept in line by a maître d'. Insofar as the clientele of the restaurant is conditioned to queue (usually the case), the maître d's function, as far as supervising queuing is concerned, is to regulate the pace of entry and to direct diners to particular tables, thereby preventing traffic jams and avoiding overloading particular waiters. The maître d' may also steer patrons whom he considers likely to disturb other diners to distant tables—inappropriately dressed couples, potential rowdies, families with children, people with physical disabilities.

One of the most important latent functions of the heterarchical queue steward is to arrange for deviations from queue norms. Deviations that fall within the exception categories are of no special interest to us now. It is the deviations that are not exceptions, deviations for bribes, for personal friends, and so on,[87] that concern us, for these deviations must be accomplished in ways that do not undermine general belief in the formal norms of the queue.

In cultures in which there are no norms prohibiting bribery, favoritism by queue stewards is accepted and expected; the only question is the fairness of the tariff. Where the elite wish to terminate such practices, special efforts will be required. My favorite example is section 44 of the Ottoman Turkish Code of Civil Procedure of 1879, which specified the following: "Parties coming to court on the appointed day will be called in the order of the queue by the court beadle according to the rule that those who arrive first are served first." People from cultures in which queues are routine and require no mention always find these efforts quaint and curious. The real purpose of section 44 was to prohibit bribery.

Because, in the United States, payments of whatever kind must be concealed, entry decisions are usually made with pretentious mystery and the self-assured authority of the maître d'. Even when there is suspicion of corruption or favoritism, other queuers are still likely to be deterred from protesting for a panoply of defensive reasons: the timidity that restrains many of us from acknowledging law violations, the uneasy suspicion that a licit reason exists for the apparent exception and that a protest will make us look ignorant and foolish, or the fear that the protest will lead the maître d' to keep us in the queue longer or even bar our entry entirely.[88] Standing in line, we note with irritation when groups inscribed on the list after us are seated first. For the most part, we express our displeasure by staring at the queue steward, but offer no other protest. We know from innumerable other heterarchical queues that if we allow our anger to overcome our caution, if we screw up our courage and protest, the maître d' can reply, "They were here first," "They had a reservation," "They needed a larger table," or, the *ultima ratio* of proprietorship, "Orders from the boss." Thus, queuers, like law-abiding citizens faced with more atrocious violations, cultivate a benign ignorance and, against all evidence, a childlike trust in the wisdom and goodness of the proximate authority figure.

The discretionary power of queue stewards can be arbitrary, yet the same people who are prone to protest violations of queue norms in coarchical queues will submit meekly to infringements by the steward. The most extreme example of this phenomenon that I have observed takes place regularly in the customs hall at Kennedy Airport in New York. Large signs direct the arriving passengers to stand in the lines marked with red if they have something to declare or in the lines marked with green if they do not. Until this point, the queue behavior is common to heterarchical and nonheterarchial queues: people wait, with at least outward patience, for their lines to advance. Meanwhile, roving customs agents move among people standing in the green lines, addressing people, apparently at random, who may be anywhere from the beginning to the end of the line. The customs officers ask whether the traveler bought things, scan the lucky traveler's customs form, and without further ado check that traveler through before all the others who are waiting in the line and have sequential priority.

These roving customs agents may have some guidelines, but those in the queue have no idea what they are. It is plain to everyone in the queue that the customs agents exercise great discretion as to whom they choose.[89] It is also clear that whomever they choose will go right through the screening process without further interference. For the lucky travelers, their intervention is a type of grace, a truly antinomian occurrence in a social institution marked by very intense nomist demands.

The submission to the deus ex machina takes place precisely because the intervener is a *deus*. And this draws attention to a rather melancholy feature of those microlegal decision structures that are heterarchical: a protest does not promise to reestablish the prescribed order. In other words, protest in heterarchical queues is not the incipient sanction that it is in the coarchical queue. On the contrary, the heterarchical queue whose microlegal situation is effectively violated presents an unpleasant situation of anomie. Queuers must acknowledge that things have been "thowed out of wack," to paraphrase Flannery O'Connor, and fixing them is not possible. To protest what is a violation brings upon the protester the wrath of the authority figure and may even lead to banishment from the distribution system entirely.[90]

Even where there is widespread suspicion of corruption and a growing and overt expression of dissatisfaction, the heterarchical queue, as opposed to the spontaneous queue, does not dissolve into stampede, for the role of the heterarch—in our example, the maître d'—is much more defined than that of the more informal queue steward. A queuer who becomes sufficiently indignant may choose to forego the good or service being distributed and withdraw.[91] In a civilization that puts a high value on material goods, the costs and even the possibilities of stepping out of line often make this only a theoretical option.

In the future, cybernetic advances may render physical queues as obsolete as the horse and buggy. Computer terminals in each home may make ordering some good or service an instantaneous operation, with supply being effected electronically. There may be waiting—it is difficult to imagine how that can be eliminated from all phases of distribution—but no waiting in line. But distribution will be more efficient at a cost of alienation, for people will be more physically separated from one another, and machines will mediate. Even lines, a weak form of community, will cease.

In the shorter run, however, we may expect more lines as popular demands—demands skillfully stoked by industries paid to focus, intensify, or, indeed, create them—rise faster than the productive, inventorying, and distributive capacities of the market to satisfy them. Someone who exercises the ultimate right of a consumer to stalk away in protest from a microlegally improper line has no choice but to go to the end of another line. As with so many other arrangements and institutions that in practice fall short of their legal promise, someone who chooses to remain in line must pretend that its law is being followed.

3

Rapping and Talking to the Boss

Except for cases of pathological incapacity one can and must communicate; it is a useful and easy way to contribute to the peace of others and one's own, because silence, the absence of signals, is in its turn a signal, but it is ambiguous and ambiguity generates anxiety and suspicion.
—Primo Levi, *The Drowned and the Saved,* trans. Raymond Rosenthal (1988)

Getting a point across is important, but talking is much more than telling someone something. The deeper satisfactions available to talkers are as important as communication. When I talk, I experience a sense of power while I hold the attention of a group. For a moment, I have the opportunity to win dividends of affection and respect. I set out my universe, the way I see things, and I confirm and validate my existence (for myself and my audience). I have the pleasure of exercising a basic skill, of displaying my ideas, my humor, and my rich vocabulary while orchestrating the complex coordinations of laryngial, labial, lingual, and facial muscular contractions and choreographing head, arm, and trunk movements. At a subconscious level, there may be residual and still profound oral gratifications, for midbrain and medulla focus much pleasure on the mouth. Talking, as Robert Louis Stevenson put it, "is a festival of ostentation." More than that. Talking is a trip.[1]

Yet talking to oneself will not do. There must be a listener. Harold D. Lasswell, America's greatest student of politics and personality, made this point with characteristic insight: "The urge to be listened to is deeply implanted in every personality, springing from the dependence of the small, weak, and inarticulate infant and child upon the environment. The frustrations which arise in the arduous process of learning an adequate set of communicating symbols emphasize the importance of speech, and the circumstance that those who listen to our verbal productions in the early years are typically those who shower care and affection upon us leads to the chronic overestimation of the emotional interest of those who listen to our verbal outpourings."[2]

It is no wonder that people will struggle—sometimes investing great resources, sometimes taking serious risks—for the right to talk, to make themselves heard, even when it is probable that their speaking will not improve their lot appreciably.[3] Some people get hooked on talking itself. Children will shriek and jump in exasperation and sometimes fight to get their two cents worth in. Adults, too, may become angry and withdraw from encounters if they are not receiving what they believe is their fair share of the pleasure of talking. That belief, as we will see, is an important indicator of normative expectations about how this pleasure is to be allocated.

Talking presupposes the interaction of at least two people, but, by its very nature, the core activity and key resource of talking must be exclusive. Only one person can talk at a time. As long as one person talks, the other must remain silent to listen. If the other talks at the same time, they may both enjoy the ecstasy of struggle, say, or gain some emotional release through self-submersion in a group, be it a Greek chorus or a mob. Shouting at each other simultaneously may involve some mediation of subjectivities. Human interaction can hardly escape that. But such mediation is not talking.[4]

Because the only way to divide talking is to share it sequentially, division, like all other processes, presupposes an effective social and political system.[5] Sharing talking is no more spontaneous, natural, or easy than sharing food. The parallel is apposite, for talkers, like eaters, are, at one level, gratifying themselves orally. Relinquishing those pleasures voluntarily is about as probable as a suckling infant's gracious surrender of the nipple to another. Waiting while another talker experiences the pleasures of talking is tantamount to expecting the same hungry infant to wait patiently in line.

Like most other social situations, mundane microsituations —even those with only two actors and of the shortest duration—have, as we have seen, three components characteristic of law. These components are, first, expectations, frequently described by the actors as the relevant "rules"; second, active demands for conformity to the rules; and, third, enforcement sanctions. People in the situation believe that there is a "right" way of acting; defections from that right way will lead to a common view that the defection was wrong; and there is a consensus that authorizes an injured party to respond in a way that at the very least will reaffirm the norm which has been violated but that may also hurt or sanction the offending actor. The response of the injured party is a form of enforcement.

Enforcement is critical, but we must be wary of the assumption that law requires centralized and formalized enforcement, for enforcement need not be effected by a formal authority. There may be no distinct, identifiable sanctioner—which is not to say that microlaw, any more than macrolaw, is self-enforcing or that a deus ex machina is maneuvering against all and sundry lawbreakers. The sanction may be embedded in the situation and may be no more than symbolic approval or disapproval, or it may be a deprivation of something more substantial, like money or time. In the first chapter, I suggested that in some circumstances a principled withdrawal from a two-person game could be an adequate sanction to support that microlegal system.

Even casual observation establishes that talking is a social organization, a microeconomy and a microlegal system in which certain important and extremely desirable but scarce resources must be divided among group members. In this chapter I explore the microlegal system of two people talking and attempt to codify its basic norms and trace the procedures for their application and sanctioning.[6] I am not concerned with how people *should* talk, although the literature on that subject may include pertinent normative material and will be consulted when appropriate. The focus here is on the rules that apply when people talk and on what happens when those rules are violated.

Talk Sessions

There is no dearth of data on talking. We talk everywhere. To be sure, people take vows of silence—significantly, sometimes as a self-inflicted punishment. Some monastic societies practice a rule of silence, and some cultures extol the practice of silence as a means of cultivating social values or associate taciturnity with strength or nobility.[7] Eccentrics may create social situations—for example, in clubs—where the implicit norm is not to talk. Thoreau and Emerson were reputed to meet regularly and to sit and smoke for several hours without exchanging a word, then to part after thanking each other for the pleasure of the other's company. These are exceptional, usually consciously cultivated, carefully staged, and lovingly recorded eccentricities. Other social activities that require intense coordination, such as certain military operations, must be preceded by talk but require the suspension of all conversation while they are being implemented. But these, too, are exceptional cases. Of course, we can and do communicate without talking; the repertory of nonverbal communication is a component of the mediation of subjectivity when people can see each other. But for the most part, talking is an indispensable and inescapable part of social activity. In popular parlance, socializing means talking.

Precisely because talking is ubiquitous, it may be useful to reserve a term for the talk features common to the diverse situations that we will be examining. I will use the term "talk session" to focus on the talking component from which we will extract and synthesize the essential talk features of more complex and mixed situations.

We can divide talk sessions according to the objects and consequences of the talking. Some talking is instrumental to the performance of another task and can be called "instrumental talking."[8] A surgeon addressing a nurse is presumably talking instrumentally. But talking is not always manifestly instrumental to the achievement of the manifest purpose of a collaboration. The act of talking is sufficiently pleasurable to most people for them to talk at times simply for the sake of talking—to gab, rap, schmooze, bullshit, shoot the breeze, chew the fat. This is "talking-for-its-own-sake."[9] It has been referred to as "casual social conversation," but I find that term potentially misleading, because informal settings often provide, and are often sought out for, instrumental talking. I have also decided not to use the term "small talk" or "chitchat" to indicate talking-for-its-own sake, because that kind of talking often imposes a burden on one of the speakers.[10]

Whether talking is instrumental or for its own sake is not always readily apparent. Two people who are ostensibly engaged in talking-for-its-own-sake may each conceal instrumental motives under the convenient cover of chatter. And even when talkers think they are engaged in nothing more than talking-for-its-own sake, an observer may conclude that things the talkers value highly, such as power, enlightenment, skill, affection, respect, health, and well-being, are being shaped and shared in the talk session.

How many times have you tried to concentrate while one of your coworkers chatters away? Many people yammer on, even when the talking undermines or retards the fulfillment of the manifest objective of the activity that it accompanies or displaces. I will refer to this as "counterproductive talk." In a sense, talking-for-its-own-sake and counterproductive talk are relatively "pure" talking, precisely because the talkers believe the talking itself is the objective and not an instrument for achieving some other objective. The relative purity of the sessions makes them particularly useful for exploration because it permits the procedures and basic rules of talking to operate with little influence from task-specific factors. In other types of talk sessions, extraneous considerations may affect the application of rules and may even suspend them or, at least, suspend protest about their violation. If one member of a sales team making a presentation to a potential client hogs the floor, the other members may suppress their indignation and refrain from protesting so as not to jeopardize the sale.

THE MICROPOLITICS OF TALKING

Nothing, one would think, could be as innocuously apolitical or, if you prefer, as spontaneously democratic as two people talking. But no serious social inquiry, whether into a brief encounter between two strangers or into a comprehensive and enduring global community, can ignore the variable of power. Power is a ubiquitous consideration in all groups, whether large or small, whether relatively stable, like the nuclear family, the clan, or a kinship group, or evanescent, like most talk sessions. The ways people talk to each other express and reflect the power relationships between them and have a profound effect on the operation of talking rules. In some circumstances, talking contributes to establishing or confirming such relationships. Consider this account from Maya Angelou's autobiography, whose moral impact defies paraphrase and summary.

At just about the same time we saw a troop of the powhitetrash kids marching over the hill and down by the side of the school. I looked to Momma for direction. She did an excellent job of sagging from her waist down, but from the waist up she seemed to be pulling for the top of the oak tree across the road. Then she began to moan a hymn. Maybe not to moan, but the tune was so slow and the meter so strange that she could have been moaning. . . .

Before the girls got to the porch I heard their laughter crackling and popping like pine logs in a cooking stove. I suppose my lifelong paranoia was born in those cold, molasses-slow minutes. They came finally to stand on the ground in front of Momma. At first they pretended seriousness. Then one of them wrapped her right arm in the crook of her left, pushed out her mouth and started to hum. I realized that she was aping my grandmother. Another said, "Naw, Helen, you ain't standing like her. This here's it." Then she lifted her chest, folded her arms and mocked that strange carriage that was Annie Henderson. Another laughed, "Naw, you can't do it. Your mouth ain't pooched out enough. It's like this." . . .

The girls had tired of mocking Momma and turned to other means of agitation. One crossed her eyes, stuck her thumbs in both sides of her mouth and said, "Look here, Annie." Grandmother hummed on and the apron strings trembled. . . .

One of the smaller girls did a kind of puppet

dance while her fellow clowns laughed at her. . . .
But the big girl turned her back, bent down and
put her hands flat on the ground—she didn't pick
up anything. She simply shifted her weight and did
a hand stand.

Her dirty bare feet and long legs went straight
for the sky. Her dress fell down around her shoul-
ders, and she had on no drawers. The slick pubic
hair made a brown triangle where her legs came
together. She hung in the vacuum of that lifeless
morning for only a few seconds, then wavered and
tumbled. The other girls clapped her on the back
and slapped their hands.

Momma changed her song to "Bread of Heaven,
bread of Heaven, feed me till I want no more.". . .

Then they were moving out of the yard, on their
way to town. They bobbed their heads and shook
their slack behinds and turned, one at a time:

" 'Bye, Annie."

" 'Bye, Annie."

" 'Bye, Annie."

Momma never turned her head or unfolded her
arms, but she stopped singing and said, " 'Bye, Miz
Helen, 'bye, Miz Ruth, 'bye, Miz Eloise." [11]

The relationship between talkers in a talk session is, like
every power relationship, either coarchical or hierarchical. At
some level of consciousness, talkers view themselves and those
to whom they are speaking in terms of relative equality (coarchy) [12] or in terms of superiority and inferiority (hierarchy). [13]
Coarchical and hierarchical sessions may be further inflected
by the social distance dividing the speakers, any expected and
demanded rituals of the situation, the degree of organization,

and so on. Coarchical talking need not be amiable. The talkers may keep each other at arm's length and may even be engaged in overt conflict—for example, as opposing counsel or as agents negotiating a deal. Hierarchy expresses itself not only in obvious rule changes in favor of the superordinated talker but also in more subtle "constitutional" matters, such as who determines or standardizes the authorized vocabulary, the acceptable images and metaphors, and the metaphysical assumptions.

The external indicia of power can be misleading. In the days of the Soviet Union, the ranking member of a foreign mission might not have been the named leader but instead someone with a lower title who, thanks to the reduced visibility of a lower rank, enjoyed greater freedom of movement. The power structures of a talk session are found in the inner images or subjectivities of the talkers.[14] Because these inner images may diverge markedly from the external behavior in the session, special care must be taken in determining whether a session is hierarchical or coarchical, for some apparently hierarchical situations may be coarchical, and vice versa. The deference and even sycophancy of a speaker do not necessarily mean that he is talking to a superordinate. It may well be his style and technique. In situations in which democratic myths conceal undemocratic power practices, elites may cultivate a mawkish style when speaking to subordinates. Conversely, the hierarchy of a talk session is sometimes concealed in a superficial social equality, as in talk between doctors and patients, especially in therapeutic interviews,[15] and in talk between men and women, where apparent equality is often infected with gender politics.[16]

Some nominally hierarchical sessions that appear to be well regulated may conceal near de facto absolutism and a frightening potential for violence: parents over children,[17] teachers over students,[18] officers over the rank and file,[19] congressional committees over witnesses.[20] Even here, however, a microlegal system is operating, and there are some potential limits that may be invoked against the hierarch.

In other situations, the micropolitical environment may appear benign. The power that professors exercise over students, based on their ability to inflict various types of career harm on those they judge insufficiently compliant, is in theory, though rarely in practice, subject to some controls. In the lecture hall, it is reinforced by the threat of public humiliation, which is easily justified as an indispensable component of routine didactic exercises. The many other nontraceable deprivations that professors can visit on students—the anodyne letter of recommendation, the pauses in a telephone consultation about a job candidate—are easy to imagine. Thus, for many students, a professor's power over them approaches the absolute.[21]

The influence of the power relationship on talking is sufficiently great to warrant precise demarcation. I will use the popular term "rapping" for coarchical talk sessions and "talking to the boss" for hierarchical talk sessions. The term "boss" will be used to designate whoever happens to be the superordinate in the session.

In coarchical or rap sessions, speakers, whatever their social status, view each other as of generally equal status. Indeed, equality is often expressed in terms of "being able to speak" to a person. Thus, Molière's M. Jourdain, an avid social climber who is acutely sensitive to the indicia of status, remarks that one of his models is "un seigneur . . . qui parle au roi tout comme je vous parle."[22] But speakers in coarchical sessions are not always equals. Ephemeral coarchical situations may be established when people who ordinarily see themselves as superior to others consciously step out of role. The extent to which the transformation takes place varies case by case.

When talking to the boss, speakers relate to each other in terms of superiority and inferiority. They may bring their relative ranks to the session as personal attributes or socially vested rights— for example, in a monarchy or bureaucracy or in a caste or sexist society. Sometimes, however, the hierarchical relationship may be only a momentary feature of the specific talk session—for example, when social equals interact in a formal meeting in which one serves as chairperson or in which one is judge or presiding arbitrator and the other the lawyer of record. For our purposes, a hierarch, a boss, is anyone in a talk session who has more power with regard to the substantive and procedural rules of the microsituation. Effective, if not formal, bosses may be observed in many otherwise ostensibly democratic situations in which all members are supposedly equal, whether we are observing boys in a school playground, athletes on a sports team, members of a sorority, company workers in the same cohort, or tenured faculty at a college.

The existence and operation of rules are generally more manifest in hierarchical situations than in coarchical ones. Indeed, in institutionalized talk sessions, rules may be authoritatively codified as "rules of procedure."[23] In the English-speaking world, *Robert's Rules of Order* is the arbiter of talking rules from parent-teacher associations to parliaments.[24] Even when the rules of the hierarchical session are not codified and are largely customary, talkers are conscious of them and may explain that "you don't talk that way to a judge/chairperson/boss/coach/cleric/teacher/parent."

Whatever the substantive and procedural rules that operate on the boss, they can be bent to the boss's will. But there are limits. The application and, to some extent, the prescription of rules of substance and procedure about talking may be more discretionary in hierarchical sessions than in rap sessions, but hierarchical sessions are not absolute despotisms—even when they look that way. The Sudanic ruler of ancient Africa, who is believed to have intentionally behaved antinomially and unpredictably in order to emphasize—by his manifest obliviousness to law—his divinity is at the most extreme pole; yet even he was probably bound by certain rules about talking. Let us consider the point in more detail.

Superordinates, even in the most absolute systems, are subject to some talk-session rules, although the procedures for their invocation are different than for rapping. When, as a lawyer in the common law system, I address a judge, her superordination in the situation is acknowledged by both of us. But she is not absolute. I have the right to speak, a right that we both acknowledge and that her superiors police either spontaneously or on my initiative. When I seek, on my own motion, to assert a right to speak, I always initiate it with some deferential statement that acknowledges her superordination: "If it pleases the Court"; "Your Honor, may I add . . ."; "With all due respect." In less formal discussions—perhaps in chambers—I preface each intervention with a nonverbal signal, such as a lowering of the head or the extension of an open hand. Still, my right to talk comes into operation only when the situational boss indicates that it is acceptable for me to speak.

For absolute despots, the general organizing principle may be that chilling Roman maxim *Quod voluit Caesar, habet vigorem legis,* "Caesar's wish is law"; but organized hierarchical situations may impose some substantive restraints on the boss as well as on the subordinate, though in different ways. The less absolute the hierarchy, the more norms apply to the boss. Saddam Hussein, the Iraqi dictator, reportedly meets his disarmed cabinet with an automatic pistol in his belt. Because he was said to execute on the spot officials who dissatisfied him, we may assume that no one, however subtly or deferentially, drew Saddam's attention to the pertinent rules of the microlaw of talking. In a court of law, too, I defer to the judge in most circumstances. But if the judge should violate critical talking rights, I may indicate that, and by direct and indirect communication I may threaten or actually impose sanctions, thus forcing the judge to comply with a judge's prescribed role. Both of us know that I may appeal to a higher authority that has the competence to enforce some talk-session rules as part of the macrolegal conception of due process. Macrolaw, then, intervenes in microlaw under conditions similar to those tracked in the preceding chapter.

Research Methodology

Microlegal systems usually operate without participants being conscious of operating under the rule of microlaw. Thus, there are very few codifications of these legal systems. Institutionalized hierarchical situations, in contrast, are more likely to have expressly codified rules. Legislative bodies have elaborate codes that manage the economy of talking by protecting the right to the floor, specifying conditions for interruption, and providing for the allocation of talking opportunities. There are even some codifications for rapping. Etiquette books and self-improvement literature on the "art of conversation" all supply some specific norms with remarkable consistency, whether the books are in English or another western European language.[25] A type of microlegal case law can be found in syndicated advice columns[26] whose self-styled experts pass daily public judgment on problem situations submitted by readers. But most of the rules of this microlegal system, whether for rapping or talking to the boss, have never been expressed. Precisely because talking is everywhere and all the time, the rules about talking prove to be more elusive than those about standing in lines, for instance, where an unusual spatial distribution serves as a vivid indicator that rules of a microlegal system are in operation or are breaking down.

As with the other microlegal studies, part of the method applied in studying talk sessions has been personal observation and what might be called, for lack of a better term, "situational" testing. For many years, I have tried to observe myself and others as we engaged in coarchical and hierarchical talk. I tried to note the deferences and self-restraints that I felt obliged to adopt in rapping or talking with the boss and, coordinately, to observe my own reactions when I thought equals were not observing comparable restraints and deferences with regard to me. A burst of irritation or suppressed anger may be an important indication of the operation of micronorms. But precisely because many subliminal factors may be irksome, it is important to be cautious in this type of inquiry. By using the technique of self-scrutiny, which I have elaborated elsewhere,[27] I tried to control for several not always separate variables: subject matter, especially that with a high emotional valence; degree of intimacy or distance; and neurotic tendencies, which we are all subject to and which may have decisive effect on how we behave in certain situations.

Once rules about expectations, demands, and sanctions in talk sessions were provisionally identified, I tried to test them in a number of internalized and externalized ways. On a number of occasions, whether rapping or talking with the boss, I realized after the conversation that my anger with a talker did not derive from the substance of the conversation but from the manner in which it had been conducted. On a few occasions I was able to correlate a burst of irritation on my part with a patent norm violation by the other speaker. In later stages of the study, I was able to test some of my hypotheses about talking rules by observing the reactions of fellow speakers when I violated a rule either intentionally or inadvertently.

I also reviewed the social science literature on talking.[28] It is rich and fascinating, but much of it is not directly relevant to the microlegal dimension of the activity, for social scientists tend to describe externally verifiable behavior without using that material to make inferences about talkers' normative subjectivities. Thus, even when the same terms are being used, the researchers are engaged in a kind of inquiry quite different from the law-oriented one pursued in this book. A number of researchers, however, have dealt with cognate issues;[29] their data and findings were helpful and are referred to in notes where appropriate. I also reviewed books on manners, how to converse, self-improvement. and *l'art de bien dire*. Because I believe that artists see things that we common mortals miss, and "explain in a new way the world unknown to you,"[30] I also consulted literary material whose verisimilitude could be verified by personal experience or by credible reports in social scientific literature.

SETTING THE STAGE

At the outset of a talk session, people must establish whether they are rapping or talking to a boss. When the parties know each other and where they stand in relation to each other, that is not likely to be a problem. If they do not know each other, the micropolitical character of their relationship must be established, at least provisionally. The determination may be made in many ways. Common methods involve preliminary verbal or nonverbal exchanges—styles of address, grammatical forms, body posture, name cards, and so on. The relative depth of a bow may be significant, as may tone of voice. A claim of superordination may be made by low voice tone and casualness, conveying the message that the other party must make the effort of communication. Sometimes the superiority of the other party may be acknowledged by speaking in a tone higher than ordinary.[31] The reasons for this are obscure and may derive from an assumed childlike role or serve as a vocalized confirmation of a stance of attention, a stiffening of muscles before a superordinate.

Languages spoken in intensely stratified societies often contain special grammatical forms or explicit modes of address that acknowledge the distribution of power and indicate whether the session is rapping or talking to the boss.[32] In Japan, where part of this chapter was written, informants explained that the Japanese language is richly inflected and requires explicit forms and signals of hierarchy. In America, where the myth of democracy prevails, the more obvious and effusive terms for conveying superordination and subordination can be viewed as fawning and can be embarrassing, offensive, and even mocking and insulting to one or the other party. But because pecking orders and political structures of inequality exist in the United States no less than in other cultures, the norms of microlegal systems of conversation are in place, although they must be teased out with patience and care.

Environmental factors, broadly understood, communicate,[33] and may often facilitate the preliminary determination of, the power relationship[34] of the talkers and, therefore, the nature of the talk session. If A comes to B's office, presumptions can be made that provisionally resolve many preliminary questions as unequivocally as would A's coming to B's bedroom. Some public settings signal that rapping or talking to the boss, as the case may be, may proceed. If I sit down close to you at a bar when there are many vacant places, the proximity I have established, which in other circumstances might be deemed aggressive, will not be taken so. The common understanding is that if you are sitting at a bar, you are making yourself available for rapping. This is, however, a presumption that you can rebut by a variety of nonverbal and verbal messages that, in this context, will not be deemed uncivil or offensive. If you sit, not at the empty bar, but at an unoccupied table, the message is quite different.

In these examples, spatial arrangements are used to signal whether the invitation is to rap or to talk to the boss. Some signals blare out hierarchy.[35] Monarchs sit on pedestals, as do judges in courtrooms. Even a desk that serves as a barrier between two potential speakers may be presumed to mean that any ensuing conversation will be hierarchical. The bigger the desk or the more elevated it is, the more superordination the person behind it wishes to convey.[36] There are, however, inherent limits on the superordinate's vanity, for too much elevation effectively precludes talking. Benito Mussolini balanced his amour propre and this unyielding limitation in an ingenious way: by sitting behind a very high desk on a pedestal at the further end of a room. A person entering the room could not help but receive an instant message of who the boss was; any residual doubts were surely dispelled as the supplicant trekked toward the elevated *Duce*. Conversely, a superordinate who abandons a desk and invites the other talker to sit at a circular table or in informal chairs helps to restore coarchy.

The physical asymmetry established when one talker is sitting and the other is standing imports hierarchy. The boss may choose to sit or to stand. When the boss sits and is lower than the subordinate, that physical asymmetry does not reflect the actual power relations. When this occurs, body language may be used to redress the situation. If the subordinate is sitting when the boss approaches, the subordinate will often awkwardly ease into a standing position, while the superordinate will frequently slump down in an ambiguous body posture that says, among other things, "I have the power to fix our physical proximity" or perhaps "I am intentionally coming down, so we are on the same level." The comical consequence of these conflicting efforts to coordinate spatial and social position can be to block the increasingly desperate subordinate from standing up. But height—being above another—is also a symbol of power: when the boss is sitting and the subordinate is standing up, the subordinate may actually crouch down so that his or her head is at least level with, if not lower than, the boss's.

Physical barriers, even when they are not elevated, can also signal hierarchy because they constrain the outsider from reaching the boss without special physical effort or contortion. Anyone behind a glass or screen operates in a situation designed to imply that that person has something the supplicant wants and, thanks to the barrier, cannot physically acquire without the other's acquiescence. In some cases, the signals are painfully clear. Consider Richard Reeves's observation of the function of barriers in Pakistan. "The windows of bureaucracy were small and built at what I would call waist level. That was on my side. On the other side, the power side, they were at the level of the eyes and ears of a clerk sitting at a desk. To deal with the clerk you had to bend to the window to be heard through the talking slot, assuming the position of a backward number '7' which was also the position for what inevitably happened next."[37] Barriers perform multiple functions, but for talking purposes, whether the person behind the barrier is a priest receiving confession, a bank teller, a pawnbroker, or a security guard, the physical structure of the situation communicates presumptions of hierarchical conversation: you are talking to a boss.

Some of these spatial arrangements may also provide signals of presumptive coarchy and thus facilitate rapping. People on the same side of the barricade, whether a desk, a fence, or a line marked on the ground, are figuratively in the same situation, and their initial presumption about the structure of a talk session will be that it is coarchical. As we saw in the previous chapter, queues are spatial conformations of democracy. Thus, people standing next to each other in a line may initiate a coarchical conversation with strangers, although they clearly would not initiate the same conversation if they happened to be walking near each other on the street.

When people encounter each other in situations in which there are no such signals, they may try to derive the information necessary for a preliminary determination of hierarchy from clothing, posture, body ornamentation, and so on.[38] Given the way different classes imitate each other's dress and style in the United States, many of the features are no longer reliable signals. In some cases, people may go out of their way to use other mobile props to facilitate identification. In David Lodge's amusing novel *Small World*, two characters sitting beside each other in an airplane are able to determine that they are members of the same subculture and to anticipate the structure and content of their rap session by displaying and surreptitiously noting that each is reading subculturally approved and fashionable arcana. "Thus it was that about one hour later Morris Zapp found himself sitting next to Fulvia Morgana in a British Airways Trident bound for Milan. It didn't take them long to discover that they were both academics. While the plane was still taxiing to the runway, Morris had Philip Swallow's book on Hazlitt out on his lap, and Fulvia Morgana her copy of Althusser's essays. Each glanced surreptitiously at the other's reading matter. It was good as a masonic handshake. They met each other's eyes."[39] When one cannot exit a situation—for example, on a long, overbooked flight—an initial misstep can mean hours of tedious, if not embarrassing, conversation. Initially, the parties may move with extraordinary indirection and caution precisely because of the costs and even risks in getting involved in a rap session with the "wrong" sort of person.[40]

When you and I talk, our conversation is made possible by complex sets of norms of substance and procedure, including constitutive or constitutional norms with their own procedures for changing the rules of the mundane conversation. If we know each other reasonably well, we take for granted which talking norms govern our exchanges. Even if we have a number of contingent conversational systems because we have different contingent relationships, the function of early signals is quickly and innocuously to establish which system obtains in the present setting. Here is an example. If A and B have not only established patterns of reciprocal joking but also held more serious talk sessions, an invitation to a rap session of joking might be gently deflected by saying "Come on, be serious" or by a gesture or facial expression. The opposite message, according to the invitation to frivolous conversation along with the different rules that it entails, can be conveyed by saying "Here we go again" or simply rolling one's eyes heavenward.[41]

Orienting signals like these function as a private language and may be inappropriate, even offensive, if used with strangers. If we do not know each other, a set of initial exchanges between us will often be indirect, aimed at determining who is who, where each of us fits in the great Chain of Being, how we relate to each other, what the common objectives of the conversation will be, whether the exchange is coarchical or hierarchical, and so on. Nor should the effect of transference in these preliminaries be discounted. Only after these have been established will the conversation proceed smoothly.

These preliminary but indispensable signals and messages are exchanged very rapidly. An invitation to flirt can be rejected by a glance, a tone of voice, even a stiffening of posture and an elevation of the pitch of the chin.[42] If the other talker does not change approach appropriately, a more explicit demurrer may follow. When would-be participants in a rap session fail to establish a common tone, the session is aborted or, in some instances, modulates into talking to the boss.

In hierarchical talk situations, initial as well as subsequent decisions about tone and subject matter are dictated by the boss. A woman talking to her boss who is subjected to talk signals with unwanted sexual overtones will find her ability to reject the advance and to participate in setting the tone of the session markedly less than when she is rapping.[43] This is an especially degrading experience because decisions about sex, a quintessential expression of self, are being taken from the individual and appropriated by the boss. Sometimes it may appear that the subordinate talking to the boss is initiating a modulation from an unwanted subject, but a closer examination of the session will usually reveal that the subordinate proposes, the boss disposes.

An agenda is the outcome of a process that sets the subject matter of a talk session. Where there is relative equality among talkers and no consensus on the topic of conversation, the agenda will be a a compromise. Its acceptance by the talkers may be the condition for initiating or continuing the rap session. Once established, an agenda is supposed to function as a reified boss, akin to the Rule of Law in macrolegal systems.

Agnes Morton, in her 1898 self-improvement book on talking, did not distinguish between rapping and talking to the boss, so she was only partly right when she wrote, "In conversation no one can independently select a subject."[44] In some relationships the agenda setting takes only a short time: the boss enjoys the power to determine the subject matter and to change it at will. A subordinate must suffer in silence the self-indulgent ramblings of the boss, even the schizophrenic disjointedness of a dictator.[45] The subordinate is constrained to ventilate irritation and seek to regain a degree of personal dignity only by fantasized responses or by subsequent mockery, prudently expressed well out of the boss's hearing range.

But it would be wrong to assume that superordination is absolute with respect to setting and changing the agenda. Power is critical in hierarchies, but not all hierarchies are absolute despotisms. Some hierarchical situations may impose significant restraints on the superordinate. A chairperson may digress, but some restraint is imposed by an agenda that has been authoritatively decided.[46] A judge may domineer and dither but is subject to substantive and procedural controls and is ultimately policed by higher levels of the judicial bureaucracy.

Constitutional Principles of Procedure

If the preliminary phase of a talk session has been successfully negotiated, the stage has been set. Now rules of substance and procedure come into operation, but they vary significantly depending on whether the speakers are rapping or talking to the boss.

Taking turns. Oscar Wilde made the point about taking turns with typically poisonous accuracy:

> "Conversation, indeed!" said the Rocket. "You have talked the whole time yourself. That is not conversation."
>
> "Somebody must listen," answered the Frog, "and I like to do all the talking myself. . . ."
>
> "You are a very irritating person," said the Rocket.[47]

The most basic rule of procedure in rapping, indeed, the practice that characterizes a rap session, is the rule of reciprocal turn-taking.[48] This has been described as an intricately collaborative process: "Turn-taking in adult conversation is normally accomplished smoothly, with few overlaps and few gaps between turns. This smooth transition of turns can be attributed to the collaborative interactional work of the participants. The listener, who is the potential next speaker, monitors the current turn for its point of possible completion. . . . At the same time, the current speaker constructs the turn in such a way that the listener can project its possible completion. Various devices may be used, such as tag questions, falling intonation contours and non-verbal cues."[49] This rule appears to be very basic and, as we will see, is not dependent on the content of communications. There is evidence that it is meticulously honored even among chronic mental patients.[50]

Coarchical talk sessions are based on several common normative premises about certain equalities of the talkers: (1) both or all parties are micropolitically equal, (2) their experience is equally valid, and (3) they each have the necessary ability to communicate. The talkers may actually believe these premises, or one or both talkers may adopt them only for the session. The talker who does not believe them must dissemble, for a patronizing attitude will either bring the rap session to an abrupt end or transform it into talking to the boss. Robert Louis Stevenson, who was brilliantly perceptive of the dynamics of two people talking, thought that a reciprocal belief in these equalities was not at all common. He viewed taking turns as an obligation on each talker to accept "the vanity of the other." Whether durable, ephemeral, or disbelieved but postulated, the premises are indispensable for a rap session and carry with them important substantive implications.[51]

In operation, the taking-turns rule requires each party to talk and to let the other talk. Where one of the parties does not comply with this rule—for example, by monopolizing the conversation—the other may characterize the violation of the micronorm in various ways: "he's lecturing me," "she doesn't let me get a word in edgewise," "he's hogging the conversation," and so on. Note that what is a violation of the microlaw when rapping would be normal and expected when talking to the boss.

Because taking turns also establishes an affirmative obligation to talk, the rule may be violated by not talking enough; in any coarchical talk session, such behavior is not interpreted as only ill-mannered haughtiness. In the epigraph to this chapter, Primo Levi notes the "anxiety and suspicion" that it generates.[52] Elsewhere he writes movingly of the pain of "the ever-repeated scene of the unlistened-to story."[53] Trial lawyers exploit this insight and intentionally violate the micronorm when interrogating hostile witnesses. William Ginsburg, a prominent trial lawyer, writes: "A technique sometimes used by plaintiffs' lawyers to attempt to prod a witness to volunteer information is the 'pregnant pause.' The deposing counsel asks a question, the witness responds, and then counsel simply stares at the witness in silence, waiting for some further response. The temptation for the witness is to fill the void with something, even if the witness has nothing to say or has completely answered the question in his or her mind. Periods of silence are uncomfortable to the average person engaged in conversation."[54] Excessive taciturnity, as we will see, violates the rules of coarchical talk sessions, unless it is accompanied by prescribed signals with which the nonspeaker waives the right to talk, thus rendering it innocuous.

The taking-turns rule does not operate when talking to the boss. Randall Jarrell's wonderful academic satire, *Pictures from an Institution,* captures the point. The president of the university was entitled, ex officio as it were, to speak interminably: "The President's conversation was . . . a lecture interrupted by silences of pure appeal. (Why didn't he say he wanted to *go back* to teaching?) He wanted you to like him, he wanted everybody to like him—it was part of being President; but talking all the time was too."[55]

This inversion of the taking-turns rule is obvious in situations that are manifestly hierarchical. It is more elusive in situations that appear to be rap sessions except that the taking-turns rule is frequently violated *and* the violations are unsanctioned. Empirical data show correlations between rates of violation and de facto power asymmetries: violations of the taking-turns rule by simultaneous talking were more likely when the initial speaker was a woman, and men were more likely to interrupt when women were talking.[56] Earlier research found that there were comparable correlations between patients and psychiatrists.[57] These studies, whose conclusions are consistent with my observations, should not be interpreted as indicating general breakdowns of the microlegal system, for many of the other rules are still observed. Rather they show that students of microlegal systems must take account of the power variable and must dig below the surface to distinguish between rapping and talking-to-the boss sessions, for different norms apply, in different ways, to each.

When the taking-turns rule does operate, it generates a number of secondary rules. Elsewhere I have used the term "structural naturalistic" for a frame of jurisprudence whose assumptions recur in Historicist legal theories, Marxist literature, and the writings of neo-Positivists like Lon Fuller. Structural naturalism assumes an inexorable causal relation between the context of an activity and its normative structure: context determines law.[58] Obviously, physical and social environment provide the context for social events. To say that they do not absolutely predetermine the arrangements that actors will select or create does not mean that they are without significant influence. Contextual factors influence the actors. Actors who are aware of context make matter-of-fact assumptions about which possible arrangements are less compatible with the dynamics of the situation and hence require a greater continuing investment and more constant policing to endure and which arrangements are likely to be more self-sustaining.

Structural naturalistic analysis is useful in drawing attention to a number of correlative or secondary norms that are associated with rapping. One such norm enjoins rappers to speak in a moderate fashion. Mary Green Conklin, in her manual of 1913 on how to converse, calls for "good humored tolerance."[59] Pounding the table and pressing a point too vigorously or heatedly imply that a view propounded by the other is without foundation. Sarcasm may chill the discussion. Such devices may be rhetorically effective, but they interfere with the smooth operation of talk sessions. William Utterback, in a more recent how-to manual, counsels: "In discussion, we should avoid all name calling words and other language tinged with emotion; it is likely to set off a chain reaction of recrimination that will make the subject too hot to handle."[60]

The violation of this norm is different from the violation of the taking-turns rule. If the taking-turns rule is violated, a rap session is transformed into talking to the boss. If these correlative norms are violated, they do not necessarily transform the session. but they do put additional stress on it. Although a violation will probably not in itself effect the transformation from rapping to talking to the boss, a cumulation of violations may have that effect. Because a single violation of these correlative norms does not ignite a sanction or stimulate a constitutional transformation, an Austinian is inclined to dismiss such norms as positive morality rather than law.[61] Yet a cumulation of these violations may reach a sort of "nodal" point and transform or disrupt the situation, indicating once again the insufficiency of the Positivist School's narrow definition of law as exclusively a product of the state.[62]

The listening corollary. Talking is interactive. While one person talks, the other takes a turn listening. In talk sessions, roles must oscillate between listening and talking. In the literature on the subject, the point is so clear that it is almost always expressed with Mosaic brevity. One popular commentator writes: "Don't Interrupt!"[63] The anonymous *Art of Conversing*, published in Boston in 1846, says: "The obligation to listen is one of the fundamental laws of the social code."[64] Almost a century later, another manual says: "Inattention is inexcusable."[65] Thoreau remarked: "It takes two to speak truth—one to speak and another to hear."[66] Protests of violations of the listening corollary, which confirm the operation of the norm, may be found in such comments as "Am I talking to myself?" and, more plaintively, "Listen!" In hierarchical sessions, one function of a chairperson is to police this rule.

Listening is not passive. The listening corollary requires that the person whose turn it is to listen conveys continuing attentiveness by "appropriate support responses."[67] As the author of *The Art of Conversing* puts it: "To consider silent immobility as attention is an erroneous interpretation of the law of politeness. You must prove that you have not only eyes but ears; and a monosyllable of approbation or interest ought, at times, to be uttered, in order to satisfy the speaker that you hear and understand all that is said. Your interlocutor requires some sign of life, to be satisfied that he is not throwing away words upon an unanimated figure."[68] Civil attention may be conveyed by periodic nods, some eye contact (but not too much and certainly not the glazed eyeball variety),[69] the head turned slightly as if an ear were cocked, nonverbal quickly raised eyebrows, grunts of "uh-huh," and so on. In telephone rapping, support responses must be nonintrusive verbalizations. Without them, the talker is likely to grow concerned and to cry out, "Hello? Hello?"or "Are you there?"

The absence of any of these support responses can constitute a sanction. Randall Jarrell in the fictional account we considered a moment ago describes one such conversation: "When he and Gertrude met they did not, shouting *A Roland! An Oliver!*

set out to see which could talk the whole time: each knew what his opponent was. One would talk for five or ten minutes while the other, all smiles and *rapport* and inattention, stared out the window or, better still, at a wonderful reflection which each of us can sometimes see in the windowpane; then they would trade parts."[70] When active or affirmative sanctions are inappropriate, the absence of manifest confirmations of listening frequently precipitates the breakup of the session or its transformation from rapping to talking to the boss.

An extreme example of the destructiveness of speaking and not being heard is Primo Levi's account of the common and unbearably painful survivor's dream of "the ever-repeated scene of the unlistened-to story." The dreamer finds himself reunited with his family and trying to tell them what has happened to him, but no one listens or understands or wants to hear.[71] Others have captured this experience as an "irrepressible need to bear witness," but with no audience that wants to listen.[72] The poet Adrienne Rich describes the attempts by historically silenced people to be heard as "the dream of a common language."[73]

Listening is necessary for talking, but even in rapping, the distribution of the obligation to listen is not always equal. Pamela Fishman found in her study of American couples' household conversations that women were doing the bulk of the work in the "division of labor in conversation."[74] As Dena Goodman writes of Fishman's study: "Women's work in conversation . . . is relative to men's needs. Sometimes the silence of a 'good listener' might be required; at other times silences need to be filled to keep conversation going."[75]

The listening corollary sheds almost all of its reciprocity and essential symmetry in a talking-to-the-boss session. Bosses have less of an obligation to listen, and whatever listening is incumbent on them declines with the increase of their absolute power. Many lawyers can recount tales of pleading before a judge who was sound asleep. On the other hand, the subordinate who is talking to the boss has a much greater listening obligation and must demonstrate it constantly by verbal formula, posture, modulation of voice, appropriate eye contact, and so on.

The yielding corollary. Rapping requires each speaker to yield the floor at regular intervals. This is the "yielding corollary." Yielding the floor does not necessarily require one talker to stop and the other to start. To be coarchical, a rap session does not have to split talk time on a straight fifty-fifty basis. But there must be some unequivocal acknowledgment of the periodic applicability of the corollary.

Speakers usually comply with the yielding rule in response to nonverbal signals,[76] for example, when A signals a willingness to yield—with a pause, an eyebrow raised,[77] a chin dropped, an inquiring "hmmm?"—and B indicates no wish to talk, giving a similar grunt or a shake of the head and a smile, thus yielding the turn to talk. This exchange may be accomplished very quickly and subtly and is often woven into the conversation.[78] In academic discussions, however, I have observed exaggerated and sometimes ritualized efforts at maintaining coarchical structure in a talk session. A confidently knowledgeable colleague who has been talking to the limits of his turn will nod in an exaggerated courtly fashion to another as if truly asking for his input though knowing that the other person is ill equipped to speak on the topic. The other must now acknowledge that she has nothing to add by saying something on the order of "No, please go ahead," or "This is very interesting." When microlegal norms are made explicit in this fashion, they are often being exploited out of sheer meanness, reasons that are distinct from the operational requirements of the microlegal system.

Neither taking-turns nor yielding rules apply to the superordinate when talking-to-the-boss.[79] The boss has no obligation to yield but does so at her discretion when the subordinate indicates that he wishes to speak. Even when the subordinate is given the opportunity to talk, it is not by right but by license, subject to immediate recall by the superordinate. The boss speaks whenever she wishes and as long as she wants; the subordinate listens. It is not unusual in instrumental talk sessions for the superordinate to deprive herself of useful and sometimes vital information that a more knowledgeable subordinate has but is denied the opportunity to express.

The corollary of self-restraint. Taking turns also imports a practice of restraint. When I do not break into your turn, unless special circumstances obtain, the self-restraint corollary is operating. "Many listeners, otherwise polite," observes the author of *The Art of Conversation,* "appear to have great difficulty in restraining their impatience to return to what they themselves were saying; forgetting that indulgence in the gratification of one's self is but a poor way of gratifying others."[80] As with all forced deferrals of gratification, it is sometimes hard to restrain oneself from breaking in. But this is an intensely demanded norm. It is often confirmed when several others are present in coarchical talk sessions. If the corollary of self-restraint is repeatedly violated, the auditors are even likely to chant spontaneously, like a Greek chorus, "Let her talk," "Give the guy a chance," and so on.

The self-restraint corollary does not necessarily mean that a speaker *must* be permitted to finish speaking. But simply breaking in is unacceptable. The proper method involves signaling that you wish to break in and waiting for permission to do so.[81] The signal may be a sharp intake of breath, conveying that one is about to speak; lifting a finger—a signal borrowed and adapted from many institutionalized hierarchical situations but substantially reduced and tempered (a more overt raised hand would convey something quite different, as we will see); expressly requesting permission to break in, with "May I?" "May I interrupt?" or, more sharply, "May I get a word in?" The restraint corollary acknowledges the competence of the speaker to decide whether to yield, but a corollary of civility, which we will examine in a moment, obliges the speaker to at least acknowledge the request. The speaker may not ignore it. To do so implies that the other person has violated the rule, and ignoring the request is a sanction.

In talking to the boss, the corollary of restraint ceases to operate reciprocally, as it does in rap sessions. But it does not cease operating entirely.[82] The subordinate may request the boss or another speaker to yield by raising a hand; in using this signal, the subordinate acknowledges that the matter is to be decided by the boss. The signal, which is widely used in Western civilization, is a two-directional connection between rapping and talking to the boss. Lift a finger gently, and you confirm that you are rapping . Raise your arm, and you may be transforming the rap session into talking to the boss, or, by the exaggeration of the gesture, be protesting a violation of the yielding rules by a speaker who has been swept away by his own eloquence. The use of this and other signals that have a constant denotation (in this case, that you wish to talk) but a potential for significantly different connotations (for example, that the other person is talking too much) can change the larger structure of conversation from coarchy to hierarchy, or vice versa.

The corollary of civility. In rapping, each speaker is entitled to indicate disagreement with what the other is saying, but there are limits to how and when this may be done. The limits are defined by the corollary of civility. Among other things, the rule of civility requires the listener not merely to listen but also to supply to the speaker unobtrusive signals of attentiveness.[83] Civility, in the sense in which I am using it, does not mean conventional politeness. Many talk sessions are marked by raillery. West African villagers or American teenage boys on a street corner may say outrageous things at each others' expense. Where joking relationships exist, the casual observer may see precious little civility; in fact, the insults may be a form of ritualized aggression. Certain secret society rituals at Yale College are reported to demand intense criticism of one of the talkers. Yet, in the context, a civility rule will still be applied.[84]

Some types of instrumental talking have civility regulations with quite varying contents. The implicit regulations of scientific discourse, for example, encourage talkers to be critical as to content, with a degree of precision and asperity that might be offensive in other settings. At an economics colloquium, I heard a commentator say that the presenter's paper was interesting but wrong in its premises and facts and flawed in the progression of certain parts of its arguments. Although hearing these criticisms was not a pleasurable experience for the presenter, the comments did not disrupt the talk session and presumably were consistent with the purpose of the meeting in helping the presenter correct her paper before publication. At the other end of the spectrum, in the advertising industry, Alex F. Osborn's technique of "brainstorming" intentionally ratchets up the threshold of civility by establishing the regulation that "adverse criticism is taboo,"[85] because criticism is presumed to stifle creativity, the desired outcome for which the talk session is the instrument.

CONSTITUTIONAL PRINCIPLES OF SUBSTANCE

Aside from the procedural rules that we have considered, there are three basic substantive rules in microlegal systems of conversation. To many people, the word "rule" suggests a rigid order. But other than the most basic and often trivial rules, most substantive rules in legal systems carve out an area and set policy in general terms, requiring of decisionmakers variation and refinement in their application of the rules in different contexts.

Respecting agendas: subject matter jurisdiction. The first rule concerns what we might call subject matter jurisdiction. It pertains to setting the scene for a talk session. Whether the talk is instrumental or talk-for-its-own-sake, the determination of subject matter in coarchical settings is relatively democratic. Once subject matter is set, speakers are expected to respect the agenda. It may not be changed without the common agreement of the participants. The rule has many different names in the literature. Probably the most colorful is Utterback's: "Follow the Ball!"[86]

English and American manners and self-improvement books on talking are unanimous in their condemnation of unilateral transformations of the subject matter of talk-for-its-own-sake or instrumental talk into anything else.[87] A serious business conversation may be introduced or lightened by a joke but may not be unilaterally transformed into a joking session. Nor may a business session be transformed into talk about an unrelated matter of some personal concern. The rapper who seeks to effect these unauthorized transitions violates a substantive norm. Being too serious in a talk-for-its-own-sake session will also violate the subject-matter rule. In the exuberantly manipulative *The Art of Conversation and How to Apply Its Technique,* a very interesting manual on talking-for-its-own sake, Milton Wright offers this advice: "Do not be too deep and do not draw one topic out to tiresome length. Keep always in mind the fact that you want to please your companion and the conversation will not lag."[88]

In some situations, changing the subject may serve as an insignia of power. On a number of occasions, I have observed manifestly coherent judges indulge themselves by wandering off into reminiscences at best tangentially related to the issue at bar. Counsel for both parties invariably waited patiently, knowing that the judge would return to the prescribed subject matter. Such vagaries may have nothing to do with momentary or impending senility. One of the latent functions of these digressions is to permit the judge to confirm his superordination to all present. If the counsel were negotiating among themselves, however, and one of them strayed in this "judicial" fashion, the other would be likely to invoke the subject-matter rule.

The degree of latitude that a boss enjoys in unilaterally changing the subject matter depends on the extent of the boss's power in a situation. The absolute despot may change the subject at will, whenever and as often as is desired. In many hierarchical situations, however, the superordinate enjoys a more limited right of unilateral change. In sessions governed by a Rule of Law, for example, prescribed procedures act as a boss and may be invoked when the superordinate violates them.

Respecting agendas does not mean that agendas cannot be changed or that talk sessions may not proceed beyond a fixed agenda. Talkers accomplish these adjustments in a microlawful and orderly fashion, thanks to what have been called conversational syntax rules.[89] One scholar has examined some of these progressions and codified the rules that seem to govern them. With respect to agendas, for example, he found that "it is appropriate to shift the topic of conversation to objects highly associated with a newly introduced object if the associated object is of interest."[90] The details of these particular rules are less important for our discussion than the evidence of their existence and operation.

Rules have their exceptions. Indeed, we say that the exception proves the rule. The exceptions to the talking rules that we are considering are particularly fascinating, for some of them provide insight into the deeper compacts of social exchange and how they operate. The most interesting of these relates to the protection of vital personal interests.

In some coarchical situations, a speaker may feel compelled to violate the rule regarding subject matter jurisdiction for important personal reasons. If a conversation approaches or touches on matters that a speaker feels are injurious to personal interests, he or she may try to deflect the conversation to a less threatening subject The talker who is unilaterally changing the subject is knowingly violating the subject matter rule.[1] The reactions to such a violation are jurisprudentially instructive. In rap sessions, other speakers will defer to this violation, behaving as if it had not occurred and no sanctions are needed. I surmise that in coarchical situations, rappers appreciate that each has certain vital interests, so a reciprocal privilege to exclude awkward items from the talk session is in their common interest. When the speaker's vital interests are threatened, he or she exercises a type of discretionary exception, akin to a "political question" privilege in a federal court, and other speakers yield to it.

When talking to the boss, however, the speaker enjoys no such privilege, and the more hierarchical the session, the weaker the subordinate's claim to vital personal interests. When talking to the boss, a unilateral effort at changing the subject is viewed as ducking the question or evading the issue, an activity described in terms that carry a strong condemnation. A speaker before a court, a legislative committee, or any other boss can be forced to respond or be sanctioned for failing to. In some hierarchical settings, to be sure, limited exceptions may be allowed. Certain rights not to self-incriminate may operate, for example. But in the more brutal of hierarchies, whether a person is standing before a totalitarian court or being put to the proof before elders, parents, teachers, or the media, no exception avails. I noted in the first chapter that in the United States the media now seem to assume that the exception does not operate with respect to the private lives of politicians. In sharp contrast, the exception is an inherent feature of rap sessions. Try to force speakers in a rap session to address a vital interest against their will, and they are likely to say, "It's none of your damned business." But if the person with vital interests to protect yields to force and allows the touchy discussion to proceed, the rap session has lost some of its coarchical character and to an extent has modulated into talking to the boss.

The rule of provisional acceptance. A coworker stops me in the hall and tells me that the bad news is that Jerusalem will be destroyed in two years; the good news is that the year after, the Messiah will arrive. I incline my head in a sign of intense interest while searching for a pretext to escape. A colleague with whom I am transacting some distasteful committee work tells me a sexist joke. I am desperate to put a seal to the committee work and get away, so, rather than jeopardize the instrumental talk session, I smile in apparent appreciation, then direct the conversation back to the agenda. In speaking to a student, I make a remark that would be unremarkable to a member of my age cohort but which the student finds alien, if not offensive. The words are scarcely out of my mouth when I realize its possible interpretation, but the student nods her head appreciatively. She, too, is desperate to conclude the transaction and be off.

These are examples of a second substantive norm in rap sessions. Common to each is a reciprocal moratorium on searching and, as a result, potentially damaging criticism. This norm requires someone to *appear* to take for granted a great deal of what the other talker says, a reciprocal provisional acceptance of, or at least a manifest pretense at accepting, the metaphysics of those with whom one is talking.

By not calling each other to account in an empirically referential way for most of the things we are saying, we create in conversations a common illusion of an objective world or at least one factually and morally common to the speakers. This norm is structurally necessary because, trite as it may sound to say so, we are all different. By holding back in this fashion and taking a lot for granted, we facilitate exchanges. Without that implied agreement to suspend substantive scrutiny, coarchical conversationalists would find it much more difficult to proceed. A number of observers have identified this agreement as an essential precondition for talking. In the scholarly literature, it has been called a "practical ethic" of conversation[92] or simply the "cooperative principle."[93]

The more congruent the universes of expectations of the talkers, the more natural and apparently spontaneous the compliance with the rule of provisional acceptance. Indicators of congruence of expectations among talkers may be found in common language and dialect, culture, class, sex or gender, age, and exposure to crises.[94] The lower the degree of convergence of the universes of expectations of the talkers, the greater the effort that at least one of the talkers must make to comply with this rule. The allocation of the burden of making the effort is determined by the relative power positions of the speakers.

Words can bridge different worlds, for talking, like good storytelling, frequently creates its own universe of expectations. Often this common universe endures no longer than the conversation, but sometimes expectations may change, permanently reshaping the lives of the talkers and many others. In other cases, provisional acceptance may be obviously strained and fragile. Then it is all the more indispensable to talking.

Although the rule of provisional acceptance facilitates talking, it does not necessarily facilitate the manifest objective of instrumental talking. Consider instrumental talking in an academic department, which requires, no less than in other groups, compliance with the rule of provisional acceptance. The rule of provisional acceptance is innocuous in talking-for-its-own-sake. But in instrumental talking in the academy, the provisional acceptance of the common assumptions of the discipline can limit or subvert the further pursuit of knowledge, which is the manifest objective of the instrumental talking. Theologians cannot have a searching discussion of the nature of God if one of the talkers harps on the idea that God does not exist, any more than jurists can explore the character of justice if one of the speakers keeps insisting that all justice reflects the interest of the stronger. The same common assumptions that make enlightened discussion possible in these settings also stifle the development of enlightenment. Innovators must violate the rule to advance a science, which is one of the reasons why they are often treated as pariahs.

The normative dissonance caused by the clash of two authoritative but inconsistent policies is not unusual. Often a policy has unintended and unsought consequences that conflict with other policies, yet it remains a critical and sometimes indispensable social objective. Consider the fundamental commitment to pluralism, which is the predicate for so many of the microlegal systems in this book. Smaller groups, which are, by definition, exclusive, establish and police their own boundaries and maintain their own esprit. Thus, they enhance contact for in-group members while reducing it for outsiders. Yet they also increase the possibility of intergroup competition and conflict and may generate feelings of insufficiency or reduced worth in the members of excluded groups. Hence a community committed to pluralism must constantly deal with the dark underside of pluralism by a variety of programs designed to minimize or mitigate undesirable consequences and to remedy the injuries that pluralism will continue to cause. The rule of provisional acceptance thus belongs to that category of norms which seem to be contextually indispensable and hence desirable from a policy standpoint but which inevitably generate social problems that must be repaired by additional normative arrangements.

Violating the rule of provisional acceptance in rap sessions brings them to a grinding halt. Conversation becomes impossible. When talking to the boss, however, the subordinate whose right to provisional acceptance has been violated does not always have the liberty of terminating the session and withdrawing. Members of groups that have known relatively permanent subordination (women, children, certain racial, religious, or caste groups) are constantly obliged to speak foreign metalanguages[95]—the languages of their superordinates' universes. In some cases, the emotional and psychological consequences can be severe.

In talking-to-the-boss sessions, the boss may consciously violate the rule of provisional acceptance as an intentional way of confusing and browbeating the subordinate. By refusing to accept provisionally, even for the limited purposes of the conversation, the metaphysics of the speaker and by insisting instead on imposing his or her own, the boss throws the subordinate into confusion, for in the deepest sense, the boss is conveying that the subordinate's reality is worthless, if it even exists. Thus the boss undermines and, in some cases, obliterates the subordinate's being. This kind of violation of the rule of provisional acceptance is a refined technique of the more violent forms of interrogation. Cleverly used, it creates the impression that the subordinate is lying. This aspect of the matter has been analyzed in some detail with regard to the taking of testimony in congressional committees.[96] It is familiar to anyone who observes the techniques of lawyers in criminal trials.

The rule of truth . . . with a variable content. Rap sessions, as we have seen, may have a wide variety of objectives. In many of them, truth—a correspondence between what speakers say and what they believe—may not be particularly important. Indeed, the rule of provisional acceptance requires a tacit and reciprocal suspension of demands for verification of many of the matter-of-fact assumptions of the speaker; if each were challenged or put to the proof by the other speaker, much talk could not proceed. In talking-for-its-own-sake, demands for truth, whether empirically verifiable statements or statements of unqualified conviction, are different from such demands in instrumental talking. All the talkers may appreciate values of companionship, human contact, and bonding far more than the manifest content of the exchange.

Where talkers vie to tell outrageous stories as a form of reciprocal entertainment, even a minimum rule of truth may seem inoperative. In fact, it never is. Because participants in such sessions are not supposed to leave with false information, fiction is always accompanied by signals marking it for what it is. The signals may come from other listeners, whose uproarious laughter or cries of disbelief unmistakably tell other, possibly more credulous listeners that what has been said is pure bull. Sometimes it will be the speaker who conveys this important metamessage.[97] When such signals come directly from the speaker, they are reminiscent of the Noh dancer who tips his mask periodically to remind the audience, already enchanted by the magic of the performance, that this is, after all, only an artistic performance.

When talking is not conducted for its own sake but is instrumental, the truth rule operates differently. Myth systems in many cultures give elaborate formal veneration to truth. Folklore may cultivate all sorts of stories and tales to reinforce that veneration, while, upscale,[98] a number of philosophers have developed elaborate systems to establish the ethics and obligations of truth in communication.[99] In fact, the operational norms in American culture manifest great variability with regard to truth requirements for both rapping and talking with the boss and suggest a much more complicated code than one modeled on George Washington and his celebrated cherry tree. Like the Viennese jurisprudential writer Rudolf Stammler's notion of "natural law with a variable content," the truth rule's requirement of truth content or "proof" varies from setting to setting.

Some settings, such as formal scientific discourse, seem to be based upon a substantive rule of extremely high, though often subculturally idiosyncratic, truth. The truth is idiosyncratic in that conventions that are believed to be fundamental and necessary premises of the discipline—for example, among economists, that the market is phenomenal rather than epiphenomenal or that all persons and their institutions are wealth maximizers—are not to be questioned. They are off bounds. To make the boundary explicit is to underline the relativity of the truth that governs within it. One of my most exhilarating and vivid childhood memories is of my Talmud teacher, at our first meeting, setting out his ground rules. "You may ask any question," he said with a gentle smile, "except about the existence of God." When the truth rule is made explicit in this fashion, it facilitates focused talking—it may well be the precondition—but it also inevitably relativizes the truth that it is placing beyond the bounds of discussion.

In other settings—for example, certain sales situations—both parties seem to expect that there will be a wide variance from the truth. An observer can infer that the variances are accepted from the terms used to describe them. Rather than calling them "lies," a term that conveys unequivocal condemnation, participants use "puffing," "exaggeration," or "hype," euphemisms that incorporate judgments about communications which depart substantially from the truth but are not deemed to be lies in the circumstances in which they are uttered. People appear to demand more proof in written communications than in oral communcations.

The truth rule is not flexible when talking to the boss. The hierarchical structure of the session permits the boss to put any statement of the subordinate to the proof, and the subordinate is expected to respond truthfully. Indeed, some hierarchical sessions drive this home by commencing with formal rituals about telling the truth. Once a ritual, such as an oath taking, has been performed, a particularly high level of proof is demanded. For the Romans, the essence of perjury was not lying as such but lying after giving an oath, for it was that which predisposed those listening to suspend normal skepticism and to rely on what they heard as the truth: "Perjuri sunt qui servatis verbis juramenti decipiunt aures eorum qui accipiunt."[100] Violations of the truth rule in such settings are subject to severe sanctions.

In the inner world of the momentary or permanent subordinate—the witness being deposed, the child being interrogated, the politician at a news conference—elaborate and pharisaical normative formulas evolve to justify defections from the truth rule: "What is not asked need not be answered"; "Executive privilege"; "It's OK to lie to an improper question." But since the power is the boss's, these essentially self-prescribed corollaries to the truth rule are fragile and contingent and may not provide immunity if the subordinate is exposed and is judged to have voluntarily misled the audience.

Paradoxically, the truth rule also operates on the boss, even on the most absolute of sovereigns. The boss who refuses to talk about a matter cannot be compelled to, the way a subordinate can. But a boss who chooses to talk is expected to tell the truth.

Special characteristics are attributed to superordinates that explain and justify their superordination and become part of their base of power. Bosses are as aware of this "institutional charisma"[101] as subordinates are. For complex reasons relating to the nature of hierarchy and the charisma attributed to superiors, bosses know that they are not supposed to lie. But bosses are also aware of the utility of lying as a strategy for preserving hierarchy. The generic boss lies (through positive assertion or passive implication) by implying, if not omniscience, then at least a knowledge and competence that are greater than the subordinate's (hence the boss's superiority) and often greater than the boss's own (hence the lie). At the same time, the boss compounds the lie by presenting to subordinates a persona or public mask that represents a high general standard of truth.

It is thus no surprise that one finds, in the Western tradition, a public celebration of the unqualified value of truthfulness; yet in a curious parallel to the tortured justifications of the subordinate, one also finds a chain of rationalizations and moralizations in interelite communications about when and why it is right for a particular elite to lie. The locus classicus of this dimension of the truth rule is in Plato, as with so many other of our ideas. In Book V of the *Republic*, Socrates observes in a poisonously clinical fashion that "our rulers will find a considerable dose of falsehood and deceit necessary for the good of their subjects."[102] This is not a reciprocative privilege. In Book III, Socrates explains: "If any one at all is to have the privilege of lying, the rulers of the State should be the persons: and they, in their dealings either with enemies or with their own citizens, may be allowed to lie for the public good. But nobody else should meddle with anything of the kind: and although the rulers have this privilege, for a private man to lie to them in return is to be deemed a more heinous fault than for the patient or the pupil of a gymnasium not to speak the truth about his own bodily illnesses to the physician or to the trainer, or for a sailor not to tell the captain what is happening about the ship and the rest of the crew."[103]

Precisely because this is such a core idea, it recurs in Western literature in many dialects and for many bosses. Dostoyevsky's Grand Inquisitor claims the same prerogative for the Church,[104] and Ibsen's Dr. Relling, with his remarkable artifact of the "life-lie," makes a comparable claim for physicians.[105] What is especially interesting about all the manifestations of this generic claim are the elaborate ratiocinations and altruisms used to justify it. These are, after all, the lies that rulers use to keep and enhance their power. Elites prefer to qualify theirs with uplifting adjectives, hence Plato's "noble lie." The very need to moralize with pretentious modifiers confirms the continuing disquiet about what is being done, as well as the continuing validity of the norm being violated.

Sanctions and Enforcement

Rules are verbal formulations. By themselves, they do not make a legal system. Neither does the mere fact that some people voluntarily comply with certain rules make a legal system. Nor does the fact that some voluntary compliers consciously reject other attractive options and reprove noncompliance make a legal system. As we have now seen in two other microlegal systems, unless there is some "bite" for noncompliance, with accepted procedures for applying that sanctioning bite, we are in the subjunctive rather than the legal mode. A legal system, whether microlegal or macrolegal, requires accepted methods for protesting and sanctioning violations of norms, methods at least effective enough to sustain belief in and demand for these norms as norms.

As we have seen, microlaw, like international law, is marked by the absence of formal, distinct, and specialized sanctioning institutions. In both systems, as a result, the injured party is often the default sanctioner. In hierarchical talk sessions, the boss can sanction, but the boss, even an absolute dictator, is still one of the talkers.

The sanctioning in microlegal systems for rapping is characterized by two sequential phases, the second of which is contingent on the failure of the first. Once a talk session is established and the substantive and procedural norms are operating, violations of the norms *must* stimulate: (1) protest-and-remedy or (2) termination. The word "must" is used advisedly, for the constitutive structure of the session will permutate if neither protest-and-remedy nor termination occurs. If, for example, one speaker constantly breaks in when the other is talking, thereby violating the fundamental rule of turn taking, the interrupted speaker *must* communicate to the rule breaker that the behavior violates a rule; failure to do so means acquiescence in the constitutive transformation of the session from coarchy to hierarchy. The one who was interrupted is no longer rapping but talking to the boss.

Protest and remedy. Although some moralists conceive of sanctions as retribution, and some of the law-abiding may look forward to the sweet ecstasy of hurting someone as a reward for a lifetime of self-repression and compliance, the pain inflicted on the norm violator is often unnecessary. Indeed, from a systemic standpoint, it may be undesirable. The key function of sanctions is not to punish but to sustain and reinforce a legal system. More often than not, the pain caused by the application of sanctions is (1) the consequence of poorly chosen sanctions, (2) a by-product of otherwise appropriate sanctions, or (3) a response to some covert psychological need of the sanctioner.

The optimum sanction is one that, in context, restores order with minimal disruption while confirming the continuing validity of the rule that was violated. In a microlegal system like a rap session, subtle indications of the violation of a norm are most desirable: the more subtle the communication, the more it contributes to the operation of the system. Such sanctions permit the talker to self-correct without losing face, for there has been no overt characterization of the talker's action as microillegal. If taking turns or one of its corollaries is violated, clearing one's throat noisily may suffice to warn the violator. Consider the following scenario.

> A violates the taking-turns rule by breaking into B's turn.
> B clears her throat or becomes "loudly" silent, or her face becomes rigid.
> A receives this communication and contains himself, mumbling, "Sorry."

Apologies are often dismissed as an unnecessary ritual. In fact, they are an important part of the sanction and enforcement system precisely because they confirm the continuing authority of the rule. As Goffman observes, one part of the person apologizing "dissociates itself from the delict and affirms a belief in the offended rule."[106] The apology reaffirms the violated norm and, thereby, the efficacy of the legal system.[107] Apologies must be graded in terms of the blameworthiness of the violator and the degree of contrition to be conveyed. The range goes from low-contrition apologies, like a mumbled "Pardon me," to statements of self-castigation, like "I feel foolish," to explicit requests for forgiveness.[108] Apologies with a higher contrition quotient may actually disrupt rap sessions by drawing attention to the violation or may transform them into talking-to-the-boss sessions.

In what are perceived as more serious or persistent violations of the yielding rule, the injured party sanctioning a rule breaker may escalate the penalty slightly by violating some of the rules of civility (1) by starting to talk and not stopping for the rule breaker to take a turn; (2) by ceasing to talk, thereby indicating dissatisfaction; or (3) by ignoring an attempt by the rule breaker to talk or by continuing to talk, even raising the voice to prevent or drown out interruption. Data indicate that increases in the sanctioner's voice volume can produce compliance without disrupting the conversation.[109] Raising the volume can function as a claim that the yielding rule has been violated and a sanction for doing so.

In other circumstances, some of these responses might be viewed as infringements of the talk-session participant's right to speak. In sanctioning contexts, however, they are viewed by members of the talk session as reprisals: manifest, purposive, and lawful violations of norms, violations that would be unlawful in other contexts but are here designed (and accepted as designed) to press an earlier norm violator to comply with the pertinent norms in the future.

Low-level, contextually integrated sanctions like these occur countless times in a single rap session. Like customary law—in the sense in which the term was used by Friedrich von Savigny, the nineteenth-century founder of the Historical School of jurisprudence [110]—they are so integrated into talking that those who demand, apply, and submit to them are unaware of them. When these low-level sanctions do not avail, talkers may escalate to more intensive ones. I may escalate by saying, "Would you please let me finish?" or by using mockery—for example, by ostentatiously raising my hand when you do not yield the floor, implying that you are bossing when you should be rapping. Or I may say facetiously, "May I interrupt?" when it is clear to all that it was you who interrupted me. In extreme circumstances, I may explicitly recall to your attention the theretofore implicit norm of the conversation: "Look, you've had your chance to talk. Now let me have mine," or, to borrow Ronald Reagan's unforgettable riposte, "I paid for this microphone."

Finding the contextually appropriate level of contrition is critical. Different levels of contrition will lead to continuity, transformation, or termination of the session. If the microviolator issues an apology that is insufficiently contrite in relation to the gravity of the infraction, the microvictim must either terminate the session or allow it to modulate to talking to the boss. If the microviolator apologizes too much, the session may also transform, and the apologizing rapper, until then an equal, may now become the subordinate. When the appropriate level of blameworthiness and contrition is not struck, an uncertainty and tension is introduced into the talk-session. If the contrition expressed is insufficient, the victim may initially resolve the tension by giving the violator the benefit of the doubt and attributing the mistake to ineptitude or boorishness. If successive violations are followed by insufficiently contrite apologies, the victim of the repeated violations must terminate the talk session or suffer subordination in a session transformed into talking to the boss.

In contrast with implicit sanctions, which restore order without damaging the fabric of the session, explicit sanctions put perceptible stress on the talk session. Indeed, a session is unlikely to survive an explicit protest, unless it is instrumental and necessitated by some common objective the talkers share and agree is imperative or unless the talkers are already bonded in some affective relationship. When a talk session is disrupted explicitly, it may strain or break a friendship or a marriage, cause psychic pain, or start a fight—or a war. But in terms of the microlegal system of talking, the disruption, through protest, of one of the many evanescent talk sessions of daily life is a sanction that benefits the system of which it is part, for it reinforces the basic expectations about this constantly recurring and indispensable microlegal system of talking.

Protest-and-remedy, like decisionmaking in all coarchical organizations, is accomplished by the actors themselves. A very different dynamic operates for infractions that occur when talking to the boss. Violations by the subordinate are punished by the boss, who uses the arsenal of deprivatory and indulgent techniques and sanctioning procedures available and, where relevant, authorized. The boss's sanctions may be quite severe. In some contexts, for example, one of Saddam Hussein's cabinet meetings, lèse-majesté in a talking context can produce a terminal sanction.

Termination. In most cases, protest, whether implicit or explicit, is sufficient to lead the other rapping party to remedy the offending behavior. Chastened by a protest, the rule breaker stops interfering, perhaps mumbles an apology, and the conversation continues. A norm was violated; as a direct response, legitimate social dissatisfaction, in a level of intensity varying with the situation and the gravity of the infraction, was expressed and directed toward the violator; the violator acknowledged the validity of the norm and the impropriety of his or her behavior with an appropriate level of contrition; and the violator corrected the offensive behavior. All of this was accomplished quickly and unobtrusively and with a minimum deprivation of respect for the violator.[111] Public order, in its microsocial dimension, was restored, and the specific objective of public order here—talking—was facilitated. The sanctioning component of a microlegal system operated effectively.

But protest-and-remedy does not always work. Substantive and procedural norms may continue to be violated, and the violator may not receive or heed the signals. Other interlocutors may terminate the conversation by withdrawing from the session and the social situation, whether with excuses or with an explicit indication that their withdrawal is a sanction. Or they may defer sanctioning the violations, suffer through the conversation, and then seek to avoid having to rap with the incorrigible micronorm violator in the future. Since rapping norms usually operate below the threshold of overt consciousness, the microsanctioners are unlikely to describe the norm violator as a talk-session scofflaw. Persistent violators are more likely to be described as "impossible to talk to," "obnoxious," "rude," "a pain in the ass." In fact, a key reason for their subsequent isolation will be their persistent violation of commonly demanded rapping norms.

Disruption of the social situation by immediate termination represents the ultimate sanction for norm violation in this microlegal system. When it operates, the conversation is ended, but, ironically, the basic rules about talking are vindicated and may even have been reinforced in the minds of those who participated in the sanction process. If there is no protest-and-remedy, the session continues, but with important transformations. Other participants in the conversation may accept the behavior of the norm violator, not as a violation, but as a constitutive change of the microlegal system. Sometimes only subject matter has been changed. It is also possible that the procedural rules will have been shifted so completely as to transform the session from rapping to talking to the boss. In some cases, one of the speakers, consciously or intuitively aware of the dynamics of the microlegal system, may seek to become the boss. Renata Adler reports the case of a more experienced counsel "encouraging" his less experienced opponent with various nonverbal compliments of professionalism until the opponent began to watch him rather than the judge and jury for cues as to how he was performing.[112] Such artful takeovers subtly transform rap sessions into talking to the boss with the now subordinated party scarcely aware of the change in status.

The utility of categories proposed here and the correspondence of this codification of the rules of the microlegal system of talking may be tested by observation and self-observation. Anyone who does so will be struck, I believe, by two apparently incompatible legal features of talking: first, that talking is unquestionably governed by a complex set of rules and procedures for their implementation and, second, that the incidence of rule violation in talk sessions is quite high but that most of the violations are quickly remedied by the violator, who reacts to a variety of nonverbal protests from the other talker.

These two features seem incompatible because they challenge one of the most common assumptions about law: that the legal system is not effective unless there is broad and regular compliance. Perhaps it is time to reexamine that assumption. Georg Simmel contended that conflict, rather than driving people apart, is one of the closest and most intimate of associations and may be socially integrative rather than disintegrative.[113] Our exploration of the microlegal system of talking provides some support for Simmel's view. Talking may provide confirmation of a jurisprudential hypothesis that is, for most of us, counterintuitive. Norm violation may be a more telling indicator of the vitality of a legal system than norm compliance. Although we tend to think of the efficacy of a legal system in terms of conformity to its rules, conformity may, in fact, conceal apathy or "natural uniformities," the type of uncoerced, spontaneously congruent social behavior that Nikolai Timasheff distinguished from law.[114] In contrast, repeated violation, protest, and penalty may indicate a continuing commitment to the legal system of which the violated norms are part. The norms are constantly put under stress by being violated, the violations are protested by those who demand compliance with the norms, and then the norms are obeyed and reaffirmed through the self-correction of the norm violators. The challenge to a putative norm requires its supporters to weigh, if only momentarily, their commitment to it. If they invest treasure and perhaps blood in its retention, it will be cherished and demanded even more intensely in the future than if it had never been challenged at all.

4

Amending Microlaw

May God bless and keep the Czar . . . far away from us.
—*Fiddler on the Roof*

That legal systems, like Mariushka dolls, occur within legal systems within legal systems is hardly rare. Legal anthropologists have demonstrated the prevalence, within the apparently unitary nation-state, of groups with effective political and legal organizations that are independent of and substantively different from those of the state. Leopold Pospisil in particular has shown that these groups need not be proto-states nor aspire to a sphere of territorial control. They may even, like gangs and other criminal organizations, work against the host society.[1]

THE PROBLEM

To those who cling to a belief in an ineluctably integrating and ultimately unitary society, apparently autonomous legal and political systems within the nation-state may seem like exotic survivals. To those prone to paranoia, they may seem like legal viruses lurking within the body politic, waiting to divide or destroy it. The totalitarian state seeks to delegitimize and suppress all the groups within its field of power, as we observed earlier. The modern liberal democratic state, with its commitment to maintaining a zone where public power does not operate—variously called the private sphere or the civic order—permits ongoing popular formation of groups. This can lead to the development of smaller, exclusive, and relatively autonomous legal systems within the political boundaries of the state. The question for the modern liberal democratic state is how to deal, if at all, with events within these lesser groups that are inconsistent with the basic norms of the state.

The answer is simple for Historicists, who view law not as the product of conscious choice by a society's current members but as the outcome of processes of growth largely shaped and constrained by previous generations or historical forces. Just as each group has its own language or dialect, it also has its own unique law. Law, in the Historicist account, should be allowed to evolve, at its own pace and according to its own preordained "logic," until it reaches the final stage of whatever it is supposed to be.[2] Historicists have curt advice for jurists, legislators, and would-be social do-gooders: Look but don't touch.

So the Historicist approach, when applied to the rich legal diversity of the many groups within a community, would allow them all to operate and evolve without external controls. In this respect, Historicism seems like a congenial theory for liberalism. Paradoxically, however, the liberal democratic state that tolerates and even encourages multiple groups within itself also proclaims certain fundamental values that may be inconsistent with some practices and microlegal arrangements within the smaller groups. Liberalism's values and toleration lock it into a continuing and never resolved quest for a balancing formula that preserves group autonomy but establishes—for all members of all groups—a commonality based on the values of human dignity.

The members of the smaller groups are caught in a paradox. On the one hand, to flourish or even to survive as an intact group, they need the civic order. On the other hand, some of the practices within their group may make the civic order a zone of injustice for them or for some of their members, for which only the intervention of the apparatus of the modern liberal state can provide a remedy. Thus, as the epigraph of this chapter sets out, members of what Judith Shklar called "permanent minorities" are torn between the desire to be left alone by the personnel and values of the macrolegal system and the need for the protection of the same macrolaw. In the West, since the Enlightenment, these conflicting interests have led to fascinating internal balance sheets as members of minorities have sought ways to maintain the integrity of their culture while incorporating some desirable secular values and accommodating group loyalty with the new opportunities for participating in the larger society: ways to be good citizens without assimilating.

For the encompassing host society, which is at once homogeneous and heterogeneous, the question of how to relate to small groups with autonomous legal and political systems operating in its midst is one of both philosophy and social engineering. The grand questions raise any number of subsidiary, practical, and even mundane questions whose larger significance is lost if they are treated separately. Should there be insistence on a national language? A national costume? Should the state establish a minimum content—scientific or otherwise—for public education and insist that all education imparted in the civic order must incorporate that minimum content? Should there be core religious values? How should the inclusive community relate to innovative religious groups or "cults," to use a term that implicitly rejects all of them? How should the broader legal system relate to the myriad microlegal systems—for example, courtship rituals that involve arranged marriages—that were formerly private but central to the smaller group, yet now affect values that are deemed important to the collective life of the entire community?

These dilemmas are not especially American. Across the globe, the issue—how larger social systems and smaller groups that resist assimilation or whose assimilation is resisted by many members of the larger group should relate to one another—has moved again to the political forefront. Internationally, the relation of states to indigenous peoples within their borders is now the subject of a number of legal initiatives to forge a common policy expressed in multilateral conventions.[3] Nor are these dilemmas uniquely modern: the history of our species is a history of interactions among individuals organized in groups in patterns of superordination and subordination.

The greatest of modern empires, the Ottoman, dealt effectively and economically with the problem of how to structure relations between groups. The Osmanlis retained political power by establishing a self-perpetuating elite and developed the *millet,* or nationality system, for all non-Osmanlis, who organized themselves or were already organized as territorial or other groups. A broad autonomy was granted to individual communities, each of which could manage itself legally and politically under indigenous institutions and leadership. The central Osmanli leadership did not, however, feel a need to establish anything akin to a common valuation of human dignity that could be used to police practices within each millet.[4]

Western civilization wrestled with the problem of the relation between greater and smaller groups in the seventeenth century. The Peace of Westphalia, with its innovative tolerance of different religions, laid the foundation for a solution in 1648, when it ended the Thirty Years War. Its implementation, however, required adaptations of both law and jurisprudence. Much of early English Positivism was an attempt to develop an appropriate psychological attitude for the new and complex system.[5] But the policy of tolerance of different systems of rectitude and religion established in the seventeenth century that allowed the liberal state to emerge may now be undergoing a far-reaching revision. As many new faiths begin to operate in the United

States, some homegrown, some imported, Islam in its various sects, Buddhism, Hinduism, Voodoo, Santería—the increasingly frequent references to "Judeo-Christian" roots (hitherto an unlikely alliance) may indicate, intentionally or not, a policy of intolerance for the newcomers.

THE METHOD

The scholar exploring the relationship that should obtain between "us" (however defined) and "them" must explicitly change role. Rather than being a disengaged observer, mapping and contemplating certain phenomena, the scholar becomes a citizen-advocate, drawing upon the results of earlier systematic inquiries; the scholar must seek to clarify the goals for which he or she, as a citizen, takes responsibility. This expansion of role requires a number of different intellectual tools, necessitated by both the cross-cultural nature of the inquiry and the thorny difficulty of the task.

Observation of others is so difficult, not because other groups —cultures, classes, castes, tribes, language and dialect communities, religious communities, gender communities, whatever— are more complex than ours, but because our own so profoundly shape us, at levels of consciousness so deep that we are often unaware of it. We observe others in our terms. In our terms, others can seem incomprehensible or stubbornly and maddeningly irrational. As Professor Higgins lamented: "Why can't a woman be more like a man?"

Legal scholars try to mitigate, if not solve, this problem with concepts borrowed from the social and natural sciences. Among them, the notion of observational standpoint is indispensable, as I explained in an earlier publication: "Both the reference and content of the term 'law' will vary, depending on whether the standpoint is that of a member of the elite or the rank-and-file, whether the observer is a member of the system observed and has internalized its folklore, is an outsider or is on the margin. Perception of the same phenomena may vary depending on the culture, class, gender, age, or crisis-experience of the observer. Even within the legal establishment, reference and content will vary depending on whether the observer is a legislator, a judge, a prosecutor, a juryman, a defense attorney, an accused or a victim. No particular standpoint is more authentic than another, but the scholar must be sensitive to the variations in perception which attend each perspective, try to disengage himself and then carefully determine and consistently maintain his own."[6] Suspending one's own categories is not easy, and complete success may be unattainable. One thing, however, is certain. Observers who fail to acknowledge the ineluctability and consequences of differences in perspective cannot help but paint a distorted picture, maybe even a complete caricature, of others.

Cross-cultural observation may also encounter terminological problems. When trying to describe other legal systems, observers must be able to identify institutions in each culture under observation that perform similar functions. At the same time, they must be able to distinguish structurally similar institutions that perform different functions. Observation of other legal systems also requires a careful balancing of verbal descriptions of what is being said and what is actually happening. Achieving this balance is especially difficult when the members of the community under study distrust and systematically exclude outside observers, as is the case with many smaller groups whose members may, quite realistically, feel threatened, or when the members are not conscious of their legal system, as is often the case with much customary law and virtually all microlaw.

Comparisons are always bedeviled by the fact that even

within a single system, there may be discrepancies between what an institution purports to do and what it actually does. Many people who have a personal investment in a system describe it as it is supposed to be rather than in terms of its actual operational codes. In addition, many people who perform indispensable functions in the systems they inhabit are sometimes unable to provide an accurate picture of what the institutions actually do. In the American legal system, for example, the word "court" is often taken to mean an institution in which rules made elsewhere are applied to specific disputes. Fundamental political compacts rest on this perception. But the courts also prescribe law, terminate existing law, provide appraisals of the performance of the aggregate political system or key sectors of it, and so on. In many legal and political systems, formal institutions ratify decisions made elsewhere. The real decisions may be made in informal and unofficial weekly lunches attended by military leaders or leading businesspeople and only then rubber-stamped by the formal institution of decision. When law students understand this, they have realized that the formal institutions are not always the effective institutions. One way of guarding against error in observations in this regard is to focus on decision functions instead of looking only at specialized and self-described institutions.[7] Making, terminating, and applying law are all different functions.

In many of the traditional legal systems that Historicists and students of customary law have studied and used to derive historical laws, members cultivate the myth that their lawmaking is spontaneous and has evolved irenically, insulated from outside forces. My friend Francis Deng, who has pioneered the mapping of the legal system among some of the Nilotic tribes of the southern Sudan, recounts an illuminating story about his own research. The vehicle for transmission of much Dinka customary law is the folktale. Tales are usually recited before people go to sleep. Most tales commence with a formula like "This is an ancient tale." Some, however, cannot be ancient, because key events—for example, participation by Arabs or Europeans or references to tobacco—can be dated rather precisely and prove to be of quite recent origin. This is an aspect of what one Dinka chief, in an interview with Deng, dubbed "the creative lies of folktales."

I do not believe that law "just grows" anywhere. Lawmaking is an ongoing process of communication; the content, the authority, and the sanction threat are modulated in many formal and informal settings.[8] It is through lawmaking as such that many decisions about who gets what are legally endorsed; lawmaking is thus at the intersection of law and politics.

If lawmaking is fundamentally political—used to decide the quintessential "who gets what"—legal systems must account for the variable of power and its operation in the system under observation. The absence of an explicit treatment of power precludes a view of the forces underlying certain decisions and leads observers to romanticize the genesis, operation, and real purpose of the legal system. A focus on power not only provides new insights into the operation of macrolaw. The custodians of smaller groups who are demanding respect for group autonomy and its law often mean to protect their own dominance as hereditary chiefs, tribal elders, fathers, husbands, and so on.

The Role of International Law

Nothing could seem further from international law than microlaw. But in an interdependent, global, technology- and science-based civilization, there are no islands. No state is sovereign; no group, no matter how durable or evanescent, is entirely autonomous. In the modern world, group autonomy is relative and is contingent on choices made by members of would-be autonomous groups, by the larger groups within which they exist, and by the larger groups within which those groups exist. Since the rise of the liberal state, as we have seen, the policy in favor of group autonomy has perforce meant an ongoing process for determining the degree to which, for certain sectors of life and through certain procedures, the elites and rank-and-file of other groups may remove themselves beyond the reach of general community norms, and fashion and apply their own.

International law now prescribes basic principles that provide legal guidelines and also serve as a moral compass for determining degree and type of autonomy and the contingencies for intervention and enforced change. This flow of decisions about the degree of group autonomy is that part of contemporary international law that concerns itself with the establishment and protection of territorially and nonterritorially organized groups and with the protection of the human rights of those who find themselves, willingly or otherwise, in the midst of such groups. Because the policies applied in this process do not derive from the law of a single state but are intended to limit and guide the choice of all state elites, the decisions that have been taken and which can emerge should be less susceptible to the sorts of abuses that have been characteristic of the perfervid nationalistic treatment of internal groups: the weird recurrence of dominant-group paranoia, of parochialism, and of xenophobia and misogyny, which appear amid nationalist and racist hysteria and generate demands for the imposition of a single language, forced name changes, official efforts to obliterate the cultures and religions of other groups and, ultimately, to purge the body politic of "foreign contamination," in an awful spiral that can conclude in genocide.[9]

In the most general terms, international law calls for the protection of individual rights and ordains a network of claims for protection and opportunity[10] that every person in the world is entitled to make against whatever government or other authority effectively exercises power over him or her. One of those claims is the right of association and group formation as an instrument for the fulfillment of personal rights. The right of group formation and, within the group, the tolerated authority of the group elite over other members, are extended insofar as they are indispensable for the achievement of individual rights. They cannot be justified under international law if their effect is to abridge or limit basic individual rights.

The legal and political practices of any group—majority or minority, state or non-state, territorially or nonterritorially based, macrolegal or microlegal—can no longer be insulated from appraisal simply and exclusively by invoking talismanic terms like "sovereignty," "domestic jurisdiction," "tradition," "history," "autonomy," by referring to the supposed will of assorted divinities, or by imputing allegedly urgent preconditions for "group continuity." I submit that the practices of all groups *must* be appraised in terms of the international code of human rights. Deviations from that code do not necessitate the termination of the group; instead, the discovery of deviations will lead to the insistence that practices inconsistent with the international standard be adjusted to come within broad margins of conformity to those standards.

Goals of Microlaw

The framework of international human rights cannot fully resolve the question of the appraisal and design of microlegal systems. The international standards do not preempt the field. They are used to appraise national practices, allowing a considerable margin of appreciation for national goals and cultural values. Because each microlegal system exists in a larger social situation whose goals and values are also respected by international law, part of the critical evaluation of its social utility will be the extent to which it contributes to those goals and values. What are the principles and priorities of accommodation?

In a liberal society, as we have seen, an abiding goal is the maintenance of personal privacy within a designated private sphere. This is why the autonomy of microlegal systems within that sphere is protected. At the same time, consistency with the most fundamental values expressed in the international human rights code must be demanded. These should set the boundaries of tolerance, and they should be applied lest pockets of grave human indignity persist in the name of tolerance. And there can be such pockets, even in microlegal systems. At least one of the microlegal systems that we have studied—looking, staring, and glaring—has been a zone of indignity for many people. Finding the right remedy, there or elsewhere, is not easy, however.

Within the boundaries of tolerance, an important criterion for appraisal of the costs and benefits of a specific type of microlegal system is its contribution to survival. Some philosophers and theologians may contemplate with easy conscience and even admiration what has come to be known as the Masada complex: the decision to perish as a group rather than depart from fundamental norms expressing key group values.[11] But students of law and policy, particularly those sensitive to the deep psychological dimensions of behavior, reject options of mass suicide. Law, by its nature, is concerned with minimum and optimum order: to enhance survival and to provide opportunities for a good life. These imperatives necessarily press the jurist to evaluate the operation of the law in terms of these fundamental social goals.

Imagine that you must design the microlegal system of a space capsule. The notion of a constitutive process, introduced at the beginning of this book—the part of every decision that is concerned with the structure of decisionmaking itself—would not present a great challenge. The astronauts are almost constantly integrated electronically with ground control, so there is a preexisting command and control system. By the same token, some of the more obvious features of the spacecraft's system of internal order would certainly be transposed, more or less consciously, from the terrestrial order.

But a good deal of attention must be given to mundane rules for interaction there. What of the less visible rules, the micronorms about shaping spheres of privacy in the cramped quarters, about self-care, about civil inattention to those things that, though perceived, are not deemed to have been socially seen or heard? Some of these micronorms might be adopted or adapted, almost without conscious decision, from cognate enclosed situations, such as railway compartments, submarines, planes, and elevators, but they would still have to be tested by some set of criteria in order to assess their appropriateness and efficacy in the new environment.

If, as part of your design task, you were called upon to appraise alternative rules, you would focus on three tests. One of the first questions to ask is whether the proposed norm contributes to the *survival and success of the mission*. The necessary preeminence of this minimum function is obvious. But obviousness should not obscure its possible negative ethical correlations: sometimes survival may require departing from critical ethical standards that would otherwise prevail. To mention only one particularly vexing example, consider survival homicide: the need to kill one member of a group in order to secure the chance, if not probability, of survival of other group members or the accomplishment of a mission.[12] However much the proposed norm conforms with more general social values, the exigency of collective survival may impose certain limits within which the ethical content of the proposed norm may come to seem an unaffordable luxury.

Many of the terms in this formula are vague. What, for example, is "success" or "survival"? Each term covers a spectrum from minimum to optimum; the ambiguity conceals a real moral peril. Even when the terms are precise, the designer of norms must take account of possible trade-offs between the degree of efficiency and the synergizing effect of a micronorm. Though not maximally efficient for mission survival and success, a norm may be so popular and so likely to call forth great personal contributions and sacrifice that, in the final analysis, it may prove more efficient than an ethically dubious but more pragmatic one. Yet somewhere there will be a limit, a minimum related to mission achievement and personal survival; when it is reached, discipline and external sanctioning must bridge the gap between voluntary compliance and expected defection from the norm. That limit or minimum will, in turn, be a factor of some weight in appraising the ethical conformity of the proposed micronorm.

A second test of a proposed rule would turn on the degree to which it contributed to the mundane functioning of the mission. Consider, for example, the minimally essential rules for the operation of a two-person sailboat. Basically, they must ensure the boat's effective operation. That imports certain features: a command structure, a distribution of functions, and so on. A microlegal norm in a friendship group that allowed for unlimited discussion until a consensus about some group decision could coalesce is appropriate. Transposed to a sailboat, it might endanger, if not doom, the sailors. We might call this the *effectiveness* test. It, too, requires complex assessments involving assumptions about the nature of the mission as well as about probable human behavior under imperfectly defined conditions.

A third test would assess the compatibility of the proposed norm with the general ethical standards of the environing culture. We might call this the *ethical conformity* test. In the relatively few social systems in which ethical standards are shared by virtually all members or in which a homogeneous elite enjoys the exclusive competence to prescribe and apply standards of rectitude, the test can be fairly simple to perform. But in divided societies or systems in transformation, where there are contending paradigms of right and wrong, there may be little or no agreement on appropriate ethical standards for critical matters.

The Operation of Microlegal Systems

It is one thing to design microlaw for innovative situations and another thing to appraise microlegal systems that are integrated into and operating in larger contexts. Where micronorms seem to fail to meet the three criteria proposed, the observer may yet discover that they derive some cogency, if not necessity, from other social arrangements that *are* beneficial. For example, in some cultures marriage functions as a technique for forging political relations between extended families or clans. Here, where wedlock is arranged by the elders, microlegal arrangements that create awkwardness and obstruct easy intimacy between young people may serve an important, even indispensable, political function. An outside observer, however, instinctively applying the criteria of another culture, is likely to appraise the resulting awkwardness and obstructions as net social losses, for they prevent opportunities for the cultivation and sharing of affection by autonomous individuals.

Consider other examples. Some micronorms may function to reflect and reinforce class or caste divisions. In some cases, this may be beneficial to the social system; in others, the norms may be viewed as problematic. Here we could contrast the costs of the almost castelike subordination of nurses to doctors and the effect that it may have on nurse recruitment, performance, and dropout rate with the castelike division between officers and ranks in a military organization and its effect on discipline and obedience. Appraisals, in short, require contextuality and caution.

A satisfactory appraisal of the social utility of microlegal systems, such as those associated with the gathering of visual information or standing in lines or talking, should also test the specific norms and their operation for consonance with general cultural values, which now include international human rights norms. In terms of one or another of these standards of appraisal, some microlegal arrangements in American society are unquestionably not functioning properly. The regime governing the gathering of visual information seems to be costly to women and to other groups that suffer from reduced status. The way some people are thought of and, hence, looked at (or not looked at) continually reduces their status. For women, many intergender looking situations may be referred to without exaggeration as recurring zones of deprivation, and the microlegal system of looking, for all its general microlegal efficiency, as a venue of injustice. Wholly aside from the wide-ranging costs incurred by the many people participating in the microlegal system, the sense of injustice generated among the victims of a recurring and socially critical microlegal norm can erode confidence in the fairness and efficacy of the microlegal system and, further, all legal and political institutions.

Thanks to the existence of common economic standards among politically potent strata of American society, microlegal arrangements that are manifestly uneconomical are more likely to be criticized than those that are manifestly economical. Recall the *New York Times* editorial that lamented the prevalence of queues in New York City. The editorial correctly identified the function of the queues as externalization of the costs of distribution: the consumer pays. The editorial proceeded to introduce a "higher law" of equitable allocation of cost between distributor and consumer as the foundation for its criticism of the microlegal system of queues: "Those lines may save the Transit Authority money, but think of the waste of everyone else's time. Banks and movie theaters may profit handsomely from the intense use of their facilities, but at what cost to the rest of us? Must one stand, docile, in line after line and take it?"[13]

I hypothesize that the sensitivity of the quotidian custodians of social ethics to noneconomic inequities in microlegal systems will be less acute, first, in proportion to the lack of consensus on the metric of appraisal and, second, when revision of the practice would be likely to deprive a dominant group whose members may be expected to resist. Thus, in the United States awareness of the unfairness and even violence of some microlegal systems and initial agitation for change have come from, and continue to come from, special interest groups composed of victims rather than from quasi-official ethics police.

MICROLEGAL PATHOLOGIES

The common law distinction between "law" and "equity," though shrouded in history, has a general analytical utility. "Legal" arrangements are generalized for an entire class; "equitable" arrangements are particularized for a specific case in order to remedy a grievance there without changing the general legal arrangement. The distinction is useful in thinking about how to deal with microlegal systems that work but sometimes produce some inequities — or often produce inequities for some.

There is an important difference between an efficient microlegal system some of whose norms and procedures are fundamentally unfair because they or their consequences are incompatible with the ethical standards of the larger political and legal community in which they occur and, in comparison, an efficient microlegal system whose norms and procedures are essentially consistent with general ethical standards but are operating ineffectively or leading to undesirable consequences for many people because of some other deeply rooted defect in society.

Consider rapping and talking to the boss. Talk sessions may be venues of aggravated indignity for oppressed groups. Recall the vivid account by Maya Angelou. Or consider again the microlegal system of looking, staring, and glaring. In Western civilization, the dynamic operation of this microlegal system certainly balances the need for gathering visual information with the need for protection of the exoself. But, as discussed above, there is ample evidence that it also allows for the victimization of women in many intergender settings. The pain that so many human beings are suffering should, in itself, be cause for a reconsideration of, if not necessarily an intervention into, a microlegal arrangement. The dissatisfaction on the part of women who are actual or potential victims may also have larger cumulative and enduring social consequences: many women may decide not to participate in or to withdraw from certain types of social arrangements or public spaces because of the acute unpleasantness of being stared at, an experience that some describe as "violation" or visual "possession." The larger social losses occasioned by the withdrawal from certain situations of human beings who might take jobs or interact in those situations to their benefit and to the benefit of others but who, because of the anticipated unpleasantness of being visually raked over, choose otherwise may push reconsideration of the microlegal system in question and lead some advocates to press for a macrolegal intervention.

Is the problem here the norms or procedures of this micro-legal system or a more general and regularly confirmed expectation that many men apparently bring to looking situations? Are the norms that many men would routinely follow with respect to looking at men optionally ignored—with impunity—when they look at women? In some social groups, men may believe that they are entitled or even expected to stare boldly at women who are unaccompanied by a man. The same men would probably not allow themselves the license of staring at the same women if those women were accompanied by a man, especially one larger and more menacing than the putative starer. But even in these strata, the practice of staring at women unaccompanied by a man is probably undertaken with the expectation that it may be done precisely because there will be no sanction.

Yet, as we have seen, contextually effective, if not 100 percent effective, sanctions are available to support the microlegal system of looking; when applied, they work often enough to sustain belief in the efficacy of the microlegal system. The license that some men allow themselves does not, then, necessarily arise from the absence of an appropriate and potentially effective sanction. It may arise from the expectation that the victim will not apply the sanction to the starer.

One possible solution may be for members of the victim group to learn a repertory of appropriate microlegal sanctions that can redress the imbalance at minimal cost to themselves. Where the problem is cross-cultural or cross-gender misunderstanding, education and instruction in the ordinary repertory of sanctions may suffice. Where the inability to wield ordinary sanctions derives from deeply rooted and possibly internalized disabilities in the environing society, where deploying the sanction will not have the sought effect, a special repertory of microsanctions may have to be developed. If the inability is created and enforced by the macrolegal system, it is obvious that it must be the target of change through the legislative intervention of the macrolegal system. But that is a major step, carrying costs of its own, and should not be undertaken hastily.

The Advantages and Problems of Microsanctions

All law requires, indeed, is characterized by, sanctions. That is not to say that everyone is law-abiding only because of sanctions. A certain number of people in any legal system are inclined to comply with the law because they are persuaded that it is the right thing to do. At some level of consciousness, the prospect of being sanctioned for deviation from the law—at the very least, being shamed for it—may play some role in their personal decision. But that prospect is not the central reason for their compliance. Many people, acting on their own behalf or for others, especially for profit-maximizing collective entities, will calculate the chance of being sanctioned and the magnitude of the prospective sanction when determining whether to comply with a norm and whether to thereby surrender certain opportunities, values, or pleasures prohibited by the norm. These are the people whom the lawmaker must consider when deciding on the indulgent or deterrent content of the sanction, especially in determining the intensity of deprivation. To review the frequency of noncompliance with an important law and then to increase the penalty from, let us say, a hundred thousand dollars per violation to one million per violation is a relatively simple legislative and implementative matter. Transforming a sanction program sustaining a particular norm from one that imposes monetary penalties to one that prescribes imprisonment is far more complex.

Increasing the severity of sanctions is in some ways akin to resorting to a more destructive military weapon. The bigger the bang, the more likely it is that innocent people will be injured or distressed. The more surgical a sanction program, the more likely it is that the sanctioning pain and disruption will be experienced only by the violator. The military analogy is also instructive for the appraisal and design of microsanctions. The application of low-level sanctions minimizes the extent of the "collateral" social disruption of a norm violation. Although X may be speaking improperly to Y or looking improperly at Y, as long as Y's response to the microlegal infraction is an effective though low-level sanction, those in their proximity will probably be unaware of the violation or, at the very least, undisturbed by it. The sanctions of microlaw tend to be surgical and nondisruptive.

Because members of a society wish to preserve the autonomy of the texture of the civic order, we have also assumed a general preference for microsanctions for microlegal systems rather than more severe sanction programs applied and sustained by the apparatus of the state. Should we reconsider the preference for microsanctions that do not disrupt a situation but are ineffective, when the cost of their ineffectiveness is largely put *on the victim of particular microlegal violations?* Let me return, for a moment, to the common but complex problem of staring at women in ways inconsistent with the pertinent microlaw. Most women who are victims of this type of violation are likely to try to exit the situation as quickly as possible. If they cannot leave, they may pretend to ignore the staring. Where a man might automatically glare to protest staring, many women, in uncertain settings, will be reluctant to exercise that microlegally appropriate response. Some may be too timid. Many may have been taught over a lifetime that it is inappropriate to disrupt a social situation for these matters. The "ladylike" thing is simply to exit the unpleasant situation as soon as possible.

Some manuals for victims of these violations have synthesized accounts of successful responses and now do not discourage strategies that include escalation through aggressive sanctioning by victims in microlegal systems with the hope that they will reduce victimizations. One cognate example of escalated microsanctions from Martha Langelan's edited collection *Back Off!* demonstrates this new, self-assertive approach:

> I'm twenty-four and work in Washington, D.C. Last July, I was on the L4 bus, heading home. The weather was hot and sticky, and it had been a long day at work. People were standing packed shoulder to shoulder in the aisle. I think lots of women and girls have probably had the experience of men using that kind of crowded bus situation to feel us up -once a guy slid his hand up under my skirt, real quick, all the way up to my crotch. Gross! I was so shocked I just stood there. Usually, my friends and I just try to move away as fast as we can, to get out of the creep's reach, although it can be hard to get away when the bus is jammed full.
>
> But this time, the most amazing thing happened. A woman about four feet in front of me suddenly reached around behind her. She was completely calm, but she gripped this guy's arm, held his hand up in the air, and in a loud, clear, commanding voice -carried all through the bus-she said, "What was this hand doing on my ass?" She held on to his arm, held his hand right up there.
>
> The man who'd harassed her—three-piece suit, looked like some junior executive type—didn't even try to deny it. Everyone knew his hand had been exactly where she said it was. He turned bright red, looked guilty as hell, and jumped off the bus at the first stop.

The women on the bus loved it. I thought, "Wow, that's terrific, I know what I'm going to do from now on! I bet he thinks twice before he feels up another woman."[14]

I believe the account and was as struck as the person reporting it, because, as Langelan remarks, "many women feel extremely self-conscious and nervous about making a public scene in a small, enclosed space."[15] But lawyers, by training, read accounts such as these as prospective generalized rules and quickly crunch them through a variety of factual variations to get a sense of the range of their implications, especially when they range a group—be it organized or spontaneous—against an individual and there is no independent trier of fact. "Everyone knew his hand had been exactly where she said it was." Suppose, even under the facts as recounted, the "perpetrator" was innocent or, if he did indeed touch the woman in question, it was an unintentional act? Suppose the woman grabbed the wrong hand? Though it is offensive to some women even to raise the question, any lawyer would be remiss if he or she did not ask if the woman had a history of reporting herself being touched and engaging in aggressive unilateral sanctions? Or consider the account in terms of the so-called "Tonkin Gulf construct:" in many international and subnational settings, individuals or groups with political agendas accelerate the inevitable by precipitating incidents in order to control the timing of their planned response. Suppose the woman "victim" in the above account had an agenda of "consciousness raising" and operated on Justice Holmes' apothegm that if hanging people deters, the deterrent effect will be just as effective even if the wrong person has been hung.

The issue here is not whether groping in crowded public places is reprehensible. It always is. Nor is the issue one of whether stopping it is a valid urgent social problem. It is. The issue is public policy about how sanctions are to be applied. In our legal system, we insist on the introduction of the protections of due process for those individuals against whom the power of a group is suddenly intensely focused and likely to be directed, whenever the sanctions that may be applied become severe. We demand many procedural safeguards, even though their operation is sure to allow some people who have done wicked things to escape conviction and punishment. We do this because we believe it is worth it.

The escalation of microlegal sanctions may begin to raise some of those concerns. The more microsanctions escalate and become more severely deprivatory, the more their application may require conformity to the general principles of the macrolegal system we call "due process." By promptly requiting a demand for justice by the victim group, immediate and aggressive microlegal sanctions may be therapeutic and have some deterrent effect. But before endorsing them as a generally acceptable practice, a civilization that is concerned with the prospect of the punishment of an innocent person to the extent that it would rather allow guilty persons to evade justice than have innocents suffer, must look hard at escalated microlegal sanctions whose contingencies and application are, by their nature, unilaterally and hastily determined. Does this rather conventional legal approach resolve the issue?

The Beam in Our Eye?

"Why," asked Matthew, "beholdest thou the mote that is in thy brother's eye, but considerest not the beam that is in thine own?"[16] It is important not to use concerns for virtue—concerns that are pretended or otherwise—as a way of evading responsibility. Sometimes escalated sanctions by victims in microlegal systems are the result of the desperation of those who suffer injustice in them. And that desperation may be caused, in no small part, by our indifference. We are all prone to a predilection of people to avoid involvement in the microdisputes of others and, insofar as possible, to try to protect, sometimes desperately, the boundaries enclosing our own relatively more pleasant if only momentary private realities. This predilection leads us to find it comfortable to maintain clearly demarked zones, whose boundaries resist making exceptions for the importance or urgency of the subject that would challenge those zones. No matter how hideous the events—for instance, the siege of Sarajevo, the massacre in Srebrenica, or the genocide in Rwanda—a man or woman who stood up in the midst of a performance at the Met and insisted on our attention and harangued us on what was occurring in one of them would not only be removed from the theater and probably arrested for disturbing the peace but would excite our indignation about the violation of the zone of entertainment that we had all established, within which such matters are not to be raised. "What a nut," we would mutter with indignation that is likely to be heightened by our uneasiness.

In the third essay, I described how each of us, in the pursuit of our own private interests, defers to, rather than challenges, the others' worldview so as not to jeopardize the short-term collaboration we need or, in some instances, just to avoid "getting involved." This cultivated indifference is often the background if not precondition of persistent and gross violations of microlaw. It is easy to say that the indifference is morally wrong, but in some contexts it may be a preferred if not mandatory course. Suppose you are negotiating with a Serb commander in Kosovo and have just about concluded a cease-fire agreement. The commander shakes your hand and whispers, "But be careful. Never trust the damned Turks." Do you say, "I don't approve of that kind of talk. It's why you're in this mess in the first place?" Or do you bite your lip and get him to sign? Lawyers and diplomats, indeed, anyone acting as an agent, face this kind of dilemma frequently.

When we act on our own behalf, we are not bound by such legal or moral obligations to refrain from intervening. Yet it is unreliable and inappropriate for each of us to undertake an individual mission to remedy every instance of a microlegal injustice. We would become a nation of "busy-bodies" and block committees, always thrusting ourselves into each other's lives; the civic order would then be threatened, not by the state, but by us. But where particular microlegal systems are regularly generating pain and injustice for a group, indifference becomes a form of complicity.

Conclusion

Microlaw and the Good Life

You are not obliged to finish the task, but you may not evade it.
—Rabbi Tarfon, The Mishnah, Fourth Tractate, N'zikin, Avot
2:16

That some micronorms, or microlegal systems, do not work or work at great cost and pain to some people prompts reflection once more about the traditional jurisprudential response to microlaw. The traditional focus of law, as we have seen, has been on mass and aggregate behavior and on the normative productions and applications of the apparatus of the state. Microlaw has been called "etiquette" or "positive morality"; it has not been viewed as law nor even as important by jurists. We have seen that rejecting the legal character of microlegal systems because they do not represent the law of the state is based on capricious and inconsistent applications of definitions. Microlegal systems have all the characteristics of law, just scaled down to small-group size. Still, are microlegal systems important enough to warrant study, appraisal, and perhaps intervention and redesign?

We can immediately dismiss the smallness of the systems as of no significance. Markets do not assign value only on the basis of size; diamonds are more valuable than coal. And who would gainsay the importance of microsurgery because it is small, or insist that macrosurgery is more important because it uses saws and axes rather than the technology of the space age?

With the exception of mobs, including the dispersed aggregate audiences of contemporary mass media, virtually all groups are subject to micronorms; social life, barring time spent in a mob, is a congeries of microsocial situations.In modern, as opposed to traditional, society, a substantial proportion of microsocial situations involve strangers. Compliance with microlaw is a prerequisite to civil interaction with those with whom we come into contact, but, as we saw, compliance is more difficult for two strangers, because neither knows which norms are appropriate to the encounter or, indeed, what the inner normative universe of the other is. Plainly, the importance of microlaw in a factory where the reciprocal hostility of different ethnic, language, dialect, or racial groups can be increased or decreased by microlegal adjustments is clear. But conflict avoidance is only one of an array of social concerns. More generally, understanding the dynamics of microlegal systems may be a prerequisite for the effective operation of a heterogeneous modern society.

An appreciation of microlegal systems may make many interactions in the workplace, the school, the family, and the most intimate of personal relationships more truly engaged and productive than they are now in terms of whatever is at stake, and less hurtful to the self-esteem and humanity of participants. One needs little imagination to appreciate the importance of appraising microlegal systems in a space capsule and modulating or terminating norms either developed or adapted holus-bolus from elsewhere, where they were contextually effective, but which now undermine the effectiveness of the space mission or the survival of its participants. Perhaps it is not so obvious that comparable microlegal adjustments in work settings that are generating sexual harassment claims may obviate many of them, as well as the further pain to victims inflicted in the harassment procedures of the law, or that the self-fulfillment of individuals in many other contexts may be aided by, if not require, an appropriately crafted microlegal system.

A fundamental tenet of liberal democracy is the effort to

maintain a line between governmental regulation and the private sphere. The effort is valuable. I am not arguing now in favor of a totalitarian organization, however benevolent, that penetrates and organizes, through innumerable normative layers, every cell of society, each with its own enforcement committee. This is not a call for a comprehensive scheme of microlegal statutes, but I certainly do not rule out macrolegal intervention where there is serious and persistent injustice. A civic order that is a zone of recurring injustice and violence is hardly compatible with the goals of a liberal society. My objective is to alert and sensitize legal scholars and the diverse official and nonofficial custodians of the private sphere to the effect that microlegal arrangements have on key aspects of individuals' lives. Individuals should become aware of the arrangements so that they can themselves appraise their operation, as they do with the other laws of society, and, where necessary, change microlaws in order to increase the contribution they make to a good life.

NOTES

Introduction

1. Mary Douglas, *Natural Symbols: Explorations in Cosmology* (New York: Pantheon Books, 1982), 2.
2. *See* in this regard Catharine A. MacKinnon, *Toward a Feminist Theory of the State* (Cambridge: Harvard University Press, 1989), 173.
3. Ray Huang, *China: A Macro History* (Armonk, N.Y.: M.E. Sharpe, 1988).
4. John Austin, *The Province of Jurisprudence Determined*, ed. Wilfrid E. Rumble (London: J. Murray, 1832).
5. Austin, *The Province of Jurisprudence Determined*, 20.
6. Henry S. Maine, *Village Communities* (New York: George H. Doran Co., 1927).
7. Leon Petrazycki, *The Twentieth-Century Legal Philosophy Series*, vol. 7: *Law and Morality: Leon Petrazycki*, trans. Hugh W. Babb (Cambridge: Harvard University Press, 1955). On Petrazycki's innovative psychology, *see* A. Meyendorff, "Leo Petrazycki," in *Modern Theories of Law* (London: Oxford University Press, 1933), 21, 35–36; Pitirim Sorokin, *Contemporary Sociological Theories* (New York: Harper & Brothers, 1928), 702–03.
8. Eugen Ehrlich, *Fundamental Principles of the Sociology of Law*, trans. Walter L. Moll (Cambridge: Harvard University Press, 1936).
9. The legal anthropology literature is extensive. *See, e.g.,* Melford E. Spiro, ed., *Context and Meaning in Cultural Anthropology* (New York: Free Press, 1965). For substantive orientations that are more compatible with the approach taken in this book, *see, e.g.,* Ray L. Birdwhistell, *Kinesics and Context: Essays on Body Motion Communication* (Philadelphia: University of Pennsylvania Press, 1970); I. Eibl-Eibesfeldt, "Similarities and Differences Between Cultures in Expressive Movements," in R.A. Hinde, ed., *Non-Verbal Communication* (Cambridge: Cambridge University Press, 1972), 297–314; Edmund Leach, "The Influence of Cultural Context on Non-Verbal Communication in Man," in R.A. Hinde, ed., *Non-Verbal Communication*, 315–47; and Patricia Pliner, Lester Krames, and Thomas

Alloway, eds., *Nonverbal Communication of Aggression*, vol. 2 of *Advances in the Study of Communication and Affect* (New York: Plenum Press, 1975), 21–75.

10. Burns H. Weston, Richard A. Falk, and Anthony A. D'Amato, *International Law and World Order: A Problem-Oriented Coursebook*, 2d ed. (St. Paul, Minn.: West Pub. Co., 1990), 14–15.

11. Walter O. Weyrauch, "The 'Basic Law' or 'Constitution' of a Small Group," *Journal of Social Issues* 27, no. 2 (1971): 49–63; *id.*, "Law in Isolation—The Penthouse Astronauts," *Transaction* 5, no. 7 (1968): 39–46; *id.*, "The Legal Structure of a Confined Microsociety—A Tentative Evaluation of the Cowan-Strickland Penthouse Experiments," University of California, Berkeley, Space Sciences Laboratory, Internal Working Paper No. 43 (1966); *id.*, "The Law of a Small Group," University of California, Berkeley, Space Sciences Laboratory, Internal Working Paper No. 54 (1967); *id.*, "The Family as a Small Group," in David A. Funk, ed., *Group Dynamic Law: Exposition and Practice* (New York: Law Arts Publishers, 1988), 153–86; *id.*, "Romani (Gypsy) Law and Its Implications for Gajikane (Non-Gypsy) Cultures," in Gudmundur Alfredsson and Peter Macalister-Smith eds., *The Living Law of Nations: Essays on Refugees, Minorities, Indigenous Peoples and the Human Rights of Other Vulnerable Groups, in Memory of Atle Grahl-Madsen* (Kehl, Germany; Strasbourg, France, and Arlington, Va.: N.P. Engel, 1996), 321; *id.*, "Governance Within Institutions," *Stanford Law Review*, vol. 22 (1969): 141; *id.*, "Autonomous Lawmaking: The Case of the 'Gypsies'" (with Maureen A. Bell), *Yale Law Journal* 103 (1993): 323; *id.*, "Island Law," *American Journal of Comparative Law* 44 (1996): 263; *id.*, "Romaniya: An Introduction to Gypsy Law," *American Journal of Comparative Law* 45 (1997): 225.

12. *See, e.g.*, Arnold Birenbaum and Edward Sagarin, *Norms and Human Behavior* (New York: Holt, Rinehart & Winston, 1976); and Arnold Birenbaum and Edward Sagarin, eds., *People in Places: The Sociology of the Familiar* (New York: Praeger, 1973); also, Nancy Henley, *Body Politics: Power, Sex, and Nonverbal Communication* (Englewood Cliffs, N.J.: Prentice-Hall, 1977), 151–67; and Mark Cook, "Gaze and Mutual Gaze in Social Encounters," in Shirley Weitz, ed., *Nonverbal Communication*, 2d ed. (New York: Oxford University Press, 1979), 77–86.

13. Erving Goffman, *Behavior in Public Places: Notes on the Social Organization of Gatherings* (New York: Free Press of Glencoe, 1963); *id.*, *Encounters: Two Studies in the Sociology of Interaction* (Indianapolis: Bobbs-Merrill, 1961); *id.*, *Forms of Talk* (Philadelphia: University of Pennsylvania Press, 1981); *id.*, *Frame Analysis: An Essay on the Organization of Experi-*

ence (Cambridge: Harvard University Press, 1974); *id., Interaction Ritual: Essays on Face-to-Face Behavior* (New York: Pantheon Books, 1967); *id., The Presentation of Self in Everyday Life* (Woodstock, N.Y.: Overlook Press, 1959); *id., Strategic Interaction* (Philadelphia: University of Pennsylvania Press, 1969); *id., Stigma: Notes on the Management of Spoiled Identity* (New York: Jason Aronson, 1963); and *id., Relations in Public: Microstudies of the Public Order* (New York: Basic Books, 1971).

14. Eric Berne, *Games People Play: The Psychology of Human Relationships* (New York: Grove Press, 1964); *id., Transactional Analysis in Psychotherapy: A Systematic Individual and Social Psychiatry* (New York: Grove Press, 1961); and *id., Beyond Games and Scripts* (New York: Grove Press, 1976).

15. *See* Georg Simmel, "Social Interaction as the Definition of the Group in Time and Space," in R. Park and E. Burgess, eds., *Introduction to the Science of Sociology,* 3d ed. (Chicago: University of Chicago Press, 1924), 348; *id.,* "The Aesthetic Significance of the Face," in Kurt H. Wolfe, ed., *Georg Simmel, 1858–1918* (Columbus: Ohio State University Press, 1959), 276–81.

16. *See* Lewis A. Coser, "Georg Simmel's Neglected Contributions to the Sociology of Women," *Signs: Journal of Women in Culture and Society 2,* no. 4 (1977): 872–73; Catharine A. MacKinnon, *Sexual Harassment of Working Women* (New Haven: Yale University Press, 1979), 3, 127, 145.

17. Phoebe C. Ellsworth and J. Merrill Carlsmith, "Effects of Eye Contact and Verbal Content on Affective Response to a Dyadic Interaction," *Journal of Personality and Social Psychology 10,* no. 1 (1968): 15–20; *id.,* "Eye Contact and Gaze Aversion in an Aggressive Encounter," *Journal of Personality and Social Psychology 28,* no. 2 (1973): 280–92.

18. *See* Paul Ekman, *Darwin and Facial Expression: A Century of Research in Review* (New York: Academic Press, 1973); Jane Van Lawick-Goodall, "A Preliminary Report on Expressive Movements and Communication in the Gombe Stream Chimpanzees," in Phyllis C. Jay, ed., *Primates: Studies in Adaptation and Variability* (New York: Holt, Reinhart & Winston, 1968), 313–74; George B. Schaller, *The Mountain Gorilla: Ecology and Behavior* (Chicago: University of Chicago Press, 1963); J. A. R. A. M. Van Hooff, "The Facial Displays of the Catarrhine Monkeys and Apes," in Desmond Morris, ed., *Primate Ethology* (Chicago: Aldine Pub. Co., 1967), 7–68.

19. Chie Nakane, *Japanese Society* (Berkeley: University of California Press, 1972).

20. Leonard Shih-Lien Hsŏu, *The Political Philosophy of Confucianism* (London: G. Routledge & Sons, 1932).

21. Some of the questions and objections regarding appropriate boundaries of legal study have their parallels in microsituation studies in sociology. *See, e.g.,* Michael L. Radelet, "The Ethnic Study of Social Control," *Urban Life* 8, no. 3 (1979): 267–74.

22. *See* Birenbaum and Sagarin, *Norms and Human Behavior, supra* note 12, at 6–7; *cf.* Randall Collins, "On the Microfoundations of Macrosociology," *American Journal of Sociology* 86, no. 5 (1981): 984–1014.

23. Bronislaw Malinowski, *Crime and Custom in Savage Society* (London: Routledge & Kegan Paul, 1926).

24. Georges A. J. Scelle, "Le Phénomène juridique du dédoublement fonctionnel," in Walter Schätzel and Hans-Jürgen Schlochauer, eds., *Rechtsfragen der Internationalen Organisation* (Frankfurt: Vittorio Klostermann, 1956), 324.

25. Lassa Oppenheim, *International Law,* vol. 1 (New York: Longmans, Green & Co., 1905). *See also* W. Michael Reisman, "Lassa Oppenheim's Nine Lives: Oppenheim's International Law," *Yale Journal of International Law* 19, no. 1 (1994): 255–84.

26. *See* W. Michael Reisman, *Folded Lies: Bribery, Crusades and Reforms* (New York: Free Press, 1979).

27. For a discussion of "techniques and strategies that conversational participants employ to prevent or reverse negative typifications of themselves . . . resulting from potential or existing violations of conversational . . . rules," *see* Margaret L. McLaughlin, *Conversation: How Talk Is Organized* (Beverly Hills: Sage Publications, 1984), 201–33. Telling an untruth, or something of questionable validity, is an example of such rule breaking. *See id.* at 206. These techniques and strategies fall into two groups: "preventatives" ("ways in which people deal prospectively" with saving face) and "repairs" (" 'detours' or 'time-outs' from ongoing talk" in order to engage in "remedial work"). Repairs can be initiated by either the talker who broke the rules or by another talker. *Id.*

Repair occurs even when the need for it is not obvious; the hearer does not have to signal the need for repair in order for the speaker to initiate it. Conversely, the hearer may see a need for remedial action even though the speaker is innocent of a rule breach. McLaughlin, *Conversation,* 208.

For a discussion of sanctions in conversation, *see generally* Marion Owen, *Apologies and Remedial Interchanges: A Study of Language Use in Social Interaction* (Berlin, N.Y.: Mouton Publishers, 1983), 17–26. *See id.* at 26–27 (Erving Goffman's rejection of judicial model as analogy of talking repairs).

28. Sir Thomas E. Holland, *The Elements of Jurisprudence*, 13th ed. (Oxford: Clarendon Press, 1924).

29. *See generally* M. H. A. Reisman, "Islamic Fundamentalism and Its Impact on International Law and Politics," in Mark W. Janis, ed., *The Influence of Religion on the Development of International Law* (Dordrecht: Martinus Nijhoff, 1991), 107–34.

30. *Quoted in* Anita Chan and Robert Senser, "China's Troubled Waters," *Foreign Affairs* 76, no. 2 (1997): 104, 115.

31. Myres S. McDougal, Harold D. Lasswell, and Lung-chu Chen, *Human Rights and World Public Order* (New Haven: Yale University Press, 1980), 815.

32. See the pathbreaking work of MacKinnon, *Sexual Harassment of Working Women, supra* note 16.

CHAPTER 1
Looking, Staring, and Glaring

1. After this essay was drafted, I discovered that Flora Davis begins chapter 8 of her book with the same example. *See* Flora Davis, *Inside Intuition* (New York: McGraw-Hill Book Co., 1973), 63–65 (describing how a gaze in a public place generates a glare). I decided to retain my example, which was drafted independently. The experience is so common that it serves to orient the reader quickly to the subject.

2. On gazing in public places, *see* Michael Argyle and Mark Cook, *Gaze and Mutual Gaze* (Cambridge: Cambridge University Press, 1976), 112–14; Erving Goffman, *Behavior in Public Places* (New York: Free Press of Glencoe, 1963).

On gazing in public and other contexts, *see generally* Michael Argyle, *The Psychology of Interpersonal Behaviour* (Harmondsworth, England: Penguin, 1967); *id., Social Interaction* (London: Methuen & Co., 1969), 105; Robert G. Harper, Arthur N. Wiens, and Joseph D. Matarazzo, *Nonverbal Communication: The State of the Art* (New York: John Wiley & Sons, 1978), 171–245; Mark L. Knapp, *Nonverbal Communication in Human Interaction,* 2d ed. (New York: Holt, Reinhart & Winston, 1972), 130; Desmond Morris, *Manwatching: A Field Guide to Human Behavior* (New York: H. N. Abrams, 1977), 71–76; David J. Schneider, Albert H. Hastorf, and Phoebe C. Ellsworth, *Person Perception,* 2d ed. (Reading, Mass.: Addison-Wesley Pub. Co., 1979); Michael Argyle and Janet Dean, "Eye Contact, Distance and Affiliation," in Argyle, ed., *Social Encounters*

(Chicago: Aldine Pub. Co., 1973), 173-86; Douglas R. Buchanan, Morton Goldman, and Ralph Juhnke, "Eye Contact, Sex, and the Violation of Personal Space," *The Journal of Social Psychology* 103 (1977): 19-25; David E. Campbell and Giulio E. Lancioni, "The Effects of Staring and Pew Invasion in Church Settings," *The Journal of Social Psychology* 108 (1979): 19-24; Mark S. Cary, "The Role of Gaze in the Initiation of Conversation," *Social Psychology* 41, no. 3 (1978): 269-71; Ralph V. Exline, "Visual Interaction: The Glances of Power and Preference," in *Nebraska Symposium on Motivation* (Lincoln: University of Nebraska Press, 1971), 163-206; Margaret Foddy, "Patterns of Gaze in Cooperative and Competitive Negotiation," *Human Relations* 31, no. 11 (1978): 925-38; B. J. Hedge, B. S. Everitt and C. D. Frith, "The Role of Gaze in Dialogue," *Acta Psychologica* 42 (1978): 453-75; G. N. Hobson, K. T. Strongman, D. Bull, and G. Craig, "Anxiety and Gaze Aversion in Dyadic Encounters," *British Journal of Social and Clinical Psychology* 12 (1973): 122-29; M. Lefebure, "Encoding and Decoding of Ingratiation in Modes of Smiling and Gaze," *British Journal of Social and Clinical Psychology* 14 (1975): 33-42; Clark McCauley, Geoffrey Coleman, and Patricia De Fusco, "Commuters' Eye Contact with Strangers in City and Suburban Train Stations: Evidence of Short-Term Adaptation to Interpersonal Overload in the City," *Environmental Psychology and Nonverbal Behavior* 2, no. 4 (1978): 215-25; Kenneth V. McDowell, "Accommodations of Verbal and Nonverbal Behaviors as a Function of the Manipulation of Interaction Distance and Eye Contact," *Proceedings,* 81st Annual Convention, American Psychological Association, 1973: 207-08; Rosalind D. Muirhead and Morton Goldman, "Mutual Eye Contact as Affected by Seating Position, Sex, and Age," *The Journal of Social Psychology* 109 (1979): 201-06; Joseph Newman and Clark McCauley, "Eye Contact with Strangers in City, Suburb, and Small Town," *Environment and Behavior* 9, no. 4 (1977): 547-58; D. R. Rutter and G. M. Stephenson, "The Functions of Looking: Effects of Friendship on Gaze," *British Journal of Social and Clinical Psychology* 18 (1979): 203-05; Brenda J. Smith, Fonda Sanford, and Morton Goldman, "Norm Violations, Sex, and the 'Blank Stare,'" *The Journal of Social Psychology* 103 (1977): 49-55; G. M. Stephenson, D. R. Rutter, and S. R. Dore, "Visual Interaction and Distance," *British Journal of Psychology* 64, no. 2 (1972): 251-58; Mary E. Valentine and Howard Ehrlichman, "Interpersonal Gaze and Helping Behavior," *The Journal of Social Psychology* 107 (1979): 193-98; and Ian Vine, "Judgement of Direction of Gaze: An Interpretation of Discrepant Results," *British Journal of Social and Clinical Psychology* 10 (1971): 320-31.

As regards the definition of such terms as "one-sided look," "face gaze," "eye gaze," "mutual look," "eye contact," "gaze avoidance," and "gaze omission," *see* Harper *et al., Nonverbal Communication,* 173.

3. Irwin Altman, *The Environment and Social Behavior: Privacy, Personal Space, Territory, Crowding,* ed. Lawrence S. Wrightsman (Monterey, Calif.: Brooks/Cole Pub. Co., 1975), 36; Harper *et al., Nonverbal Communication, supra* note 2, at 181–88; Knapp, *Nonverbal Communication in Human Interaction, supra* note 2, at 131–32. Such a one-sided look may become a mutual look, which may be the first step to a social encounter. *See* Argyle and Cook, *Gaze and Mutual Gaze, supra* note 2, at 113. Since I do not want a social encounter, I find myself torn between looking and looking away, an ambivalence sometimes expressed in a series of back and forth glances. *See* Morris, *Manwatching, supra* note 2, at 71. How I resolve this conflict depends on a number of factors, including my own objective and my target's response.

4. James J. Gibson and Anne D. Pick "Perception of Another Person's Looking Behavior," *American Journal of Psychology* 6 (1963): 386–94 (people can sense, with a high degree of accuracy, when someone is looking at them).

5. Sigmund Freud, "Notes upon a Case of Obsessional Neurosis," in *The Standard Edition of the Complete Psychological Works of Sigmund Freud,* trans. James Strachey, vol. 10 (London: Hogarth Press, 1955), 153–57. On ascription of sexual connotations to certain types of eye contact, especially if the contact is prolonged and intergender, *see* Davis, *Inside Intuition, supra* note 1, at 66. Analysts have suggested that the connotations exist partly because eye contact is an important sexual signal (*see* Argyle and Cook, *Gaze and Mutual Gaze, supra* note 2, at 4) and partly because eye contact plays an important role in sexual exploration. Davis, *Inside Intuition, supra* note 1, at 66 and 74.

6. The link between the eye and sex is illustrated by the use of the eye as a symbol for the sex organs. On eye contact ("making eyes") between lovers, *see* Morris, *Manwatching, supra* note 2, at 71–72. On nonverbal signals in general and their role in attraction, *see* David B. Givens, "The Nonverbal Basis of Attraction: Flirtation, Courtship, and Seduction," *Psychiatry* 41 (1978): 346–59. *See* Knapp, *Nonverbal Communication in Human Interaction, supra* note 2, at 130.

7. *See* Davis, *Inside Intuition, supra* note 1, at 64–65.

8. Gaze aversion is a common way of letting another know that the communication channel is not open. Harper *et al., Nonverbal Communication, supra* note 2, at 181–88; Knapp, *Nonverbal Communication in Human Inter-*

action, *supra* note 2, at 132. As elaborated *infra*, gaze aversion also allows us to avoid the obligations of an encounter. *See* Argyle and Cook, *Gaze and Mutual Gaze, supra* note 2, at 113 and 171.

9. *See* Argyle, *Social Interaction, supra* note 2, at 105–06; Harper *et al., Nonverbal Communication, supra* note 2, at 181.

10. *See* Argyle, *Social Interaction, supra* note 2, at 105. On the effect of smiling and gaze on attempts to ingratiate, *see* Luc M. Lefebure, "Encoding and Decoding of Ingratiation in Modes of Smiling and Gaze," *British Journal of Social and Clinical Psychology* 14 (1975): 33–42. On the significance of "second glances," one study (described in Harper *et al., Nonverbal Communication, supra* note 2, at 181) found that it was a second glance from females watching males enter a room that seemed to determine whether conversation would occur between the two.

11. Knapp states that a look—which I have referred to as instrumental scouting—of more than ten seconds is usually enough to make a target uncomfortable. Knapp, *Nonverbal Communication in Human Interaction, supra* note 2, at 135. Many would consider a look of shorter duration the threshold of tolerance. On the other functions of looking, *see* Argyle and Cook, *Gaze and Mutual Gaze, supra* note 2, at 115–23; Argyle, *Social Interaction, supra* note 2, at 107–09; Mark Cook, *Interpersonal Perception* (Harmondsworth, England: Penguin, 1971), 76–78; Harper *et al., Nonverbal Communication, supra* note 2, at 181–88; Knapp, *Nonverbal Communication in Human Interaction, supra* note 2, at 131–35; Argyle and Dean, "Eye Contact, Distance and Affiliation," *supra* note 2. Naturally, too much scouting may set off a negative response in the target. Argyle, *Social Interaction, supra* note 2, at 107.

12. On the role of gaze with respect to the initiation of conversation, *see* Cary, "The Role of Gaze in the Initiation of Conversation," *supra* note 2. In some cases, of course, gaze creates an obligation to respond—for example, where a restaurant patron catches a waiter's eye. *See* Knapp, *Nonverbal Communication in Human Interaction, supra* note 2, at 132.

13. Besides signaling that the communication channel is closed, gaze aversion can also serve, as we will see below, as a defensive measure against an overly long or unwarranted gaze. Other defensive measures may include turning away, changing body orientation, or even seeking to place a physical barrier between looker and target (*e.g.*, a hand, an arm, a pile of books). *See* Argyle and Cook, *Gaze and Mutual Gaze, supra* note 2, at 112–13. Also, glaring may be used to defend against an intrusive gaze. *Id.* at 112.

In a two-person interaction, the visual behavior of the participants is extremely interdependent, and the rate of change of gaze direction is very highly correlated. Adam Kendon, "Some Functions of Gaze-Direction in Social Interaction," *Acta Psychologica* 26 (1967): 22-63.

14. On the normative regulation of this activity, *see* Argyle and Cook, *Gaze and Mutual Gaze, supra* note 2, at 112-14. Most of us understand that we are "expected to gaze in certain ways," *id.* at 112, if only because to violate this norm, in Argyle's words, disturbs the social equilibrium. *Id.* Goffman has coined the wonderful phrase "civil inattention" to describe the most fundamental of our norms with respect to looking at strangers. *Id.* at 83; *see also* Harper *et al., Nonverbal Communication, supra* note 2, at 203-06. This is less true in small towns than it is in large cities. Argyle, *id.; see also* McCauley *et al.,* "Commuters' Eye Contact with Strangers in City and Suburban Train Stations," *supra* note 2; Newman and McCauley, "Eye Contact with Strangers in City, Suburb and Small Town," *supra* note 2.

15. *See* Davis, *Inside Intuition, supra* note 1, at 94-103; Edward T. Hall, *The Silent Language* (New York: Doubleday & Co., 1959); Argyle and Dean, "Eye Contact, Distance and Affiliation," *supra* note 2; Gary W. Evans and Roger B. Howard, "Personal Space," *Psychological Bulletin* 80, no. 4 (1973): 334-44; Nancy Jo Felipe and Robert Sommer, "Invasions of Personal Space," *Social Problems* 14, no. 2 (1966): 206-14.

16. Ethologically, a steady direct gaze among nonhuman primates is characteristic of aggressive behavior. Jane Van Lawick-Goodall, "A Preliminary Report on Expressive Movements and Communication in the Gombe Stream Chimpanzees," in Phyllis C. Jay, ed., *Primates: Studies in Adaptation and Variability* (New York: Holt, Rinehart & Winston, 1968); George B. Schaller, *The Mountain Gorilla: Ecology and Behavior* (Chicago: University of Chicago Press, 1963); J.A.R.A.M. Van Hooff, "The Facial Displays of the Catarrhine Monkeys and Apes," in Desmond Morris, ed., *Primate Ethology* (Chicago: Aldine Pub. Co., 1967).

Such a gaze is often a prelude to or a substitute for an attack. Reaction to a direct gaze is fight, flight, or submission. Gaze aversion is a common submissive or defensive reaction. Stuart A. Altmann, "The Structure of Primate Communication," in Altmann, ed., *Social Communication Among Primates* (Chicago: University of Chicago Press, 1967).

Some primatologists have said that the fixed stare is also a form of threat in man (Schaller, *The Mountain Gorilla;* Van Hooff, "The Facial Displays of the Catarrhine Monkeys and Apes"; Van Lawick-Goodall, "A Preliminary Report on Expressive Movements and Communication in the Gombe Stream Chimpanzees") or a form of anger (Paul Ekman, *Dar-*

win and Facial Expression: A Century of Research in Review [New York: Academic Press, 1973]; Paul Ekman, Wallace V. Friesen, and Phoebe Ellsworth, *Emotion in the Human Face: Guidelines for Research and an Integration of Findings* [New York: Pergamon Press, 1972]).

Among humans, a stare has negative or threatening properties and therefore will elicit fight or flight reactions. If fight (a return glare, stare, or move) is not desired or possible (*e.g.*, in a elevator), the tension will build. When flight does become possible, it will be exaggerated, *e.g.*, by leaving the scene of the stare faster than normal. Phoebe C. Ellsworth, J. Merrill Carlsmith, and Alexander Henson, "The Stare as a Stimulus to Flight in Human Subjects: A Series of Field Experiments," *Journal of Personality and Social Psychology* 21, no. 3 (1972): 302–11 (drivers at a red light drove off faster than normal when stared at). Once a person knows he or she is being stared at, the flight response is turned on, not gradually, as with a rheostat, but all at once, as with an on-off switch. Staring leads to flight. As soon as a person realizes that he or she is being stared at, the target expects the starer to avert his or her gaze — or to mitigate the stare by, *e.g.*, a smile, a remark, or something else to indicate a lack of hostility. If there is no such disarming accompaniment to the stare, the gaze immediately elicits the flight response, regardless of the duration of the stare. People who know they are being stared at become nervous and fidgety if they cannot escape.

The presence or absence of eye contact has the effect of intensifying or exaggerating the feelings, positive or negative, that a person has in a situation. In an experimental study, Phoebe Ellsworth demonstrated that when the content of a conversation was neutral or positive, subjects liked the interviewer significantly more when the interviewer looked them in the eye. But if the conversation was even indirectly critical of the subject, the effect was the reverse, and subjects liked the interviewer less if there was eye contact. Subjects considered the same critical conversation as worse if there was looking as well. Phoebe C. Ellsworth and J. Merrill Carlsmith, "Effects of Eye Contact and Verbal Content on Affective Response to a Dyadic Interview," *Journal of Personality and Social Psychology* 10, no. 1 (1968): 15–20.

If the content of the conversation is negative, *e.g.*, firing someone, confessing to a priest, admitting innermost secrets to a psychiatrist, then often eye contact is avoided; *see* Harry S. Sullivan, *The Psychiatric Interview*, ed. Helen S. Perry and Mary L. Gawel (New York: W.W. Norton, 1954).

If the communication is negative, the communicator's lack of eye contact does not necessarily worsen the impact of the content of the communication, because the addressee may see it as an attempt to be tactful or or a signal that the communicator "feels sorry" to have to say those things. *See generally* Ekman *et al.*, *Emotion in the Human Face,* especially chap. 18, "What Is the Relative Contribution of Facial Behavior and Contextual Information to the Judgment of Emotion?" at 135–51.

17. Crowding involves physical contact that, in some Western cultures and strata, would otherwise be unacceptable; toucher and touched, as participants in a crowd, should hardly be surprised at contact. But since any touching may have aggressive or offensive implications, the muttering serves to interpret the touching as innocuous, to disarm it.

18. "The Talk of the Town," *The New Yorker,* 16 Nov. 1981, pp. 45–49.

19. *See, e.g.,* Phoebe C. Ellsworth, "Direct Gaze as Social Stimulus: The Example of Aggression," in Patricia Pliner, Lester Krames, and Thomas Alloway, eds., *Advances in the Study of Communication and Affect,* vol. 2 (New York: Plenum Press, 1974), 53, 59.

20. Dirk Johnson, "Home on the Range (and Mighty Lonely, Too)," *New York Times,* 12 Dec. 1995, sec. A, p. 20.

21. A number of social psychologists have concluded that eye contact, smiling, interaction distance, and verbal content are continuously adjusted until an equilibrium is reached: Kendon, "Some Functions of Gaze-Direction in Social Interaction," *supra* note 13; Michael Argyle and Janet Dean, "Eye-Contact, Distance and Affiliation," *Sociometry* (1965): 289–304. Different types of intimacy are substituted for each other until a contextually appropriate equilibrium is found. Each nonverbal variable is interdependent, and so, for example, as interaction proximity increases, the amount of eye contact decreases to maintain the equilibrium. (Of the situation in an elevator it is said that because we are compelled to stand closer to strangers than we normally would, eye contact decreases.)

Although the use of eye contact may often be singled out for inquiry and appraisal, it is but one of the entire package of visual cues of nonverbal communication. Some psychologists maintain that it is impossible to distinguish the effects of eye contact from among those of other nonverbal cues and communications. Mehrabian states that our likeability for strangers is determined by all nonverbal cues, including eye contact, distance, body orientation, and body relaxation. Albert Mehrabian, "Relationship of Attitude to Seated Posture, Orientation, and Distance," *Journal of Personality and Social Psychology* 10, no. 1 (1968): 26–30; *id.,* "Significance of Posture and Position in the Communication of Attitude and Status Relationships," *Psychological Bulletin* 71, no. 5 (1969): 359–72.

22. The way we respond to this type of anomic crisis is considered in the next chapter. The hypothesis here is that the integrality of nonlegal variables notwithstanding, the careful observer can discern a distinct, microlegal system for looking.

23. On the notion of sanctioning goals, *see* Harold D. Lasswell and Richard Arens, *In Defense of Public Order: The Emerging Field of Sanction Law* (New York: Columbia University Press, 1961). For an application, *see* W. Michael Reisman, *Systems of Control in International Adjudication and Arbitration: Breakdown and Repair* (Durham, N.C.: Duke University Press, 1992).

24. *See* E. Adamson Hoebel, *Anthropology: The Study of Man,* 3d ed. (New York: McGraw-Hill Book Co., 1966), 440; Max Rheinstein, ed., *Max Weber on Law in Economy and Society,* trans. Edward Shils and Max Rheinstein (New York: Simon & Schuster, 1954), 5; Edwin W. Patterson, *Jurisprudence* (Brooklyn: Foundation Press, 1953), 169; Giorgio Del Vecchio, *Philosophy of Law,* 8th ed., trans. Thomas O. Martin (Washington, D.C.: Catholic University of America Press, 1953), 305; Michael Barkun, *Law Without Sanctions: Order in Primitive Societies and the World Community* (New Haven: Yale University Press, 1968). *See generally* W. Michael Reisman, "Sanctions and Enforcement," in *The Future of the International Legal Order,* ed. Cyril E. Black and Richard A. Falk, vol. 3: *Conflict Management* (Princeton: Princeton University Press, 1971), 273–335, *reprinted in* Myres S. McDougal and W. Michael Reisman, *International Law Essays: A Supplement to International Law in Contemporary Perspective* (Mineola, N.Y.: Foundation Press, 1981), 381–436.

25. A stare may be perceived as a threat. As such, it can cause the person being stared at to move away (*see* Argyle and Dean, "Eye Contact, Distance and Affiliation," *supra* note 2) or even flee (*see* Ellsworth *et al.,* "The Stare as a Stimulus to Flight in Human Subjects," *supra* note 16). But a stare may also provoke a counterattack. *Id.* at 311. Thus, in some respects, responses to staring are similar to responses to the invasion of personal space. *See* Smith *et al.,* "Norm Violations, Sex, and the 'Blank Stare,'" *supra* note 2, at 49, 50.

26. Walter Benjamin, "The Work of Art in the Age of Mechanical Reproduction," in Walter Benjamin, *Illuminations,* ed. Hannah Arendt, trans. Harry Zohn (New York: Harcourt, Brace & World, 1968), 224.

27. J.P. Mayer, *Sociology of Film: Studies and Documents* (London: Faber & Faber, 1972), 21.

28. Marshall McLuhan, *Understanding Media: The Extensions of Man* (New York: McGraw-Hill Book Co., 1964), 87.

29. *See* note 2 *supra;* and *see also* Gibson and Pick, "Perception of Another Person's Looking Behavior," *supra* note 4.

30. Rudolf von Jhering, *Der Kampf um's Recht* (*The Struggle for Law*), 2d ed., trans. John J. Lalor (Chicago: Callaghan and Co., 1915).

31. W.H. Auden, "Postscript" to "Prologue: The Birth of Architecture," in W.H. Auden, *Collected Poems*, ed. Edward Mendelson (New York: Random House, Vintage International, 1991), 688.

32. I prefer "exoself" to "mask" or "persona" here because the latter term focalizes on the face. Much looking and staring is not concerned with the face, yet it may be as much, if not more, of an invasion.

33. *See generally* Davis, *Inside Intuition, supra* note 1, at 94–103; *see also* Julius Fast, *Body Language* (New York: M. Evans, 1970), 16–65.

34. Martin Buber, *Between Man and Man,* trans. Ronald G. Smith (London: Kegan Paul, Trench, Trubner & Co., 1947), 27.

35. Felipe and Sommer, "Invasion of Personal Space," *supra* note 15.

36. C.S. Lewis, *That Hideous Strength* (New York: Macmillan Co., 1946).

37. Jude Colter, *quoted in* Stefan Bechtel, *The Practical Encyclopedia of Sex and Health* (Emmaus, Pa.: Rodale, 1993), 287.

38. Schneider *et al., Personal Perception, supra* note 2, at 120.

39. Amy Vanderbilt, *Amy Vanderbilt's New Complete Book of Etiquette: The Guide to Gracious Living* (Garden City, N.Y.: Doubleday & Co., 1971), x.

40. Empirical and clinical evidence indicate that eye contact is "a parabolic function of the attitude towards the addressee." Mehrabian, "Relationship of Attitude to Seated Posture, Orientation, and Distance," *supra* note 21.

41. *See generally* Robert Harrold, *Cassadaga: An Inside Look at the South's Oldest Psychic Community with True Experiences of the People Who Have Been There* (Miami: Banyan Books, 1979).

42. For a review of the scant literature on gaze in these sort of groups, *see* Argyle and Cook, *Gaze and Mutual Gaze, supra* note 2, at 106–07.

43. Patricia Williams, "Spirit-Murdering the Messenger: The Discourse of Fingerpointing as the Law's Response to Racism," *University of Miami Law Review* 42, no. 1 (1987): 127–57, 149. *See also* her *Alchemy of Race and Rights* (Cambridge: Harvard University Press, 1991).

44. Mehrabian, "Relationship of Attitude to Seated Posture, Orientation, and Distance," *supra* note 21.

45. Some cultures are quick to invest the eyes of another with the power to hurt. *See* Davis, *Inside Intuition, supra* note 1, at 65. In South Africa, for example, certain Bushmen believe that the look of a menstruating woman can fix a man where he stands and turn him into a tree. *See* Knapp, *Non-*

verbal Communication, supra note 2, at 130. In the Mediterranean "belief in the evil eye is still strong." *See* Morris, *Manwatching, supra* note 2, at 141. Many mothers in these regions protect their children from the dangers of the evil eye by pinning a "horned hand" amulet to their clothing. For an illustration, see *id.* at 140.

46. *Cf.* Susan Sontag, *On Photography* (New York: Farrar, Straus & Giroux, 1977). Jacqueline Onassis sued a photographer for violating a 1975 court order barring him from getting closer than twenty-five feet to Mrs. Onassis and thirty feet to her children. *See* David Bird and Robert McG. Thomas, Jr., "Notes on People," *New York Times,* 17 Dec. 1981, sec. B, p. 11.

The ambivalent treatment of paparazzi in the United States is, in many ways, a paradigm of looking and staring problems. A total prohibition of unauthorized looking and photographing would permit the public figure to exploit the media, hence the assumption of a kind of waiver of privacy on the part of those who make themselves notorious or become so; I will codify this assumption later in this chapter. A blanket waiver would have negative public policy consequences, for many talented people, animated by a desire to serve the public, might shun public service because of the likelihood of a fishbowl existence. But a blanket prohibition would conflict with the fundamental policy on freedom of expression, virtually hallowed in the First Amendment to the Constitution. Legislative and judicial efforts to accommodate these interests have foundered on one or the other consideration.

A number of recent initiatives to limit the activities of paparazzi have encountered constitutional problems. One, submitted by Senators Feinstein and Hatch in February 1998, would make it a federal crime to chase someone in a way that might cause bodily harm to that person in order to photograph or record that person for commercial purposes. Trespass is to be defined to include the use of a telephoto lens if the picture that the lens would secure could not otherwise be taken without setting foot on private property. Significantly, the sponsors of the bill introduced it at the Screen Actors Guild in Hollywood, for actor-celebrities are often stalked by paparazzi. But to accommodate the public policy with respect to gathering visual information, the Feinstein-Hatch bill sought distinguish between the public sphere and personal or family activities conducted in a physically private sphere. In introducing the bill, Senator Feinstein said: "There is a line between legitimate news-gathering and invasion of privacy, between snapping a picture of someone in a public place and chasing them to the point where they fear for their safety." "Paparazzi Abuses,"

17 Feb. 1998, Federal Document Clearing House, Congressional Press Release. *See also* Todd S. Purdum, "Two Senators Propose Anti-Paparazzi Law," *New York Times*, 18 Feb. 1998, sec. A, p. 16.

47. *See* Morris, *Manwatching, supra* note 2, at 71–72. Such gazing restrictions spring from the fact that "eye contact . . . heightens intimacy, expresses and simultaneously escalates emotions, and is an important element in sexual exploration." Davis, *Inside Intuition, supra* note 2, at 66. On staring taboos in general, see *id.* at 65–69.

48. *See* Morris, *Manwatching, supra* note 2, at 72–74.

49. It is not always entirely clear which signal is intended. Where people do not share the same cultural expectations, the potential for miscommunication and misunderstanding is substantial. For an illustration, *see* Fast, *Body Language, supra* note 33, at 136–39.

50. Comment of William Fields at a conference entitled "The Sacred and the Profane: Second Annual Academic Symposium in Honor of the First Americans and Indigenous Peoples Around the World," held at St. Thomas University, Miami, Fla., 18 Jan. 1996.

51. Yoram Binur, *My Enemy, My Self,* trans. Uriel Grunfeld (New York: Doubleday, 1985), 69–70.

52. Vanderbilt, *New Complete Book of Etiquette, supra* note 39.

53. Indeed, many handbooks seem to assume the social and economic homogeneity of would-be interactants—or at least the homogeneity of their pretensions. *See, e.g.,* Barbara Cartland's often humorous book *Etiquette for Love and Romance* (Bath: Chivers Press, 1985).

54. Stephen A. Richardson, Barbara Snell Dohrenwend, and David Klein, *Interviewing: Its Forms and Functions* (New York: Basic Books, 1965), 117. These and other manipulative techniques will be considered in the third chapter.

55. C. Wright Mills, *The Power Elite* (New York: Oxford University Press, 1956).

56. See descriptions of such encounters in Erving Goffman, *Relations in Public: Microstudies of the Public Order* (New York: Basic Books, 1971), 32, 131.

57. *See* McCauley *et al.,* "Commuters' Eye Contact with Strangers in City and Suburban Train Stations," *supra* note 2.

58. Businesspeople have long been aware of the importance of nonverbal signals to success. They employ consultants who teach them how to behave both at home and abroad, enlighten them on business customs overseas, and teach them to project a contextually appropriate image of success. For examples of these consultants' ideas, *see* John T. Molloy, *Dress for Success*

(New York: H. Wyden, 1975); Edward T. Hall, "The Silent Language in Overseas Business," *Harvard Business Review* 38, no. 3 (1960): 87–96; Alison Lurie, *The Language of Clothes* (New York: Random House, 1981).

CHAPTER 2
Standing in Line and Cutting In

1. Observers have noted that the enforced queues for undesirable results produce queuing rules that are mirror images or reciprocals of rules for voluntary, "positive" queues. For example, in a positive queue, the rule of sequential priority allows individuals to move backward in a line (by either going to the end of the line or allowing one or more people immediately behind to move ahead) while prohibiting moves forward in the line. Conversely, in negative queues the rule of sequential priority allows forward moves but no deferral of one's place in line. Erving Goffman, *Relations in Public: Microstudies of the Public Order* (New York: Basic Books, 1971), 36.

2. But not in all situations; consider, for example, lines of automobiles, which are considered further on in this chapter. David A. Wiessler, "Why People Are Rude—How It Harms Society," *U.S. News and World Report*, 22 Aug. 1983, pp. 54–55.

3. *See* Leon Mann, "Learning to Live with Lines," in John Helmer and Neil A. Eddington, eds., *Urbanman: The Psychology of Urban Survival* (New York: Free Press, 1973), 43.

4. *See* Georgia Dullea, "On the Pressures and Politics of Waiting in Line," *New York Times*, 11 Feb. 1982, sec. C, p. 1.

5. *See* Edward T. Hall, *The Silent Language* (Garden City, N.Y.: Doubleday, 1959), 151.

6. Some members of a queue may temporarily step out of the line far enough to see the size of the line or, for especially long lines, may hire "line watchers." *See* Mann, "Learning to Live with Lines," *supra* note 3, at 55. Queue members may also receive information regarding the entire line by monitoring reactions of observers or passersby. *See, e.g.,* David A. Karp and William C. Yoels, *Symbols, Selves and Society* (New York: J.B. Lippincott, 1979), 99.

7. *Id.* at 44. Mann notes that these number queues often are instituted when especially long lines develop regularly. *See generally* Leon Mann, "Queue Culture: The Waiting Line as a Social System," *American Journal of Sociology* 75, no. 3 (1969): 340–54.

8. *See* Charles B. Goodsell, "Welfare Waiting Rooms," *Urban Life* 12, no. 4 (1984): 467–77 (describing one typology of waiting room).

9. *Time,* 10 Aug. 1981, p. 36 (article by Thomas A. Sancton).
10. *See* Robert G. Bill and William F. Herrnkind, "Drag Reduction by Formation Movement in Spiny Lobsters," *Science* 193, no. 4258, 17 Sept. 1976, pp. 1146-48. The sociobiological model of human territoriality and spatial behavior "incorporates concepts drawn from spatial organization among other animal species." Rada Dyson-Hudson and Eric Alden Smith, "Human Territoriality: An Ecological Reassessment," *American Anthropologist* 80, no. 1 (1978): 21-41, 36-37.
11. As I mentioned earlier, the study of microlegal systems finds useful data in ethnographic studies. *See, e.g.,* James P. Spradley, *The Cultural Experience: Ethnography in Complex Society* (Chicago: Science Research Associates, 1972). Yet ethnographic studies describe generally cultural patterns of behavior or beliefs; the study of microlegal systems, in contrast, focuses on those shared expectations that contain norms or rules and are enforced by sanctions. Some sociological work describes microsituations in terms of rules and sanctions. *See, e.g.,* Goffman, *Relations in Public, supra* note 1; Erving Goffman, *Behavior in Public Places: Notes on the Social Organization of Gatherings* (New York: Free Press of Glencoe, 1963); Georg Simmel, "Social Interaction as the Definition of the Group in Time and Space," in Robert E. Park and Ernest W. Burgess, eds., *Introduction to the Science of Sociology,* 2d ed. (Chicago: University of Chicago Press, 1924), 348; and, in particular, Walter O. Weyrauch's seminal study "The 'Basic Law' or 'Constitution' of a Small Group," *Journal of Social Issues* 27, no. 2 (1971): 49-63. However, a legal study of a microsituation goes beyond description by analyzing the policy implications of a microlegal system and its contribution to public order.
12. *See* Barbara G. Katz and Joel Owen, "Disequilibrium Theory, Waiting Costs, and Saving Behavior in Centrally Planned Economics: A Queueing-Theoretic Approach," *Journal of Comparative Economics* 8, no. 3 (1984): 301-21.
13. Hedrick Smith, *The Russians* (New York: Quadrangle / New York Times Book Co., 1976), 64-65.
14. Excerpt from Andrei Voznesensky, "A Chorus of Nymphs," in Andrei Voznesensky, *Nostalgia for the Present,* ed. Vera Dunham and Max Hayward, trans. Vera Dunham and H. W. Tzalsma (Garden City, N.Y.: Doubleday, 1978). Morrow comments, "The Soviets have turned waiting into a way of life. . . . Almost perversely, when Soviet shoppers see a line forming, they simply join it." Lance Morrow, "Waiting as a Way of Life," *Time,* 23 July 1984, p. 65. The reporter Serge Schmemann noted from Moscow that "so common and pervasive are the lines that they have

evolved their own etiquette, even their own slang." Serge Schmenann, "Standing in Line Persists as Scourge of Soviet Life," *New York Times*, 6 Feb. 1985, sec. A, p. 10. Lines even gave rise to their own psychology, as a Soviet reporter observed: "The line takes on its own magic significance. . . . The mere existence of a line . . . means that at the end of it, there must be something that is in short supply. Getting it becomes a goal in itself, a kind of hunt, a game." *Id., quoting* L. Ivanova (reporter for *Sovetskaya Rossiya,* a Moscow daily).

15. Charles Holt and Roger Sherman acknowledge that queues formed to distribute a limited number of fixed-price commodities to consumers on a first-come, first-served basis are "pervasive in countries with price controls," but "common in other countries as well." Examples that they offer are "rationing tickets to sporting events like the World Series or college basketball games, . . . theater tickets, theater seats for ticket holders, access to retail sales, work through labor exchanges, certain classes of airline tickets, seats in many travel modes or even in college classrooms." Charles A. Holt and Roger Sherman, "Waiting-Line Auctions," *Journal of Political Economy* 90, no. 1 (1982): 280–94; *see also* Dulles, "On the Pressures and Politics of Waiting in Line," *supra* note 4, at 1 (reporting that Dr. Thomas Saaty, University of Pittsburgh, estimates that Americans spend five years of their lives waiting).

16. "Beating the Line," *New York Times,* 8 Sept. 1981, sec. A, p. 22.

17. *See generally* Hall, *The Silent Language, supra* note 5, at 28–41, 166–77, 184–85; Julius T. Fraser, ed., *The Voices of Time: A Cooperative Study of Man's Views of Time as Expressed by the Sciences and the Humanities* (New York: G. Braziller, 1966). *Cf.* Eviatar Zerubavel, "The Standardization of Time: A Sociohistorical Perspective," *American Journal of Sociology* 88, no.1 (1982): 1–23, 20–21 (standardization of time by anchor other than nature is key characteristic of modern civilization).

18. *See* N.S. Timasheff, *An Introduction to the Sociology of Law,* vol. 3 of *Harvard Sociological Studies* (Cambridge: Harvard University, Committee on Research in the Social Sciences, 1939), 7.

19. Hall, *The Silent Language, supra* note 17, at 145; Michael Lipsky, *Street-Level Bureaucracy: Dilemmas of the Individual in Public Services* (New York: Russell Sage Foundation, 1980), 98; Barry Schwartz, *Queuing and Waiting: Studies in the Social Organization of Access and Delay* (Chicago: University of Chicago Press, 1975), 94.

20. Gene I. Maeroff, "Offering Public School to Three- and Four-Year-Olds," *New York Times,* 24 May 1983, sec. C, p. 1.

21. *See* Pierre Moessinger, "Developmental Study of the Idea of Lining Up,"

The Journal of Psychology 95 (1977): 173–78 (eight-year-olds had developed priority rule, but "hold-my-place" rule was observed only in older children).

22. *See, e.g.,* Irvine R. Levine, *Main Street, U.S.S.R.* (Garden City, N.Y.: Doubleday, 1959), 338–39; Schwartz, *Queuing and Waiting, supra* note 19, at 108, 200 n. 11.

   Hall relates a society's spatial behavior to its cultural values of equality (Hall, *The Silent Language, supra* note 17, at 158) and of order (Edward T. Hall, *The Hidden Dimension* [Garden City, N.Y.: Doubleday, 1966], 128, 162). The prevalence of queuing behavior in the Soviet Union is generally explained by economic scarcity or administrative incompetence. *See, e.g.,* Holt and Sherman, "Waiting-Line Auctions," *supra* note 16; Schmenann, "Standing in Line Persists as Scourge of Soviet Life," *supra* note 14. Many writers refer to the British as having a "queuing culture" but view it as a quality of the people rather than the economy. Mann, "Learning to Live with Lines," *supra* note 3, at 56.

23. Hans Kelsen, *General Theory of Law and State* (New York: Russell & Russell, 1961).

24. People tend to underestimate the number of people in front of them if a commodity is scarce, even in very short lines. Leon Mann and K.F. Taylor, "Queue Counting: The Effect of Motives upon Estimates of Numbers in Waiting Lines," *Journal of Personality and Social Psychology* 12, no. 2 (1969): 95–103.

25. Franz Kafka, "Before the Law," in Kafka, *Parables and Paradoxes* (New York: Schocken Books, 1946), 60–61.

26. *See supra* note 9; *see* Schmenann, "Standing in Line Persists as Scourge of Soviet Life," *supra* note 14.

27. Similarly, expectations of first come, first-served queues may be so common that officials will explain alternative systems. Goodsell, "Welfare Waiting Rooms," *supra* note 8, at 473.

28. Stanley Milgram, "The Experience of Living in Cities," *Science* 167, no. 3924, 13 Mar. 1970, pp. 1461–68 ("norms of non-involvement"). *See generally* Goffman, *Behavior in Public Places, supra* note 11.

29. "Other, more mundane settings, because of their special ecology and social structure, encourage social mingling . . . [including] most lines if the wait is long enough." Jacqueline P. Wiseman, "Close Encounters of the Quasi-Primary Kind: Sociability in Urban Second-Hand Clothing Stores," *Urban Life* 8, no. 1 (1979): 23–51, 26.

30. George Nash, "Waiting in Movie Lines Achieves Status Rating," *New York Times*, 25 Apr. 1970, sec. A, p. 31.

31. Mann, "Learning to Live with Lines," *supra* note 3, at 340–41.
32. Schwartz, *Queuing and Waiting, supra* note 19, at 15, 92–93.
33. Schwartz, *Queuing and Waiting, supra* note 19, at 3–4. Queuing theory originated in 1913 with a mathematical model for Copenhagen's telephone system. *Id.* at 3. The theory has since been applied to a wide range of problems in operations research. On traffic, *see* R. Akçelik and M.J. Maher, "Route Control of Traffic in Urban Road Networks: Review and Principles," *Transportation Research* 11, no. 1 (1977): 15–24; Brian L. Allen and Gordon F. Newell, "Some Issues Relating to Metering or Closing of Freeway Ramps—Part II: Translationally Symmetric Corridor," *Transportation Science* 10, no. 3 (1976): 243–68; Arnold I. Barnett, "Control Strategies for Transport Systems with Nonlinear Waiting Costs," *Transportation Science* 12, no. 2 (1978): 119–36; Frederick J. Beutler and Benjamin Melamed, "Decomposition and Customer Streams of Feedback Networks of Queues in Equilibrium," *Operations Research* 26, no. 6 (1978): 1059–72; Werner Brilon, "Queueing Model of Two-Lane Rural Traffic," *Transportation Research* 11, no. 2 (1977): 95–108; Guy L. Curry, Arthur De Vany, and Richard M. Feldman, "A Queueing Model of Airport Passenger Departures by Taxi: Competition with a Public Transportation Mode," *Transportation Research* 12, no. 2 (1978): 115–20; Carlos F. Daganzo, "Traffic Delay at Unsignalized Intersections: Clarification of Some Issues," *Transportation Science* 11, no. 2 (1977): 180–89; Rajat K. Deb, "Optimal Dispatching of a Finite Capacity Shuttle," *Management Science* 24, no. 13 (1978): 1362–72; Z. Eshcoli and I. Adirir, "Single-Lane Bridge Serving Two-Lane Traffic," *Naval Research Logistics Quarterly* 24, no. 1 (1977): 113–25; David G. Hoel and George H. Weiss, "Properties of Noise Emitted by Vehicular Queues," *Transportation Research* 11, no. 1 (1977): 39–44; Panos G. Michalopoulos and George Stephanopoulos, "Oversaturated Signal Systems with Queue Length Constraints—I. Single Intersection," *Transportation Research* 11, no. 6 (1977): 413–22; Katsuhisa Ohno, "Computational Algorithm for a Fixed Cycle Traffic Signal and New Approximate Expressions for Average Delay," *Transportation Science* 12, no. 1 (1978): 29–47; S. Chandana Wirasinghe, "Determination of Traffic Delays from Shock-Wave Analysis," *Transportation Research* 12, no. 5 (1978): 343–48; Sam Yagar, "Minimizing Delays for Transient Demands with Application to Signalized Road Junctions," *Transportation Research* 11, no. 1 (1977): 53–62; Jonathan Halpern, "The Accuracy of Estimates for the Performance Criteria in Certain Emergency Service Queueing Systems," *Transportation Science* 11, no. 3 (1977): 223–42;

Augustine O. Esogbue and Amar J. Singh, "A Stochastic Model for an Optimal Priority Bed Distribution Problem in a Hospital Ward," *Operations Research* 24, no. 5 (1976): 884-98; A.A. Sissouras and B. Moores, "The 'Optimum' Number of Beds in a Coronary Care Unit," *Omega* 4, no. 1 (1976): 59-65. On airplane seat and motel reservations, *see* M.F. Driscoll and N.A. Weiss, "An Application of Queueing Theory to Reservation Networks," *Management Science* 22, no. 5 (1976): 540-46; James J. Solberg, "A Tenant Vacancy Model," *Decision Sciences* 7, no. 2 (1976): 202-18. On inventory systems, *see* Chandrasekhar Das, "The (S-1,S) Inventory Model Under Time Limit on Backorders," *Operations Research* 25, no. 5 (1977): 835-50; D.P. Heyman, "Optimal Disposal Policies for a Single-Item Inventory System with Returns," *Naval Research Logistics Quarterly* 24, no. 3 (1977): 385-405. On police patrol cars and ambulances, *see* Jan M. Chaiken and Peter Dormont, "A Patrol Car Allocation Model: Background," *Management Science* 24, no. 12 (1978): 1280-90; Kenneth Chelst and James P. Jarvis, "Estimating the Probability Distribution of Travel Times for Urban Emergency Service Systems," *Operations Research* 27, no. 1 (1979): 199-204; Carlos F. Daganzo, "An Approximate Analytic Model of Many-to-Many Demand Responsive Transportation Systems," *Transportation Research* 12, no. 5 (1978): 325-33; Ernest Koenigsberg and Richard C. Lam, "Cyclic Queue Models of Fleet Operations," *Operations Research* 24, no. 3 (1976): 516-29. On equipment repair facilities, *see* Bezalel Gavish and Paul J. Schweitzer, "The Markovian Queue with Bounded Waiting Time," *Management Science* 23, no. 12 (1977): 1349-57. On public facilities, *see* Norbert Oppenheim, "Maximum Fluctuations in Mass Demand for Service at Public Facilities," *Transportation Research* 11, no. 1 (1977): 33-37. On community correctional centers, *see* Carl M. Harris and T.R. Thiagarajan, "Queueing Models of Community Correctional Centers in the District of Columbia," *Management Science* 22, no. 2 (1975): 167-71. And on drive-in banking, *see* B.L. Foote, "A Queuing Case Study of Drive-In Banking," *Interfaces* 6, no. 4 (1976): 31-37.

34. Mann, "Learning to Live with Lines," *supra* note 3, at 45.
35. For an application of queuing theory to this problem, *see* J. Teghem, "Use of Discrete Transforms for the Study of a GI/M/S Queue with Impatient Customer Phenomena," *Zeitschrift für Operations Research* 23, no. 3 (1979): 95-106.
36. Plato, *Gorgias*, trans. Terence Irwin (Oxford: Clarendon Press, 1979), 57.
37. Friedrich W. Nietzsche, *The Genealogy of Morals* (New York: Macmillan Co., 1924).

38. But contrast Jean-Jacques Rousseau's affirmative formulation of the insight, in Rousseau, *The Basic Political Writings,* trans. Donald A. Cress (Indianapolis: Hackett Publishing Co., 1987), 69.

39. Schwartz, *Queuing and Waiting, supra* note 29, at 137.

40. *See, e.g.,* D. Nichols, E. Smolensky, and T.N. Tideman, "Discrimination by Waiting Time in Merit Goods," *The American Economic Review* 61 (1971): 312–23, 313 (queues can be used to ration government-subsidized merit goods by imposing a "price"—the opportunity cost of the time spent waiting—that the poor can afford more than the less poor).

41. Schwartz, *Queuing and Waiting, supra* note 19, at 21–24.

42. Lipsky, *Street-Level Bureaucracy, supra* note 19, at 89–95.

43. Murray Edelman, *Political Language: Words That Succeed and Policies That Fail* (New York: Academic Press, 1977), 135.

44. Morrow, "Waiting as a Way of Life," *supra* note 14, at 65. The symbolic connections between queuing and social control and class stratification can be seen in this and other examples in the English language. *See, e.g.,* Arnold Birenbaum and Edward Sagarin, *Norms and Human Behavior* (New York: Holt, Rinehart & Winston, 1976), 18, 49. *See generally* Schwartz, *Queuing and Waiting, supra* note 19, at 181.

45. Lines can be connected with affluence and leisure, such as those connected with passports and airports. *See* Mann, "Learning to Live with Lines," *supra* note 3, at 45; Morrow, "Waiting as a Way of Life," *supra* note 14, at 65. But the waiting areas tend to be more pleasant. Jeffrey M. Prottas, *People-Processing: The Street-Level Bureaucrat in Public Service Bureaucracies* (Lexington, Mass.: Lexington Books, 1979), 24–25; Goodsell, "Welfare Waiting Rooms," *supra* note 8. Additionally, the rich can often hire people to stand in line for them. Mann, "Learning to Live with Lines," *supra* note 3, at 55. These added considerations mitigate the theory that the rich are faced with a greater opportunity cost per unit time waiting than the poor simply because of their greater earning power.

46. Editorial, *New York Times,* 8 Sept. 1981, sec. A, p. 22.

47. *See* Dulles, "On the Pressures and Politics of Waiting in Line," *supra* note 4, at 7 (reporting Dr. Stanley Milgram's study showing that only those immediately next to line jumpers will react to violation).

48. *See supra* text accompanying notes 29–30.

49. 43d Knesset, Draft law of member of the Knesset Abraham Porez, 1848-P, 22 Dec. 1997; my translation.

50. *Id.*

51. These "situational supports" not only are important in signaling queue formation but also deter violations. Schwartz, *Queuing and Waiting, supra*

note 19, at 99. Where physical barriers are not present, members of the queue may set them up to protect their line. Mann, "Learning to Live with Lines," *supra* note 3, at 340, 347.

52. *See infra* text accompanying notes 72–74.

53. Morrow, "Waiting as a Way of Life," *supra* note 14. Patience while waiting is not necessarily related to the amount of time that one is willing to wait. *See, e.g.,* Schwartz, *Queuing and Waiting, supra* note 19, at 122, 161, 163.

54. *Time,* 10 Aug. 1981, p. 36.

55. For an examination using queuing theory of customer impatience and queue leaving, *see* Celik Parkan, "A Note on Reneging Decisions," *Decision Sciences* 10, no. 3 (1979): 487–92. For "an analysis of the optimal reneging decision of a customer who joins a G/M/1 queue and has imperfect information about the queue," *see* Celik Parkan and E.H. Warren, "Optimal Reneging Decisions in a G/M/1 Queue," *Decision Sciences* 9, no. 1 (1978): 107–19.

56. *See generally* Michael Argyle, *Bodily Communication* (London: Methuen, 1975), 66–68.

57. Dullea, "On the Pressures and Politics of Waiting in Line," *supra* note 4, at 7.

58. Calvin Trillin, "Profiles: Making Adjustments," *The New Yorker,* 28 May 1984, pp. 50–51.

59. Signs at Six Flags Magic Mountain, an amusement park near Los Angeles, read: "Warning. Breaking lines is cause for removal from the park. No refunds." "Why People Are Rude," *supra* note 2, at 54, 55.

60. Schwartz, *Queuing and Waiting, supra* note 19, at 101–07 (queue panic; exit and entrance disorder).

61. Norms of social control may be most readily self-enforcing in situations in which the members of the group are self-selected and the good is not a "necessity." *See, e.g.,* Norman Trondsen, "Social Control in the Art Museum," *Urban Life* 5, no. 1 (1976): 105–20.

62. Simply by virtue of its distributive function, the line must always be tangent to the distribution point. A line cannot grow from an outside point inward to the distribution point because this reverses the first-come, first-served sequential rule basic to the operation of a queue.

63. The norm of sequential priority has been related to the broader value of "distributive justice." George C. Homans, *Social Behavior: Its Elementary Forms* (New York: Harcourt, Brace & World, 1961).

64. *See generally* Birenbaum and Sagarin, *People in Places, supra* note 44, at 51.

65. This verbalizing of excuse or justification plays an important role in re-

ducing sanctioning behavior. *See* Dullea, "On the Pressures and Politics of Waiting in Line," *supra* note 4, at 7 (reporting studies by D. Mary Harris, University of New Mexico, finding less anger at queue violators who said "Excuse me," gave a "hard-luck story," or were admitted by queue members next to them).

66. *See supra* note 7. In children's concepts of queuing rules, development of a place-holding ethic occurs later than the basic ethics of standing in line.

67. *See* Robert Sommer and Franklin D. Becker, "Territorial Defense and the Good Neighbor," *Journal of Personality and Social Psychology* 11, no. 2 (1969): 85–92; *see also* Franklin D. Becker, "Study of Spatial Markers," *Journal of Personality and Social Psychology* 26, no. 3 (1973): 439–45 (high demand for space decreases effectiveness of markers).

68. *Id.*

69. Queuing theory has been applied to queuing systems with "interruptions." *See* M.J. Fischer, "An Approximation to Queueing Systems with Interruptions," *Management Science* 24, no. 3 (1977): 338–44.

70. Smith, *The Russians, supra* note 13, at 85–86.

71. *See, e.g.,* "Why People Are Rude," *supra* note 59 (reporting Washington, D.C., woman who stands in supermarket line while children fill cart and meet her at head of line).

72. Smith, *The Russians, supra* note 13, at 80. Mann notes that there are time limits imposed on "holding a place." He postulates the "rule" involved not as sequential priority but as "serving time." Mann, "Learning to Live with Lines," *supra* note 3, at 345–46.

73. Smith, *The Russians, supra* note 13, at 80.

74. *See generally* Karp and Yoels, *Symbols, Selves and Society, supra* note 6, at 170.

75. *See generally* Schwartz, *Queuing and Waiting, supra* note 19, at 96–98 (preemptive priorities).

76. Smith, *The Russians, supra* note 13, at 66.

77. Vladimir Vysotsky, *Hamlet with a Guitar,* trans. Sergie Roy (Moscow: Progress Publishers, 1990).

78. Trillin, "Profiles," *supra* note 58, at 71.

79. A queue steward tends to be the people immediately behind the violator. Dulles, "On the Pressures and Politics of Waiting in Line," *supra* note 4, at 7; Mann, "Learning to Live with Lines," *supra* note 3, at 54.

80. Mann, "Learning to Live with Lines," *supra* note 3, at 347–49 (physical action is rare, used only when people believe that line jumping threatens their ability to receive service). Recent research indicates that nonverbal sanctions, such as staring, can have the effect of a more forceful physical

sanction. Mutual gazes cause greater physiological arousal than non-mutual gazes. An actor can manipulate another's physiology by gazing in one way or another. The response to mutual gazes is a good predictor of the gazer's degree of influence in social interactions. Allan Mazur, Eugene Rosa, Mark Faupel, Joshua Heller, Russell Leen, and Blake Thurman, "Physiological Aspects of Communication via Mutual Gaze," *American Journal of Sociology* 86, no. 1 (1980): 50–74. *See also* Chapter 1, *supra.*

81. *See* Dulles, "On the Pressures and Politics of Waiting in Line," *supra* note 4, at 7.

82. Mann, "Learning to Live with Lines," *supra* note 3, at 54. Jane Prather also notes that queuers close up lines to reduce the amount of body space between members as the line grows longer. Prather, "Sociological Observations of Privacy Behavior in a Bank Lobby," Paper presented at the Annual Meeting of the American Sociological Association, 28–31 Aug. 1972, *quoted in* Schwartz, *Queuing and Waiting, supra* note 19, at 206 n. 3. *See generally* Karp and Yoels, *Symbols, Selves and Society, supra* note 6, at 94–96 (the greater the number of bystanders, the less likely that any will intervene).

83. Oliver Wendell Holmes, Jr., *The Common Law* (Boston: Little, Brown, 1881).

84. Rule breaking is as necessary to social life as rules themselves are, for it is only through the sanctions accompanying violations that people can confirm norms. Birenbaum and Sagarin, *People in Places, supra* note 44, at 5. *See generally,* Kai T. Erikson, *Wayward Puritans; A Study in the Sociology of Deviance* (New York: Wiley, 1966).

85. On the general breakdown of expectations of compliance with social-interaction norms, *compare* Wiessler, "Why People Are Rude," *supra* note 2, at 54 ("Rudeness is becoming a common occurrence in American life."), *with* Ann Hulbert, "Why Manners Matter," *New Republic,* 6 Dec. 1982, pp. 24–27 (noting resurgence of interest in etiquette).

86. On the distinction between myth systems and operational codes, *see* W. Michael Reisman, *Folded Lies: Bribery, Crusades and Reforms* (New York: Free Press, 1979).

87. A server may discriminate among customers in a line, not just as a result of bias or in order to gain personally, but also in order to heighten the line's efficiency. It was found in a queuing-theory study that servers did not necessarily serve customers according to their sequential order in line, because "if customers with shorter service times were served first, . . . the mean queuing time could be reduced considerably." *International Abstracts*

in Operations Research 20, no. 2 (1979): 189. The study concluded that such discrimination among customers could be built into the system. "In a comparison with the 'optimal' shortest-service-time rule, a simple queue discipline involving only two non-preemptive priority classes fares very well." *Id. See* D.E. Matthews, "A Simple Method for Reducing Queuing Times in M/G/1," *Operations Research* 27, no. 2 (1979): 318–23; Derek Robinson, "Optimization of Priority Queues—A Semi-Markov Decision Chain Approach," *Management Science* 24, no. 5 (1978): 545–53.

88. "Institutionalized evasion," or "winking," serves two purposes: first, it allows "quiet" norm-breaking and, second, it latently benefits norm upholders by maintaining their preferences as the "existing social order." This minimizes conflict in those societies where group values and behaviors are widely divergent. Patricia A. Adler and Peter Adler, "Dry with a Wink: Normative Clash and Social Order," *Urban Life* 12, no. 2 (1983): 123–40, 134–36.

89. *See, e.g.,* Prottas, *People-Processing, supra* note 45, at 74–77, 134–35.

90. Norm upholders "fear that thorough enforcement would so outrage the objects of reform that they will threaten the norm." Adler and Adler, "Dry with a Wink," *supra* note 88, at 137.

91. Distributors often count on this "rationing" effect. *See* Lipsky, *Street Level Bureaucracy, supra* note 19, at 95–97.

CHAPTER 3
Rapping and Talking to the Boss

1. Robert Louis Stevenson, *Talk and Talkers* (Westport, Conn.: Redcoat Press, 1962), 7. For exploration of why people generally enjoy talking, *see* Donald Allen and Rebecca Guy, *Conversation Analysis: The Sociology of Talk* (The Hague: Mouton, 1974), 27 ("verbal exchange is satisfying and rewarding to both actors because it tends to reduce dissonance, give social support, and provide further information for future action"), 31 ("Most real people actively seek out occasions where they can expend their energy in talking to others.)"; *but see* Philip Zimbardo, *Shyness: What It Is, What to Do About It* (Reading, Mass.: Addison-Wesley Publishing Co., 1977) (for some talking is an uncomfortable activity). In the epigraph to this essay, Primo Levi suggests that talking is a necessary form of anxiety abatement precisely because one is heard, registered, and confirmed by another human being. Primo Levi, *The Drowned and the Saved,* trans. Raymond Rosenthal (New York: Summit Books, 1988), 68–69.

2. Harold D. Lasswell, *World Politics and Personal Insecurity* (New York: McGraw-Hill Book Co.; London: Whittlesey House, 1935), 119.
3. For a discussion of the right to speak, the power to control this right (*e.g.*, censorship), and the right not to speak (*e.g.*, the Fifth Amendment), *see* Ronald Wardhaugh, *How Conversation Works* (Oxford: B. Blackwell, 1985), 50–51.
4. *But see* the intriguing report of K. Reisman, *Contrapuntal Conversations in an Antiguan Village,* in Richard Bauman and Joel Sherzer, eds., *Explorations in the Ethnography of Speaking* (London: Cambridge University Press, 1974).
5. Harvey Sacks, Emanuel A. Schegloff, and Gail Jefferson, "A Simplest Systematics for the Organization of Turn Taking for Conversation," in Jim Schenkein, ed., *Studies in the Organization of Conversational Interaction* (New York: Academic Press, 1978), 7–55.
6. *See* in this regard Starkey Duncan, Jr., "Toward a Grammar for Dyadic Conversation," *Semiotica* 9, no. 1 (1973): 29–46.
7. *See, e.g.,* Keith H. Basso, " 'To Give Up On Words': Silence in Western Apache Culture," *Southwestern Journal of Anthropology* 26, no. 3 (1970): 213–30.
8. *See generally* Nathaniel Cantor, *Learning Through Discussion* (Buffalo: Human Relations for Industry, 1951), 45–55 (hierarchy in group discussions and among discussion leaders), 56–108 (dynamics of discussion meetings); Robert S. Cathcart and Larry A. Samovar, *Small Group Communication* (Dubuque, Iowa: W.C. Brown Co., 1970), 341–429 (leadership in discussion); Thomas Fansler, *Creative Power Through Discussion* (New York: Harper & Brothers, 1950), 148–75 (accomplishing goals in meetings and conferences), 179–85 (leadership in discussion); John Hasling, *Group Discussion and Decision Making* (New York: Crowell, 1975); Irving Lee and Laura L. Lee, *Handling Barriers in Communication* (New York: Harper, 1957) (handbook on conducting lecture-discussions and conferences); William S. Smith, *Group Problem-Solving Through Discussion,* rev. ed. (Indianapolis: Bobbs-Merrill Co., 1965), 144–48 (theory of discussion-group leadership); Theodore M. Mills, *Group Transformation: An Analysis of a Learning Group* (Englewood Cliffs, N.J.: Prentice-Hall, 1964); National Society for the Study of Education, Committee on the Dynamics of Instructional Groups, "The Dynamics of Instructional Groups," in *Yearbook of the National Society for the Study of Education* (Chicago: University of Chicago Press, 1960), vol 59, part 2; Ernest G. Bormann, *Discussion and Group Methods* (New York: Harper & Row,

1969); William M. Sattler and N. Edd Miller, *Discussion and Conference* (New York: Prentice-Hall, 1954); J. Maxwell Atkinson and John Heritage eds., *Structures of Social Action: Studies in Conversation Analysis* (Cambridge: Cambridge University Press, 1984); Jaime Bulatao, *The Technique of Group Discussion* (Manila: Aetneo University Press, 1966), 17–23 (discussion leaders); William E. Utterback, *Group Thinking and Conference Leadership* (New York: Rinehart, 1954), 162 (examples of discussion conferences; Utterback generally uses the term "group discussion" for instrumental talking); Halbert E. Gulley, *Discussion, Conference and Group Process* (New York: Holt, Rinehart & Winston, 1968), 52, 171–244 (discussion leadership).

For discussion of lectures, *see* Erving Goffman, *Forms of Talk* (Philadelphia: University of Pennsylvania Press, 1981), 137–40 (subordination of audiences), 185 (difference between lectures and friendly talk), 187, 192–93 (ways lecturers mitigate hierarchical distinction between themselves and audiences by enhancing appearance of their accessibility and common ground with audience), 188 (contextualizing a lecture).

For discussion of verbal signals for making a transition from non-instrumental talk to instrumental talk, *see* M.A. Atkinson, E.C. Cuff, and J.R.E. Lee, "The Recommencement of a Meeting as a Member's Accomplishment," in Jim Schenkein, ed., *Studies in the Organization of Conversational Interaction* (New York: Academic Press, 1978), 133–53, 134, 136.

Examples of goals in conversation are (1) inducing the hearer to perform some action; (2) manipulating the hearer's inference process; (3) conveying information about a known entity; (4) creating a new conceptual element to correspond to an entity already in hearer's knowledge store; and (5) directing the hearer's attention. T.A. Winograd, *A Framework for Understanding Discourse,* in M.A. Just and P.A. Carpenter, eds., *Cognitive Processes in Comprehension* (Hillsdale, N.J.: Erlbaum, 1977), 69, *noted in* Margaret L. McLaughlin, *Conversation: How Talk is Organized* (Beverly Hills: Sage Publications, 1984), 41. For more on pragmatic conversation, *see* McLaughlin, *Conversation,* 81–87.

A speaker's goals in instrumental talk are not necessarily overt. An example is the successful carrying out of "an action of dubious social standing," such as boasting. In fact,such goals as maintaining coherence in the conversation or simply avoiding lapses in the conversation underlie non-instrumental talk. McLaughlin, *Conversation,* 41–42.

9. *See, e.g.,* Amos B. Alcott, *Table-Talk* (Boston: Roberts Brothers, 1877); Charles Bucke, *The Book of Table-Talk* (London: Charles Knight, 1836);

Frank P. Wilson, *Table Talk* (San Marino, Calif.: Henry E. Huntington Library and Art Gallery, 1940); Otto Bismarck, *Bismarck's Table-Talk* (London: H. Grevel and Co., 1895); Samuel T. Coleridge, *Specimens of the Table Talk* (New York: Harper & Brothers, 1835); Leigh Hunt, *Table Talk: To Which Are Added Imaginary Conversations of Pope and Swift* (London: Smith, Elder, 1851); Edward Hussey, ed., *Extracts from Various Authors; and Fragments of Table-Talk* (Oxford: H. Hart, 1891); Samuel Johnson, *Table-Talk: Containing Aphorisms on Literature, Life and Manners* (Boston: J. Greenleaf, 1809); Samuel Rogers, *Recollections of the Table-Talk of Samuel Rogers*, 3d ed. (London: Edward Moxon, 1856); John Seldon, *The Table Talk of John Seldon* (Birmingham, Ala.: Legal Classics Library, 1989); G. Bernard Shaw, *Table Talk of George Bernard Shaw* (New York: Harper & Brothers, 1925); André Morellet, *Éloges de Madame Geoffrin* (Paris: H. Nicolle, 1812); Jonathan Swift, *A Complete Collection of Genteel and Ingenious Conversations* (London: Printed for B. Motte & C. Bathurst, 1738).

For a definition of non-instrumental talk as used in sociological study, see Goffman, *Forms of Talk, supra* note 8 at 14.

10. Utterback, *Group Thinking and Conference Leadership, supra* note 8, at 7.

11. Maya Angelou, *I Know Why the Caged Bird Sings* (New York: Random House, 1969), 29–31.

12. For an example of a coarchical conversation, *see* Goffman, *Forms of Talk, supra* note 8, at 143 (two mechanics).

13. Studies of the ends of conversations, when the conversers prepare to part company ("closings"), show hierarchy among conversers ("status-discrepant dyads"). Nonverbal behavior in hierarchical closings differed from nonverbal behavior in coarchical closings. In hierarchical ones, the lower-status partner tended to emit more "short sociocentric sequences like 'Uh' and 'Well.'" McLaughlin, *Conversation, supra* note 8, at 176–77.

For a mention of "social stratum characteristics" in conversation, *see* Allen and Guy, *Conversation Analysis, supra* note 1, at 45–46 ("sex, education, age, social class, and power"). For a discussion of some effects of status in conversation, *see id.* at 117–19. *See also* Aaron V. Cicourel, "Basic and Normative Rules in the Negotiation of Status and Role," in Hans P. Dreitzel, ed., *Patterns of Communicative Behavior*, vol. 2 of *Recent Sociology* (New York: Macmillan Co., 1970); William Labov and David Fanshel, *Therapeutic Discourse: Psychotherapy as Conversation* (New York: Academic Press, 1977), 127, 347 (therapist and patient conversations as conversations "between speakers of unequal status"); Goffman, *Forms of Talk, supra* note 8, at 142 (sociological studies of physician-patient consultations).

See generally Robert Brown and Albert Gilman, "The Pronouns of Power and Solidarity," in Thomas A. Sebeok, ed., *Style in Language* (Cambridge, Mass.: MIT Press, 1960), 253–76. *But see* Mills, *Group Transformation, supra* note 8, at 22 (assumes hierarchy in all two-person associations).

14. *See* Goffman, *Forms of Talk, supra* note 8, at 147 ("words are heard as representing in some direct way the current desire, belief, perception, or intention of whoever animates the utterance"); *but see id.* at 146 ("it is not true to say that we always speak our own words and ourself take the position to which these words attest").

15. *See,* as a good example, Labov and Fanshel, *Therapeutic Discourse, supra* note 13.

16. *See* in particular Goffman's stunning analysis of this, *supra* note 8, at 124–26. *See also* the useful essays in Barrie Thorne and Nancy Henley, eds., *Language and Sex: Difference and Dominance* (Rowley, Mass.: Newbury House Publishers, 1975). Males and females "differ in story reception behavior in ways consistent with traditional sex-role stereotypes." In studies, men "were more likely to display interest tokens and add or predict details, while the more supportive appreciation behaviors were characteristically female." McLaughlin, *Conversation, supra* note 8, at 191. *See generally* Allen and Guy, *Conversation Analysis, supra* note 1, at 88, 107–12, 116, 119–24, 128–33, 134–60 (range of somatic behavior), 179–89, 196–202.

17. *See generally* Peter French and Margaret MacLure, eds., *Adult-Child Conversation* (London: Croom Helm, 1981); Michael McTear, *Children's Conversation* (Oxford: B. Blackwell, 1985); Lynne Feagans, Catherine Garvey, and Roberta Golinkoff, eds., *The Origins and Growth of Communication* (Norwood, N.J.: Ablex Pub. Co., 1984). For ways in which parent-child conversations are hierarchical, *see* Labov and Fanshel, *Therapeutic Discourse, supra* note 13, at 84–85 (parents tend to aggravate the harshness of requests to their children regarding rights and obligations). *See generally* Allen and Guy, *Conversation Analysis, supra* note 1, at 35; Goffman, *Forms of Talk, supra* note 8, at 54 (teacher-student conversations are examples of roles determined by context), 150–51.

18. A study on the violation of the turn-taking rule, a fundamental rule in talk sessions, which is examined *infra,* in conversations between elementary school teachers and students showed that teachers frequently broke the rule. Although in most other types of conversations a "summons" placed "strong demands for a response . . . upon its addressed recipient," in the elementary classroom, teachers repeatedly ignored students' requests for the teachers' attention. McLaughlin, *Conversation, supra* note 8, at 218–19.

19. *See* Mills, *Group Transformation, supra* note 8, at 22 (hierarchy based on "difference in authority," for example, parents and children, therapist and group members, army officer and unit members).

20. Harvey L. Molotoch and Deirdre Boden, "Talking Social Structure: Discourse, Domination and the Watergate Hearings," *American Sociological Review* 50, no. 3 (1985): 273–88.

21. For one perspective from the victim's point of view, *see* Martha J. Langelan, *Back Off! How to Confront and Stop Sexual Harassment and Harassers* (New York: Simon & Schuster, 1993), 267 ff.

22. Molière, *Le Bourgeois Gentilhomme,* 2d ed., ed. M. Pellisson (Paris: Librairie Ch. Delagrave, 1892), 3.

23. *See* Atkinson *et al.,* "The Recommencement of a Meeting as a Member's Accomplishment," *supra* note 8, at 146–47 ("institutional framework" for meetings).

24. Henry M. Robert, *The Scott, Foresman Robert's Rules of Order,* ed. Sarah C. Robert (Glenview, Ill.: Scott, Foresman, 1981).

25. *See, e.g.,* John J. Gumperz, *Discourse Strategies* (Cambridge: Cambridge University Press, 1982); *The Polite Gentleman; or, Reflections upon the Several Kinds of Wit* (London: Printed for R. Basset, 1700); *The Art of Conversation; or, The Polite Entertainer* (London: R. Withy & J. Ryall, 1757); Society of Gentlemen, *The Art of Conversing,* 9th ed. (Boston: James French, 1850); William D. Basse, *A Helpe To Discourse; or, A Messelany of Seriousnesse with Merriment* (London: Thomas Brudenel, 1630); John Constable, *The Conversation of Gentlemen Considered* (London: J. Hoyles, 1738); Horatio S. Krans, *The Lost Art of Conversation* (New York: Sturgis & Walton Co., 1910); Alan Marshall, *Speak for Yourself* (New York: Hillman-Curl, 1937); Donald Carroll, *Why Didn't I Say That? The Art of Verbal Self-Defense* (New York: Watts, 1980); J. Starkey, *The Art of Complaisance: or, The Means to Oblige in Conversation* (London: Printed for J. Starkey, 1673); Giovanni Della Casa, *Galateo; or, The Book of Manners,* trans. R.S. Pine-Coffin (Harmondsworth, England: Penguin Books, 1958); Samuel A. Foot, "An Address Delivered Before the Euglossian and Alpha Phi Delta Societies of Geneva College, Aug. 1, 1832" (Geneva: J.C. Merrell & Co., 1832); Adrienne Lehrer, *Wine and Conversation* (Bloomington, Ind.: Indiana University Press, 1983); Charles G. Leland, *The Art of Conversation* (New York: Carleton, 1864); Justin McCarthy, *Con Amore* (London: Tinsley Brothers, 1868); Agnes H. Morton, *Our Conversational Circle* (New York: Century Co., 1898); Member of the Aristocracy, *Society Small Talk; or, What to Say and When to Say It,* 2d ed. (London: F. Warne

& Co., 1879); Jonathan Swift, *A Complete Collection of Genteel and Ingenious Conversation* (London: Printed for B. Motte & C. Bathurst, 1738); Henry W. Taft, *An Essay on Conversation* (New York: Macmillan Co., 1927); Daniel Tuvill, *The Dove and the Serpent* (London: Printed by T.C., 1614); Henry Thomas, *The Complete Book of English* (Garden City, N.Y.: Garden City Publishing Co., 1938); D.A. Gent, *The Whole Art of Converse* (London: Printed for Joseph Hindmarsh, 1683); Milton Wright, *The Art of Conversation and How to Apply Its Technique* (New York: McGraw-Hill Book Co.; London: Whittlesey House, 1936); Elinor Ochs, *Acquiring Conversational Competence* (London: Routledge & Kegan Paul, 1983).

26. For an explicit example, *see, e.g.,* "Dear Abby Column," *Los Angeles Times,* 28 Dec. 1975, part 8, p. 7.

27. W. Michael Reisman and Aaron M. Schreiber, *Jurisprudence: Understanding and Shaping Law* (New Haven: New Haven Press, 1987), 12–13.

28. *See generally* Allen and Guy, *Conversation Analysis, supra* note 1; Robert F. Bales, *Interaction Process Analysis* (Cambridge, Mass.: Addison-Wesley Press, 1950) (systematic approach to verbal interaction); Lauri Carlson, *Dialogue Games: An Approach to Discourse Analysis* (Dordrecht: D. Reidel Pub. Co., 1983); David D. Clarke, *Language and Action: A Structural Model of Behaviour* (Oxford: Pergamon Press, 1983); Teun A. van Dijk, *Prejudice in Discourse: An Analysis of Ethnic Prejudice in Cognition and Conversation* (Amsterdam: J. Benjamin Pub. Co., 1984); Charles Goodwin, *Conversational Organization: Interaction Between Speakers and Hearers* (New York: Academic Press, 1981); Labov and Fanshel, *Therapeutic Discourse, supra* note 13; McLaughlin, *Conversation, supra* note 8; Marion Owen, *Apologies and Remedial Interchanges: A Study of Language Use in Social Interaction* (Berlin, N.Y.: Mouton Publishers, 1983); Atkinson and Heritage, *Structures of Social Action, supra* note 8; Wardhaugh, *How Conversation Works, supra* note 3; Florian Coulmas, ed., *Conversational Routine: Explorations in Standardized Communication Situations and Prepatterned Speech* (The Hague: Mouton, 1981); Jim Schenkein, ed., *Studies in the Organization of Conversational Interaction* (New York: Academic Press, 1978); Paul Werth, ed., *Conversation and Discourse: Structure and Interpretation* (London: Croom Helm, 1981); Feagans *et al., The Origins and Growth of Communication, supra* note 17; Robert F. Bales, "A Set of Categories for the Analysis of Small Group Interaction," *American Sociological Review* 15, no. 2 (1950): 257–63; Robert F. Bales, Fred L. Strodtbeck, Theodore M. Mills, and Mary E. Roseborough, "Channels of Communication in Small Groups," *American Sociological Review* 16, no. 4 (1951): 461–68.

29. *See* in particular Allen and Guy, *Conversation Analysis, supra* note 1, at 206–17.

30. Dziga Vertog, *quoted in* John Berger, *Ways of Seeing* (London: British Broadcasting Corp. & Penguin Books, 1972), 17.

31. For mention of how high pitch indicates subordinate status, *see* Labov and Fanshel, *Therapeutic Discourse, supra* note 13, at 129. For a discussion of how body gestures, intonation, pitch, and other voice qualifiers in conversation signal status, *see id.* at 22–27, 29–30, and 355–56. *See also* Goffman, *Forms of Talk, supra* note 8, at 128 (pitch change); Dwight L. Bolinger, "A Theory of Pitch Accent in English," *Word* 14, nos. 2–3 (1958): 109–49; Philip Lieberman, "On the Acoustic Basis of the Perception of Intonation by Linguists," *Word* 21, no. 1 (1965): 40–54; Robert P. Stockwell, "The Place of Intonation in a Generative Grammar of English," *Language* 36, no. 3 (part 1) (1960): 360–67; Jo Ann Goldberg, "Amplitude Shift: A Mechanism for the Affiliation of Utterances in Conversational Interaction," in Jim Schenkein, ed., *Studies in the Organization of Conversational Interaction* (New York: Academic Press, 1978), 199–218.

32. Such styles of address as signs of subordination are easier for Americans to spot outside the United States. *See, e.g.,* Wardhaugh, *How Conversation Works, supra* note 3, at 50–51.

33. *See generally* Jurgen Ruesch, *Nonverbal Communication: Notes on the Visual Perception of Human Relations* (Berkeley: University of California Press, 1956).

34. For the importance of context in conversation, *see generally* Wardhaugh, *How Conversation Works, supra* note 3, at 101–15; and Labov and Fanshel, *Therapeutic Discourse, supra* note 13, at 352.

35. For examples of physical barriers suggesting hierarchy in conversation, *see* Wardhaugh, *How Conversation Works, supra* note 3, at 82.

36. On physical barriers, *e.g.,* pedestals, *see* Goffman, *Forms of Talk, supra* note 8, at 165 (platforms).

37. Richard Reeves, *Passage to Peshawar: Pakistan Between the Hindu Kush and the Arabian Sea* (New York: Simon & Schuster, 1984), 43.

38. On clothing, posture, and body ornamentation indicating hierarchy or coarchy in the absence of other environmental clues, *see* Jim Schenkein, "Identity Negotiations in Conversation," in Schenkein, ed., *Studies in the Organization of Conversational Interaction* (New York: Academic Press, 1978), 57–78, 61–62 ("appearance, carriage, and gesture" and "interactional grace" reveal such biographical details as place of residence, occupation, education, and personal wealth); R. de Beaugrande, "Text,

Discourse, and Process: Towards a Multidisciplinary Science of Texts," in R.O. Freedle, ed., *Advances in Discourse Processes,* vol. 4 (Norwood, N.J.: Ablex Publishing, 1980), 243- 44, *quoted in* McLaughlin, *Conversation, supra* note 8, at 34 (five ways in which talkers orient themselves to environment of conversation: (1) "typical and determinate concepts and relations in world knowledge," (2) "cultural and social attitudes," (3) "conventional scripts and goals," (4) traits of the current context, and (5) episodic knowledge of shared experiences). For more on the context of conversations and the necessity for common ground for the speakers, *see* McLaughlin, *Conversation, supra* note 8, at 49–52.

39. David Lodge, *Small World: An Academic Romance* (London: Secker & Warburg, 1984), 117–18.

40. For an amusing account, *see* Anne Tyler, *The Accidental Tourist* (New York: Knopf, 1985).

41. Shift in topic can be signalled verbally. *See* Sally Planalp and Karen Tracy, "Not to Change the Topic But . . . : A Cognitive Approach to the Management of Conversation," in Dan Nimmo, ed., *Communication Yearbook,* vol. 4 (New Brunswick: Transaction Books, 1980), 237–58; Allen and Guy, *Conversation Analysis, supra* note 1, at 230–33.

   For discussion of studies done on the conversation triggers to change turn-by-turn talk into a story, *see* McLaughlin, *Conversation, supra* note 8, at 186–94; Gail Jefferson, "Sequential Aspects of Storytelling in Conversation," in Jim Schenkein, ed., *Studies in the Organization of Conversation Interaction* (New York: Academic Press, 1978), 219–48, 220. *See generally* Alan L. Ryave, "On the Achievement of a Series of Stories," in Jim Schenkein, ed., *Studies in the Organization of Conversation Interaction* (New York: Academic Press, 1978), 113–32, 123; Goffman, *Forms of Talk, supra* note 8, at 152.

42. *See* Wardhaugh, *How Conversation Works, supra* note 3, at 83 (eye contact); Goffman, *Forms of Talk, supra* note 8, at 59–60 (examples of conversations in which strangers are flirting).

43. *See generally* Catharine A. MacKinnon, *Sexual Harassment of Working Women* (New Haven: Yale University Press, 1979); Carroll M. Brodsky, *The Harassed Worker* (Lexington, Mass.: Lexington Books, 1976), 40 (psychological effects of harassment); A. Astrachan, *How Men Feel* (Garden City, N.Y.: Anchor Press / Doubleday, 1986), chap. 5; Eliza G.C. Collins and Timothy B. Blodgett, "Sexual Harassment . . . Some See It . . . Some Won't," *Harvard Business Review* 59 (1981): 76–94; Langelan, *Back Off! supra* note 21.

44. Morton, *Our Conversational Circle, supra* note 25, at 49.
45. *See* Goffman, *Forms of Talk, supra* note 8, at 78–122 (response cries uttered by individuals in isolation).
46. Atkinson *et al.,* "The Recommencement of a Meeting as a Member's Accomplishment," *supra* note 9, at 146 (chairing or controlling talk involves such talk practices as scheduling the topic or items of discussion into recordable episodes to reflect the business discussed, and using attention-getting prefaces — "machinery which shapes the talk in predesigning ways"); Fansler, *Creative Power, supra* note 8, at 152 (conference procedure); Hasling, *Group Discussion and Decision Making, supra* note 8, at 108 (procedure for meetings); Gulley, *Discussion, Conference and Group Process, supra* note 8, at 336–48 (procedure rules for discussion at conferences and conventions); Bulatao, *The Technique of Group Discussion, supra* note 8, at 14–16 (discussion procedure).
47. Oscar Wilde, *The Remarkable Rocket* (Boston: Roberts Brothers, 1888), 108–09.
48. *See* McLaughlin, *Conversation: How Talk is Organized, supra* note 8, at 15 (the whole book is a handbook on conducting lecture-discussions and conferences); for an early inquiry, *see* Victor H. Yngve, "On Getting a Word in Edgewise," *Papers from the Sixth Regional Meeting, Chicago Linguistic Society* (Chicago: Chicago Linguistic Society, 1970), 567–78. For discussion of cognitive studies of taking turns, *see* McLaughlin, *Conversation,* at 91–131; Sacks *et al.,* "A Simplest Systematics for the Organization of Turn Taking for Conversation," *supra* note 5 (organization of turn taking as distributive mechanism). For discussion of conversational repairs addressed to violations of the turn-taking rule, *see* McLaughlin, *Conversation,* at 216–19; Sacks *et al.,* "A Simplest Systematics for the Organization of Turn Taking for Conversation," at 39–40 ("turn-taking system . . . favors . . . smaller numbers of participants"). For mention of lapses in conversation, *see* Wardhaugh, *How Conversation Works, supra* note 3, at 139–56; Owen, *Apologies and Remedial Interchanges, supra* note 28, at 31–33; Harvey Sacks, Emanuel A. Schegloff, and Gail Jefferson, "A Simplest Systematics for the Organization of Turn-Taking for Conversation," *Language* 50, no. 4 (part 1) (1974): 696–735; Sacks *et al.,* "A Simplest Systematics for the Organization of Turn Taking for Conversation," *supra* note 5, at 7, 45 (chairperson at meetings "partially preallocate[s] turns," "has rights to talk first, and to talk after each other speaker, and can use each such turn to allocate next speakership"), 48 n. 6 (quoting anthropologist Ethel M. Albert: "The order in which individuals speak in

a group is strictly determined by seniority of rank."), 49 n. 8 (the degree to which turn taking is sensitive to context), 53 n. 27 ("relative distribution of turns . . . is an index of, or medium for, power, status, influence, etc.").

49. McTear, *Children's Conversation, supra* note 17, at 159.

50. Harry Stack Sullivan, *Conceptions of Modern Psychiatry* (Washington, D.C.: Wm. Alanson White Psychiatric Foundation, 1945).

51. Stevenson, *Talk and Talkers, supra* note 1. *See* discussion of the rule of provisional acceptance *infra.*

52. Primo Levi, *The Drowned and the Saved, supra* note 1.

53. Primo Levi, *Survival in Auschwitz: The Nazi Assault on Humanity* (New York: Collier Books, 1961), 60.

54. William H. Ginsburg, "Preparing for Depositions" *For the Defense* 32, no. 11 (November 1990): 27–30, at 28.

55. Randall Jarrett, *Pictures from an Institution* (New York: Knopf, 1954), 28.

56. Frank N. Willis and Sharon J. Williams, "Simultaneous Talking in Conversation and Sex of Speakers," *Perceptual and Motor Skills* 43 (1976): 1067–70. *See also* Jessie Bernard, *The Sex Game* (Englewood Cliffs, N.J.: Prentice-Hall, 1968).

57. Starkey Duncan, Jr., "Some Signals and Rules for Taking Speaking Turns in Conversations," *Journal of Personality and Social Psychology* 23, no. 2 (1972): 283–92.

58. Reisman and Schreiber, *Jurisprudence, supra* note 27.

59. Mary G. Conklin, *Conversation: What to Say and How to Say It,* 2d ed. (New York: Funk & Wagnalls Co., 1913), 27.

60. Utterback, *Group Thinking, supra* note 8, at 56.

61. John Austin, *The Province of Jurisprudence Determined,* ed. Wilfrid E. Rumble (London: J. Murray, 1832).

62. Austinian thought is considered with reference to conversational replies and responses in Goffman, *Forms of Talk, supra* note 8.

63. Utterback, *Group Thinking, supra* note 8, at 54.

64. *The Art of Conversing* (Boston: James French, 1850), 23.

65. Wright, *The Art of Conversation, supra* note 25, at 311.

66. Henry D. Thoreau, *A Week on the Concord and Merrimack Rivers* (New York: Thomas Y. Crowell Co., 1911), 28.

67. Charles Derber, *The Pursuit of Attention: Power and Individualism in Everyday Life* (Boston: G.K. Hall, 1979), 29–33.

68. Society of Gentlemen, *The Art of Conversing, supra* note 25, at 24–45.

69. Indeed, licenses to gaze as part of listening appear to be subject to a complex code. *See* Geoffrey W. Beattie, "Contextual Constraints on the Floor-Apportionment Function of Speaker-Gaze in Dyadic Con-

versations," *British Journal of Social and Clinical Psychology* 18 (1979): 391–92.

70. Jarrett, *Pictures from an Institution, supra* note 55, at 28.

71. Levi, *Survival in Auschwitz, supra* note 53, at 60.

72. Alain Finkielkraut, *Remembering in Vain: The Klaus Barbie Trial and Crimes Against Humanity* (New York: Columbia University Press, 1992), 18.

73. Adrienne Rich, *The Dream of a Common Language: Poems, 1974–1977* (New York: W.W. Norton & Co., 1978); Adrienne Rich, *On Lies, Secrets, and Silence: Selected Prose, 1966–1978* (New York: W.W. Norton & Co., 1979), 243.

74. Pamela M. Fishman, "Interaction: The Work Women Do," in Barrie Thorne, Cheria Kramarae and Nancy Henley, eds., *Language, Gender and Society* (Rowley, Mass.: Newbury House, 1983), 99.

75. Dena Goodman, *The Republic of Letters: A Cultural History of the French Enlightenment* (Ithaca, N.Y.: Cornell University Press, 1994), 103–04.

76. For an impressive systematization, *see* Duncan, "Some Signals and Rules for Taking Speaking Turns in Conversations," *supra* note 57. For data indicating subtle distinctions between nods as listening confirmations and nods as signals to yield, *see* Allen T. Dittman and Lynn G. Llewellyn, "Relationship Between Vocalizations and Head Nods and Listener Responses," *Journal of Personality and Social Psychology* 9, no. 1 (1968): 79–84.

77. Curiously, available empirical research indicates that gaze per se does not function as a yielding signal. *See* Beattie, "Contextual Constraints on the Floor-Appointment Function of Speaker-Gaze in Dyadic Conversations," *supra* note 69, at 391–92.

78. Starkey Duncan, Jr., and George Niederehe, "On Signalling That It's Your Turn to Speak," *Journal of Experimental Social Psychology* 10 (1974): 234–47.

79. Utterback, *Group Thinking and Conference Leadership, supra* note 8, at 55.

80. Wright, *The Art of Conversation, supra* note 25, at 23–24.

81. *See* Sacks *et al.,* "A Simplest Systematics for the Organization of Turn Taking for Conversation," *supra* note 5, at 29 ("an important, perhaps the central, general technique whereby current speaker selects next" speaker is an "addressing" technique, which includes directing gaze toward selected speaker); Wardhaugh, *How Conversation Works, supra* note 3, at 78–88 (gazing). For a discussion of violations of the yielding rule, *see* Allen and Guy, *Conversation Analysis, supra* note 1, at 170–73. For a discussion of verbal signals for yielding the floor in coarchical conversation,

see Gail Jefferson and Jim Schenkein, "Some Sequential Negotiations in Conversation: Unexpanded and Expanded Versions of Projected Action Sequences," in Jim Schenkein, ed., *Studies in the Organization of Conversational Interaction* (New York: Academic Press, 1978), 155–72, 158 ("passes"). For a discussion of exceptions to the yielding rule, *see* Goffman, *Forms of Talk, supra* note 8, at 29.

For treatments of nonverbal behavior in conversations, *see generally* Mark Knapp, *Nonverbal Communication in Human Interaction* (New York: Holt, Rinehart & Winston, 1978); Desmond Morris, *Manwatching: A Field Guide to Human Behaviour* (New York: H.N. Abrams, 1977); R.A. Hinde, ed., *Non-Verbal Communication* (Cambridge: Cambridge University Press, 1972); Adam Kendon, "Movement Coordination in Social Interaction: Some Examples Described," *Acta Psychologica* 32 (1970): 101–25; Albert E. Scheflen, *How Behavior Means* (New York: Gordon & Breach, 1973); Michael Argyle, *Non-Verbal Symbolic Actions: Gaze, Life Sentences—Aspects of the Social Role of Language,* ed. R. Harre (London: John Wiley, 1976); Michael Argyle and Mark Cook, *Gaze and Mutual Gaze* (Cambridge: Cambridge University Press, 1976); Charles Goodwin, *Conversational Organization: Interaction Between Speakers and Hearers* (New York: Academic Press, 1981); Adam Kendon, "Some Functions of Gaze Direction in Social Interaction," *Acta Psychologica* 26, no. 1 (1967): 22–63. For discussion of body language in conversation, *see* Allen and Guy, *Conversation Analysis, supra* note 1, at 134–60; Goffman, *Forms of Talk, supra* note 8, at 12, 33 (facial gestures and body orientation), 153–54 (shift to whisper or hand gestures changes meaning of talk).

82. For a discussion of yielding the floor in hierarchical conversations, *see* Goffman, *Forms of Talk, supra* note 8, at 176 (question-and-answer sessions after lectures). *See, e.g.,* Sacks *et al.,* "A Simplest Systematics for the Organization of Turn Taking for Conversation," *supra* note 5, at 15 (conversations where "overwhelmingly one party talks at a time," which can happen because "the system allocates single turns to single speakers, any speaker getting, with the turn, exclusive rights to talk to first possible completion of an initial instance of a unit-type, rights that are renewable for single next instances of a unit-type").

83. Goffman wrote: "Listeners are obliged to avoid staring directly at the speaker too long lest they violate his territoriality, and yet they are encouraged to direct their visual attention so as to obtain gesticulatory cues to his meaning and provide him with evidence that he is being attended. . . . It is as if they must look at the speaker, but not see him." Goffman, *Forms of Talk, supra* note 8, at 140, 141. I am uncertain of the accuracy of Goff-

man's observation. Speaking may involve a waiver to listeners of some of the prohibitions on protracted observation. Correlatively, failing to accord the speaker the visual indicators of close attention may itself violate the pertinent talking norms. For some speakers, the waiver is an additional reward; for them, speaking is a way of saying "Look at me!" For others, the waiver is an additional disincentive, for speaking becomes a license to be looked at in ways they find painful. In public performances, the degree of permissibility of staring increases greatly, perhaps in part because the speaker-victim, cannot stare back at the pack of eyes.

84. For discussion of the use of insults in conversation, *see, e.g.,* Alan Dundes, Jerry W. Leach, and Bora Özkök, "The Strategy of Turkish Boys' Verbal Dueling Rhymes," in John J. Gumperz and Dell Hymes, eds., *Directions in Sociolinguistics: The Ethnography of Communication* (New York: Holt, Rinehart & Winston, 1972); Claudia Mitchell-Kernan, "Signifying and Marking: Two Afro-American Speech Acts," in John J. Gumperz and Dell Hymes, eds., *Directions in Sociolinguistics: The Ethnography of Communication* (New York: Holt, Rinehart & Winston, 1972); Iona A. Opie and Peter Opie, *The Lore and Language of Schoolchildren* (Oxford: Clarendon Press, 1959).

85. Arthur M. Coon, "Brainstorming—A Creative Problem-Solving Technique," in Robert S. Cathcart and Larry A. Samovar, eds., *Small Group Communication* (Dubuque, Iowa: W.C. Brown Co., 1970), 160.

86. Utterback, *Group Thinking and Conference Leadership, supra* note 8.

87. *See, e.g.,* Conklin, *Conversation: What to Say and How to Say It, supra* note 59, at 24–26; Morton, *Our Conversational Circle, supra* note 25.

88. Wright, *The Art of Conversation, supra* note 25, at 107.

89. Roger Schank, "Rules and Topics in Conversation," *Cognitive Science* 1, no. 4 (1977): 421–41. *See also* Labov and Fanshel, *Therapeutic Discourse, supra* note 13, at 120 (conversations between family members, close associates, and members of ethnic groups—people with common background and high degree of shared knowledge—appear cryptic to outsiders); Goffman, *Forms of Talk, supra* note 8, at 67 (context can recast meaning of speech), 74 (familiar conversers less pressured to articulate thoughts).

90. Schank, "Rules and Topics in Conversation," *supra* note 89.

91. For a discussion of "masking" and "resistance" in conversation, *see* Labov and Fanshel, *Therapeutic Discourse, supra* note 13, at 334–36 (use of speech devices to mitigate abrasiveness of conversational interaction, thereby undermining accuracy of speech content, *e.g.,* euphemisms, vague references, intonation, narrative responses, leaving things unsaid).

For discussion of how subject matter is controlled in conversation, *see*

Goffman, *Forms of Talk, supra* note 8, at 61–62 (directive "aimed at inducing the hearer to impart verbal information on a particular matter"), 19 (ritual constraints on subject matter "preserve orderly communication").

92. Harold Garfinkel, *Studies in Ethnomethodology* (Englewood Cliffs, N.J.: Prentice-Hall, 1967), 74, *cited in* Molotoch and Boden, "Talking Social Structure," *supra* note 20.

93. H. Paul Grice, "Logic and Conversation," in Peter Cole and Jerry L. Morgan, eds., *Syntax and Semantics,* vol. 3 (New York: Academic Press, 1975), 41–58. For mention of the cooperative principle, *see also* McLaughlin, *Conversation, supra* note 48, at 206; Allen and Guy, *Conversation Analysis, supra* note 1, at 12. For a discussion of the cooperative principle, *see* Wardhaugh, *How Conversation Works, supra* note 3, at 49–77, especially 63–66. For a discussion of seeming violations of the cooperative principle, *see* Wardhaugh, *How Conversation Works, supra* note 3, at 55–57.

94. *See* Allen and Guy, *Conversation Analysis, supra* note 1, at 214–15 ("the words and the referents used are in many cases uniquely determined by specific cultures so that it is impossible to fully equate the thought processes of two persons from different cultures even though they appear to be saying the same thing," making it difficult for "people to talk in a cross-cultural relation and maintain full congruence of terms and referents"); Goffman, *Forms of Talk, supra* note 8, at 68 (each culture has its own reinterpretive framework). For an allusion to metalanguages, *see* Wardhaugh, *How Conversation Works, supra* note 3, at 61; Goffman, *Forms of Talk, supra* note 8, at 128–56 ("coding switching" or changing "footing"). For an account of a hierarchical conversation in which a subordinate was forced out of her natural role into one dictated by the superordinate, *see* Goffman, *Forms of Talk, supra* note 8, at 124–25 (press conference exchange between Nixon and female reporter). *See also* van Dijk, *Prejudice in Discourse, supra* note 28 at 76–77 ("Racist discourse"— how majorities talk to minorities: "discriminatory sets of the white majority members . . . may be accompanied or executed (para) verbally").

95. Molotoch and Boden, "Talking Social Structure," *supra* note 20.

96. Schank, "Rules and Topics in Conversation," *supra* note 89; *see also* Derber, *The Pursuit of Attention, supra* note 67.

97. *See* Goffman, *Forms of Talk, supra* note 8, at 174–75, 189–90.

98. Charles E. Merriam, *The Making of Citizens: A Comparative Study of Methods of Civic Training* (Chicago: University of Chicago Press, 1931); *id., Systematic Politics* (Chicago: University of Chicago Press, 1945).

99. *See, e.g.,* Sissela Bok, *Lying: Moral Choice in Public and Private Life* (New York: Pantheon Books, 1978); John Rawls, *A Theory of Justice* (Cam-

bridge, Mass.: Belknap Press of Harvard University Press, 1971). *But cf.*
W. Michael Reisman, *Folded Lies, Bribery, Crusades, and Reforms* (New
York: Free Press, 1979).

100. 3 Inst. 166.
101. Ferdinand Tonnies, *Community and Society*, trans. and ed. Charles Loomis
(East Lansing: Michigan State University Press, 1957).
102. Plato, *Republic*, Book V (Jowett translation 1901).
103. Plato, *Republic*, Book III (Jowett translation 1901).
104. Fyodor Dostoyevsky, *The Brothers Karamazov*, trans. Constance Garnett
(New York: Modern Library, 1949).
105. Henrik Ibsen, *The Wild Duck*, trans. Peter Hall and Inga-Stina Ewbank
(Bristol, Englang: Longdunn Press, 1990).
106. Erving Goffman, *Relations in Public: Microstudies of the Public Order* (New
York: Basic Books, 1971), 143.
107. *See generally* Owen, *Apologies and Remedial Interchanges*, *supra* note 28.
108. Barry R. Schlenker and Bruce W. Darby, "The Use of Apologies in Social
Predicaments," *Social Psychology Quarterly* 44, no. 3 (1981): 271–78.
109. Leo Melzer, William N. Morris, and Donald P. Hayes, "Interruption
Outcomes and Vocal Amplitude: Explorations in Social Psychophysics,"
Journal of Personality and Social Psychology 18, no. 3 (1971): 392–402.
110. Friedrich K. von Savigny, *Of the Vocation of Our Age for Legislation and
Jurisprudence*, trans. Abraham Hayward (New York: Arno Press, 1975).
111. For discussion of the repair of disruption caused by violation of conversational norms, *see* Goffman, *Forms of Talk*, *supra* note 8, at 16, 19 (repair
and termination for breach of turn-taking rule), 21 (conditions for tolerating and not tolerating "lapses in maintaining the ritual [conventional]
code"), 26–27 (self-help used to secure "justice"). For mention of the termination sanction, *see* Wardhaugh, *How Conversation Works*, *supra* note 3,
at 49.
112. Renata Adler, *Reckless Disregard* (New York: Alfred A. Knopf, 1986).
113. Georg Simmel, *Conflict*, trans. Kurt H. Wolff (Glencoe, Ill.: Free Press,
1955), 17–18. For a discussion of Simmel's theory in this regard, *see* Lewis
A. Coser, *The Functions of Social Conflict*, ed. W.J.H. Sprott (London:
Routledge & Kegan Paul, 1956).
114. N.S. Timasheff, *An Introduction to the Sociology of Law*, vol. 3 of *Harvard
Sociological Studies* (Cambridge: Committee on Research in the Social
Sciences, Harvard University, 1939).

CHAPTER 4
Amending Microlaw

1. *See* Leopold Pospisil, "Legal Levels and Multiplicity of Legal Systems in Human Societies," *The Journal of Conflict Resolution* 11, no. 1 (1967): 2–26.

2. For classic statements of Historicist jurisprudence, *see generally* Frederick Charles von Savigny, *Of the Vocation of Our Age for Legislation and Jurisprudence*, trans. Abraham Hayward (London: Littlewood & Co. Old Bailey, 1986). For criticism, *see* Morris Raphael Cohen, "History vs. Value," *The Journal of Philosophy, Psychology and Scientific Methods* 11 (1914): 701–16, 705; Friedrich A. von Hayek, "Scientism and the Study of Society: The Historicism of the Scientistic Approach," in Friedrich A. von Hayek, *The Counter-Revolution of Science: Studies of the Abuse of Reason* (Glencoe, Ill.: Free Press, 1952).

3. *See, e.g.*, Discrimination Against Indigenous Peoples: First Revised Text of the Draft Universal Declaration on Rights of Indigenous Peoples, U.N. Doc. E/CN.4/Sub.2/1989/33 (1989). For the leading U.N. study on indigenous communities, *see* J. Cobo, Study of the Problem of Discrimination Against Indigenous Populations, U.N. Doc. E/CN.4/Sub.2/1986/7/Add.4, U.N. Sales No. E86 XIV.3 (1986).

4. *See* Bernard Lewis, *The Jews of Islam* (Princeton: Princeton University Press, 1984).

5. W. Michael Reisman, "The Tormented Conscience: Applying and Appraising Unauthorized Coercion," *Emory Law Journal* 32 (1983): 499–544.

6. W. Michael Reisman, "Theory About Law: The New Haven School of Jurisprudence," *Wissenschaftskolleg Jahrbuch 1989/90* (1991), 28, 233.

7. *See generally* Harold D. Lasswell, *The Decision Process: Seven Categories of Functional Analysis* (College Park: University of Maryland Press, 1956); *see also* Myres S. McDougal et al., "The World Constitutive Process of Authoritative Decision," *Journal of Legal Education* 19, no. 3 (1967): 253–300 and 403–37, *reprinted in* Myres S. McDougal and W. Michael Reisman, eds., *International Law Essays* (Mineola, N.Y.: Foundation Press, 1981), 191.

8. These ideas are set out in W. Michael Reisman, "International Lawmaking: A Process of Communication," Lasswell Memorial Lecture, American Society of International Law, 24 Apr. 1981, in *Proceedings of the American Society of International Law* (1981): 101; and Myres S. McDougal and W. Michael Reisman, "The Prescribing Function in the World Constitutive Process: How International Law Is Made," *Yale Studies in World*

Public Order 6, no. 2 (1980): 249–84, *reprinted in* Myres S. McDougal and W. Michael Reisman, *International Law Essays, supra* note 7, at 355.

9. Raul Hilberg, *The Destruction of the European Jews* (New York: Octagon Books, 1961), 760–62.

10. *See, e.g.,* Universal Declaration of Human Rights, G.A. Res. 217A, U.N. GAOR, 3d Sess. pt.1, at 71, U.N. Doc. A/810 (1948); International Covenant on Civil and Political Rights, 16 Dec. 1966, G.A. Res. 2200, U.N. GAOR, 21 Sess., Supp. No. 16, at 52, U.N. Doc. A/6316 (1967) (entered into force on 23 Mar. 1976); International Covenant on Economic, Social and Cultural Rights, 15 Dec. 1966, G.A. Res. 2200, U.N. GAOR, 21st Sess., Supp. No. 16, at 49, U.N. Doc. A/6316 (1967) (entered into force on 3 Jan. 1976).

11. *See, e.g.,* Mary Wright, *The Last Stand of Chinese Conservatism: The T'ung-Chih Restoration, 1862–1874* (Stanford, Calif.: Stanford University Press, 1962).

12. *See, e.g.,* P.P. Read, *Alive: The Story of the Andes Survivors* (Philadelphia: Lippincott, 1974), describing how the marooned survivors of an airplane crash were compelled to eat the flesh of their dead companions in order to keep from starving.

13. "Beating the Line," *New York Times,* 8 Sept. 1981, sec. A, p. 22.

14. Martha J. Langelan, *Back Off! How to Confront and Stop Sexual Harassment and Harassers* (New York: Simon & Schuster, 1993), 21.

15. Langelan, *Back Off! supra* note 14, at 241.

16. Matthew 7:3.

Acknowledgments

I have been interested in microlegal systems for more than two decades. In part, this interest has been a reaction and corrective to the very large and often abstracted focus that international law, my major scholarly concern, forces on those who study, write about, or practice it. Curiously, however, the informal character and unorganized decision structure of the bulk of international law is a key to microlaw. In part, my interest in microlegal systems has been driven by a general interest in jurisprudence, on which I have also lectured. In part, the interest arose as a conscious defense against a feeling of awkwardness or inadequacy in many microsocial situations. I moderated these feelings of inadequacy by disengaging at one level of consciousness and observing and testing myself and my own reactions, as well the reactions of those with whom I was interacting, in an investigative and intellectual rather than spontaneous social fashion. Methodology, I acknowledge, grew out of personal experiences and the search for a defense. Although this is a legitimate reason for scientific inquiry, there are, as I am well aware, research problems in using the self as a source of information and ethical problems in exploiting others even at a microsocial level.

Over the years I have benefited from discussions with many friends, colleagues, and students. I would particularly like to acknowledge the assistance of Mahnoush Arsanjani, Myres S. McDougal, Andrew R. Willard, Walter Weyrauch, Eisuke Suzuki, André Bétaille, and James Jacobs. Andrew Willard read the entire manuscript in several versions. Owen Fiss, Stanton Wheeler, Felix Lopez, Paula Montonye, Walter Weyrauch, Guy Lesser, Russell Caplan, and Mark Eisenberg read early drafts of Chapter 1 and made many comments that helped me establish and clarify the initial focus on microlaw. Barbara A. Glessner and Tahirih Lee helped me enormously in thinking through Chapter 2. Tahirih Lee helped me with Chapter 3. Natalie Nenadic, in the course of editing the final manuscript, raised many challenging points that occasioned reconsideration and new perspectives. Once again, Cheryl A. DeFilippo skillfully managed the preparation of the manuscript, with the assistance of Stacy Ho and Rosemary Chieppo. Law librarians in New Haven, Berlin, Geneva, and Tokyo concealed their bewilderment and were very helpful. In particular, the help of Gene Coakley, at the Yale Law School, was indispensable.

INDEX

Civic order: as microlaw, 16–17; in the private sphere, 16–17, 149; and the state, 16

Coarchical situations: in queues, 71–75; sanctions in, 85–91, 141–146; in talking 104–107

Codes: of looking, 45–48, 54; in queues, 92

Context: importance of, in looking, 49–56

Constitutional principles: of procedure, 118–128; of substance, 128–140

Constitutive process, 2, 159; in talking, 98–100, 111–118

Etiquette: looking and, 40; as microlaw, 19, 174; micronorms in, 33, 109

Exoself, 31–32, 165

Eye contact, 29–38. *See also* Looking

Glaring, 1, 34, 47. *See also* Looking; Staring

Grundnorm, 60

Heterarchical situations: sanctions in, 91–96. *See also* Power

Hierarchical situations: in talking, 104–107; truth in, 138–139. *See also* Power

Historicists, 150, 155

International law: as microlaw, 6, 15, 140, 156–158

Jurisprudence: implications of talking for, 147–148; and law of the state, 2–3, 5–6; resistance to study of microlaw in, 13

Law, international. *See* International law

Law: "real" law, 2, 5, 6; in Roman, 6, 16; totalitarian system, 15

Lawyers and microlaw, 19–20

Legal Positivism, 5–6, 7, 121, 122, 152

Legal systems: comparison of, 154–155; development of, 155–156; reference points for, 153–154; requirements, 54; social inequities and, 164

Legal theory. *See* Jurisprudence

Looking: code for, 45–48; context of, 49–50; etiquette of, 33, 40; eye contact in, 33–38; microlegal system of, 39–45, 165; norms of, 21–24; sanctions for, 25–29; sexual element of, 21; social dynamics of, 29–38; unlawful, 23–25. *See also* Staring

Macrolaw, 12, 69. *See also* State

Microlaw, 2, 9; amending, 149–176; appreciation of, 3–4, 17–20, 174–

Microlaw (continued)
176; constitutional dimension of, 2; economic study of, 163-164; effectiveness of, 160-161; ethics of, 162; etiquette as, 19; function of, 2-3, 19-20, 175-176; goals of, 158-162; importance of context in, 49-50; international law and, 15, 140, 156-158; as law, 12; lawyers and, 19-20; of looking, 39-48; and macrosystems, 17; norms in, 9-10, 39-43, 160-162; operation of, 162-167; pathologies of, 164-167; sanctions in, 43-44, 167-171; social utility of, 40, 162-164; and statists, 12

Micronorms. *See* Norms
Microsanctions. *See* Sanctions
Microsituations, 53-55. *See also* Microlaw

Norms, 9-10, 15, 166, 174-175; of looking, 24, 39-50; in microsituations, 53-55, 160-162; in queues, 55, 76-84; in social situations, 39-43; in talking, 115-118; violation of, 147

Patience: in queues, 65, 74-75
Power, 35, 156. *See also* Hierarchical situations
Protest: as remedy in conversation, 141-145

Queues: behavioral adaptation to, 59-61; coarchical, 71-75; community aspect of, 51; corruption in, 92-95; deferral of satisfaction in, 58-59; distributive function of, 62-67; economic justification of, 66-67; ethics of, 59, 67-69;

formation and transformation of, 71-75; heterarchical, 71-72, 85, 91-96; macrolaw and, 69; microlaw and, 52, 69-71; norms in, 55, 76-84; operational code in, 92; patience in, 65, 74-75; priority in, 76-84; ritual purpose of, 59-61; role of steward in, 71-75, 88-89, 92-96; sanctions in, 85-96; service model of, 64; social distribution of, 67-69; socializing in, 61-62; structure of, 51-53, 63; supertanker dilemma, 69-70; types of, 52-53; violation of rules in, 65-66

Rapping, 101, 106. *See also* Talking Rules. *See* Norms

Sanctions: in coarchical situations, 85-91, 141-146; in heterarchical situations, 91-96; in microsituations, 12-13, 14, 15, 43-44, 167-171; nonverbal, 26-29; in queues, 85-96; in talking, 140-146; verbal, 27-28
Skoaling, 34
Standing in line. *See* Queues
Staring: code for, 45-48; improper, 1; permissible, 46-48; power basis for, 35; sanctions for, 25-29; as unlawful, 23-25. *See also* Looking
State: and civic order, 16; in jurisprudence, 2, 4, 5-6, 8-9; liberal-democratic, 149-150; limitations of, 15-16; and microlaw, 12; "partial," 15; small groups in, 149-153; totalitarian, 15, 149
Supertanker dilemma, 69-70. *See also* Queues

Talking: coarchical, 104-107, 114, 136-138; constitutive principles of, 118-140; etiquette and, 109; for-its-own-sake (rapping), 101; hierarchical, 104-107, 114, 116-118, 138-139; instrumental, 101, 134, 136; jurisprudential implications of, 147-148; norms in, 101, 107, 115-118, 135-136; pathologies of, 165; process of, 98-100, 111-118; rules of procedure, 118-128; rules of substance, 128-140; sanctions in, 140-146; truth in, 136-140

Truth: rule of, in talking, 136-140